P9-DCI-434

THE SKY RAINED
HEROES

A JOURNEY FROM WAR TO REMEMBRANCE

FREDERICK E. LaCROIX

Synergy Books

The Sky Rained Heroes: A Journey from War to Remembrance
Published by Synergy Books
P.O. Box 80107
Austin, Texas 78758

For more information about our books, please write to us, call 512.478.2028, or visit our website at www.synergybooks.net.

Printed and bound in Canada. All rights reserved. No part of this book may be reproduced in any form or by any electronic or mechanical means including information storage and retrieval systems without permission in writing from the copyright holder, except by a reviewer, who may quote brief passages in review.

Copyright© 2009 by Frederick E. LaCroix

Publisher's Cataloging-in-Publication
(Provided by Quality Books, Inc.)

LaCroix, Frederick E.
    The sky rained heroes : an Asian journey from war to remembrance / Frederick E. LaCroix.
    p. cm.
    Includes bibliographical references.
    LCCN 2008909606
    ISBN-13: 978-0-9821601-3-8
    ISBN-10: 0-9821601-3-5

    1. LaCroix, Frederick E. 2. LaCroix, Robert Edward.
3. Ishizuka, Yasuyuki, d. 1945. 4. World War, 1939-1945
--Campaigns--Pacific Ocean. 5. World War, 1939-1945--
Japan. 6. United States. Air Force--Officers--
Biography. 7. Japan. Rikugun--Officers--Biography.
8. Fathers and sons--United States--Biography.   I. Title.

D767.9.L33 2009   940.54'25
                         QBI08-600313

Front cover design by Daniel Will-Harris.

10 9 8 7 6 5 4 3 2 1

So it was that the war in the air began. Men rode upon the whirl-wind that night and slew and fell like archangels. The sky rained heroes upon the astonished earth...

—H. G. Wells, *The World Set Free*

To my Father:
His was the humility of true courage.

CONTENTS

PART I

BRAVE MEN AND VALOROUS

Brave men were living before Agamemnon
And since, exceeding valorous and sage,
A good deal like him too, though quite the same none;
But then they shone not on the poet's page,
And so have been forgotten...

—Byron, Don Juan [1819–1824] canto 1, st. 5

1

THE SPLENDOR AND THE GRIEF

On the wall of my rowing club at Cambridge University is a plaque on which are inscribed the names of every member of the club who perished in the mad chivalric contest that was WWI. Half a decade of young rowers were consumed in a technological Acheron whose malevolence surpassed imagination. The only signification of their passing is the living memory of mortal men and an inscription on a fading memorial.

An elderly don, a former colleague of Bertrand Russell, recounted to me that not a single of his pre-war friends was living upon his return to England from the Western Front in 1918. Robert Graves, in his cathartic *Good-Bye To All That*, writes of everybody singing and rejoicing at the Armistice in 1918, but that "'everybody' did not include me…cursing and sobbing and thinking of the dead." He quotes the French essayist and poet Georges Duhamel: "It was ordained that you should suffer without purpose and without hope, but I will not let all your sufferings be lost in the abyss."[1] In plaque upon plaque, village upon village, train terminus upon boat quay, stoic age-encrusted cenotaphs stand in mute proxy for a generation obliterated by God, King, Country, and idealism subverted.

The Second World War, a mere twenty years after the carnage of the first, was less mindless in its human sacrifice but more premeditated, compensating in scale, efficiency, and ferocity for the sangfroid with which the first had spawned the Lost Generation. The tombstones of the nameless would not have appreciated the distinction. Near Cambridge in Madingley, a corner, forever America, slumbers.

The incandescence of the Cambridge War Memorial's white Portland stone is a vaunting paean to the anguish of loss for which it was erected. Years have subdued the resonance but not the poignancy of the memorial's message. Stone-upon-stone keening "Here Rests in Honored Glory a Comrade in Arms Known But to God" yearn for the recognition owed a life. Ten thousand "white hotels," in DM Thomas's memorable metaphor, each of whom "had dreamed dreams, seen visions and had amazing experiences."[2] My father ran his fingers over names of lost fellow aviators and shuddered involuntarily with each resuscitated image of a comrade in flight training or combat. Each name was an inferred rebuke of his own completeness of life, and tears welled in his eyes—the only outward emotional expression of his defining life experience I was ever privileged to share.

I had witnessed similar elegiac rights at war memorials around the world. The sight never failed to evoke a melancholic envy. Envy of camaraderie tempered in a crucible of conflict. Envy of self-knowledge won in the shadow of tenuous, fleeting mortality. Envy of moral certitude and self-assurance, unsought offspring of visceral aggression forced on virginal courage. But what of your recurring anxieties, the physical restiveness, the uneasy sleep punctuated by intense, sweat-enveloped flashbacks? What of the reflexive leaping from a childhood bed to grasp your mother in a hammerlock six months after the war's end as she crept into your sleeping world to close a storm-threatened window? What of unspoken memories, unspeakable to any but fellow combatants, emotional scars dim-proofed against the otherwise irresistible dermabrasion of time? "Young men with eyes which did not match their age, shaken beyond speech or tears by the splendour and the grief of [their memories]."[3]

2

2

ALL DISCORD, HARMONY

In 1945, two men, impelled by historical tides against which they had neither inclination nor ability to swim, met and fought in Asia. One died; the other became my father. The dead Japanese warrior was wrapped in a battle flag retrieved and presented to my father, an officer, as a memento of victory. The flag, at the time, was nothing more or less than a totem of evil vanquished. Over the ensuing decades, the flag's conflictual connotations, like its blooded Rising Sun, faded. Hostility glazed, blurred, and transmuted to grudging recognition of shared experience and unspoken loss.

My father passed the flag to me shortly before his death, ruing how little he knew of the soldier who died in its name. The flag, a historical curiosity to which I gave little thought, hung for several years on my library wall opposite a full-length Japanese wedding kimono. The contraposition mirrored to me the balancing force of opposites in the Japanese (or more generally the human) character. On one wall the tattered, bloodied, Kanji-inscribed Japanese battle flag, relic of an ethic at once passionately honorable and insensately brutal, noble and primordial, devoted to order yet self-destructively rigid. On the other the luminous white silk kimono, intricately, delicately, and with mesmerizing sensuality embroidered with the symbols of longevity, steadfastness, eternal youth, happiness, and good fortune: pines, bamboo, cranes, wave-riding rabbits, and algae-trailing tortoises. The same nameless tension that spawned the nihilistic kamikaze and the timeless artistic sensibility of the kimono had, on a larger scale, driven two civilized peoples to mutual slaughter.

3

The flag would likely have remained an object of idle musing had I not, a year after my father's death, come upon a trove of his wartime correspondence while helping my mother sift through old files. Poring over the yellowed letters, preserved by my grandparents as wartime surrogate for an absent son, I glimpsed a remarkable universe of intersecting, entwined coincidence. As I followed leads suggested by the letters, the seemingly chance points at which my life and the wartime lives of my father and the dead Japanese officer converged challenged credulity. I thought of Pope's dismissal of coincidence in his *Essay on Man*:

All nature is but art, unknown to thee;

All chance, direction which thou canst not see;

All discord, harmony not understood;

All partial evil, universal good;

And, spite of pride, in erring reason's spite,

One truth is clear, whatever is, is right.[4]

In 1942, Sergeant Yasuyuki Ishizuka, already a veteran of Japan's horrific China campaign, landed in northern Malaysia,[5] bicycled and marched the length of the peninsula, crossed the Johor-Singapore causeway, and conquered the fortress of Singapore with the Fifth Division of General Yamashita's Twenty-fifth Army. In the bombardment preceding the fall of the island citadel, the maternal grandparents of a girl born twenty-two years later were killed. In combat at a place called Kent Ridge in Singapore, one of her uncles was killed fighting Sergeant Ishizuka's division. In the occupation that ensued, her grandfather was sent to work on the Thai-Burma railway, the famous *The Bridge on the River Kwai*. Her uncle was arrested twice and tortured by the Kempetai, Japanese counterpart to the German Gestapo, and her father and another uncle were beaten by Japanese soldiers for stealing fruit and neglecting to bow. With Japan ascendant, Sergeant Ishizuka returned home to teach school and resume his competitive judo training. Two years later, now-Lieutenant Ishizuka was battling the Americans in the Philippines.

In 1942, my father, Robert Edward LaCroix, joined the Army Air Force, flying a P-51 fighter plane with the Third Air Commandos after completing flight training in Texas and Florida. First Lieutenant, later

Captain, LaCroix served in the Pacific Theater from New Guinea to the Philippines, supporting Douglas MacArthur's Leyte invasion task force and fighting up to Manila and beyond. In a combat strafing mission in northern Luzon, he was shot down over water and later rescued. After recovering from his wounds, he participated in a pitched battle against retreating troops of General Yamashita's Fourteenth Army, including Lieutenant Ishizuka, around Yamashita's headquarters in the Philippines' hill station of Baguio. The destinies of two lives, mirroring the greater conflict, collided. One was extinguished in the miasma of defeat; the other learned to live with his victory.

Forty years later I moved to Singapore to teach law at the National University of Singapore, built on the site of the Kent Ridge battlefield. I met and later married a graduate of this law school, the granddaughter, niece, and daughter of the family whose fates had been so entwined with Lieutenant Ishizuka's and who was now legal counsel overseeing an American semiconductor firm's Baguio-based plant. As CEO of a start-up venture engaged in rural electrification and development in Asia, I worked to provide educational and economic opportunities to villagers of the same provinces whose liberation, I later discovered, my father had shared in—Batanes, Leyte, Samar, Palawan, and parts of Luzon. I witnessed veterans of Lieutenant Ishizuka's army in Burma, Saipan, and Guam, returning to renascent battlefields to complete Shinto burial rites for long-gone comrades.

Spurred by my father's wish and navigating by his letters and the flag, I traveled to Japan to unearth the identity and the surviving family of the lost Japanese soldier. With the willing support of Japanese city, prefectural, and national authorities, I searched from one end of Honshu to the other end of Kyushu, scouring veterans' records and Imperial Japanese Army histories. In my naivety I discovered how emotionally laden a symbol is a sixty-year-old flag, whether to revisionist nationalists or determined pacifists. After months of fruitless searching, a tentative clue unveiled Lieutenant Ishizuka and led ultimately to his surviving family. At an emotional ceremony in Tokyo, I returned to his family the flag that had cost them so dearly sixty years earlier. Perhaps two absent soldiers would have been reconciled in the symbolic act of remembrance.

3

"AND TIME REMEMBERED IS GRIEF FORGOTTEN"

If all progress is the product of reconciled conflict, not all reality is "purified by the passage of time," as the poet Czeslaw Milosz wrote. Traveling Asia in search of two men's closure, I witnessed remembrance and reconciliation crash repeatedly against the rocks of atonement and accountability. In Japan there was little interest to recall or confront a painful national humiliation. In China, Korea, and parts of Southeast Asia, reconciliation with a former colonial overlord was anathema. Lieutenant Ishizuka and his flag were emblematic. Underneath the remarkable veneer of modernization and growth simmered unforgiven, unforgotten, and undimmed passions. And like the geological rim of fire on which the region rests, ageless stresses erupted with little notice and toxic consequence.

It is said that we study history to rid ourselves of it. It seemed a simple enough issue to me, an American, to build a bridge between two former enemies on the shared experience of loss. Yet in Asia even the basic facts of the war are disputed. The lenses of collective experience, fogged with the passage of time and the ossification of prejudice, produce contrasting versions of the same events. The loss of the Second World War was epic, surpassing our grasp of loss. Where I saw honorable remembrance, others saw forgiveness without accounting. Where, I was asked, was the attribution of responsibility, the atonement? Was I so naïve as to think that mere symbolism and goodwill could salve the searing experience of atrocity? Blame has at least the merit of emotional vindication. Blame is the catharsis by which the demons of loss are exorcised. But blame is as fatal to progress as it is illusory solace.

Whether at Nuremberg or in the Tokyo trials of Class A war criminals or, more contemporarily, at The Hague, justice struggles to calibrate the balance between individual guilt and collective exoneration. It runs to the root of forgiveness and reconciliation. Tolstoy, in *War and Peace*, weighed the balance when he wrote of the "two aspects to the life of every man: the personal life, which is free in proportion as its interests are abstract, and the elemental life of the swarm, in which a man must inevitably follow the laws laid down for him. Every man [makes] use of his free-will for attainment of his own objects, and feels…that he can do or not do any action…But he serves as an unconscious instrument in bringing about the historical ends of humanity…[A]s soon as he does anything, that act…becomes irrevocable and is the property of history, in which it has a significance, predestined and not subject to free choice. Every action…that seems…an act of…free-will is in an historical sense not free at all, but in bondage to the whole course of previous history, and predestined from all eternity."[6]

Certainly the victor has less cause to feel aggrieved than the victim. Was my "grand gesture" complacently impervious to the pain it might cause those who suffered horribly under Japanese wartime occupation? Or did irretrievable loss and the passage of time require just such resolute steps to reconciliation? I admittedly enjoyed the luxury of comfortable distance. Nevertheless, when emotion has leached from a conflict, the residue is the memory of individuals striving to survive. That struggle merits remembrance. Lieutenant Ishizuka's flag, initially a symbol of division, ultimately proved a catalyst for reconciliation. In a properly ordered world, the poet's wish would father the deed:

> …And time remembered is grief forgotten,
> And frosts are slain and flowers begotten…
> Blossom by blossom the spring begins.[7]

4

A Pantheon of Heroes

Despite desire, resource, and opportunity, my father never returned to Asia after 1945. There would always be time but there never was. A close friend of his flew with General Chennault's Flying Tigers[8] in China during the early days of the Japanese invasion, was wounded in combat, and was recuperating in Singapore when Sergeant Ishizuka's division crossed the causeway. My father heard he was in the Alexandra Road Hospital when the Japanese, infuriated at the unforeseen British Commonwealth forces' resistance, went berserk, bayoneting bedridden patients, among whom was the former Flying Tiger. He was believed to have been buried in Singapore's Kranji War Cemetery, along with many of the defenders of Kent Ridge.

Nestled in the far north of the island close to the Johor-Singapore causeway across which Ishizuka's men pedaled to conquest, the Kranji War Memorial is a sentinel of the past standing post for a world that has moved on. But it is a cemetery of heroes, and I had come to redeem a promise to my father. Like any cemetery, Kranji's entrance might be emblazoned with the epigram: "To be is to be remembered." After the febrile buzzing of Singapore's business district, Kranji's calm is preternatural. Befitting rest as release, one wonders "how anyone could ever imagine unquiet slumbers for the sleepers in that quiet earth."[9] Suffusing all is a plaintive mournfulness, the collective resonance of premature death.

It is impossible not to empathize with Siegfried Sassoon's sentiment *On Passing the New Menin Gate* in Belgium, erected for the slaughtered multitudes from the allies' Pyrrhic victory at Ypres in the First World War.

Who will remember, passing through this gate,
The unheroic dead who fed the guns?
Who shall absolve the foulness of their fate—
Those doomed, conscripted, unvictorious ones?

As with all war cemeteries, it is the sheer scale of loss that eludes ready comprehension. The cascading anonymity of symmetrically aged headstones. A wretched, leveling sameness, a faux uniformity obscuring the deserve-to-be-remembered authenticity of life stories abridged mid-plot. Against unsought seclusion and the remorseless amnesia of nature, one struggles to discern the uniqueness that was a life.

Recollection is to renewal as indifference is to abandon. Only conscious remembrance gives enduring meaning to sacrifice; to remember "while the crowded years between remove their battles...as far from us as the fights in Homer," in Kipling's words from his masterful *The Irish Guards in the Great War*[10]. Remembrance is the soundest surety against the demeaning oblivion of unremarked loss and the inadvertence of an indifferent age. Everything has already been said but nobody pays attention, so each morning it has all to be said again, Proust observed. Truly we repeat what we elect to forget.

The lives of my father and other veterans have relevance beyond their emotionally cauterizing war experiences. They "are a bridge to our future," as Bernhard Schlink writes in *The Reader*.[11] Their history is an antidote to that unlucky propensity of which Tolstoy spoke: "the faculty of seeing and believing in the possibility of good and truth, and at the same time seeing too clearly the evil and falsity of life to be capable of taking a serious part in it."[12] It models for emulation the nobility of the human spirit. That circumstance more often than not thrusts this nobility unasked for on its favorites does nothing to diminish their heroism.

And what is wrong with lionizing heroes? My father, like most veterans, would have rejected any such characterization. He, like they, would have been mistaken. Steinbeck believed that men require monsters in their personal oceans, for life without nameless creatures is like sleep without dreams. Are heroes in our personal pantheons any less essential? For if dreams are just yearning uncloaked, heroes are their waking form.

PART II

BEFORE THE FLOOD

The Fathers before the flood and their Generations when seen remote they appear as One Man.

—William Blake, *Vision of the Last Judgement*

5

THE AWAKENING

What, then, is Japan's policy in the Far East? In a word...national safety and prosperity...Without colonies and emigration on a large scale she cannot attain to economic independence and cannot secure to her people the means of livelihood. Raw materials and markets are essential...If peace is to be preserved in the Pacific, she will...have to have other outlets for her population and other markets for her goods.[1]

—Lt.-Comdr. Tota Ishimaru, Imperial Japanese Navy, 1936
Author of *Japan Against the World* and *Japan Must Fight Britain*

A story is recounted of the Russo-Japanese War in 1905. Russian trains bound for the Manchurian front via Vladivostok were laden with decorations and prize money. Officers and men traveled in the highest of spirits, celebrating, toasting victory, and making light of their small-statured enemy—all before the conflict began. Outside of Japan it was inconceivable that a civilized Western power could do anything but eradicate a presumptive Asiatic power. The Russian high command had boasted of the invincible strength of the fortress at Port Arthur on the Manchurian peninsula. In an appalling glimpse of the future, in a battle described by George Kennan as "the shriek of the lowest hell on this earthly abode of ours," the Russian military suffered the most ignominious military defeat in its history, precipitating the Russian Revolution of 1905. Just thirty-five years later, the Western powers were about to pay the price of inattention.

Japan had never lost a war, and its first war against a Western power fired the national conviction that *Nippon seishin*, "Japanese spirit," would sweep its soldiers to victory where all others would fail. The exceptionalist vigor of an ordained manifest destiny was not uniquely American. A Japanese soldier had written on receiving notice of mobilization for the Manchurian front, "We...felt our bones crackle and our blood boil up...A mysterious kind of spiritual electricity seemed to permeate [us], the flower of the Land of the Gods."[2] "To die under the flying flag of the Rising Sun, and to die while doing a splendid service to one's country, was the wish and resolve of every heart,"[3] recorded a young officer. A female student rhapsodized over "the thrilling beauty of...intellectual young men...in their twenties driven to die, contrary to their own intentions."[4]

In the infamous Manchurian Incident of September 1931, a group of Japanese Army officers of the Kwantung Army blew up part of the South Manchuria Railway, a Japanese concession, furnishing the militarist faction in Tokyo the pretext of Chinese instability and lawlessness needed to justify the total annexation of Manchuria. Colonial control was quickly consolidated through the puppet Manchuko regime, replete with puppet Emperor Pu Yi, portrayed in Bertolucci's *The Last Emperor*. The adventure whetted Japan's Western-emulating colonial appetite. Having annexed Taiwan and southern Manchuria after the 1895 First Sino-Japanese War, Korea in 1910, and the rest of Manchuria in 1931, China was the fulcrum on which Japan would wrest Asia from European and American dominance. In bizarre counterpoint, while Japanese diplomats labored to achieve an amicable settlement with China, one supposedly based on an exclusive fraternity of shared racial affinity, the Kwantung Army, called "the divine sword" at home, worked feverishly to supplant the civilian government in Japan and brutally to absorb the whole of China as a "supercolony."

Yasuyuki Ishizuka, a fifth-degree black belt judo master whose life's wish was to teach school, was exhilarated by Japan's awakening as a great World Power. He quaffed the narcotic brew of burgeoning national pride, Confucian respect for authority, cult-of-the-emperor religiosity, and strongest of all, irresistible peer expectation. In 1938, he turned

14

twenty, the average minimum age for military service, and anxiously awaited the standard "Letter of Instruction from Military Authorities." The Japanese equivalent of the U.S. Selective Service System's Vietnam-era "Greetings" letter from the president, the conscription letter, in part, read:

> *Greetings to the Father,*
>
> *We have learned that your son will shortly experience the greatest joy and satisfaction possible to one of our nation by joining soon our company. We congratulate you.*
>
> *When your son enters the barracks, the officers…will be to him as a stern father and a loving mother. We will always be concerned with his two-fold training, body and mind, so that…he may be able to realize the highest hope of a member of our race [i.e., to die for the emperor]…*
>
> *With the company and your home forming a complete circle we wish to cooperate with you to the fullest extent in order to administer his education and guidance along the most rational lines…*
>
> *On the day your son enters the barracks, we trust that you will accompany him in order that we may meet you and have an intimate talk with you.*
>
> *Respectfully yours,*
> *(Commanding Officer)*
> *Imperial Japanese Army*[5]

6

THE SHANTYMAN'S DREAM

Life at Cornell University in the summer of 1940 had the somnolent quality of any American college campus in August. Sunk in the blue-hazed lassitude of New York's Catskill Mountains, it fostered the illusion of self-containment, isolated and unaffected by the world outside. Yet it was tinged with poignancy imparted by looming change. As in the country at-large, a sense of precious impermanence gave every pleasure the heightened savor of a farewell dinner: unspoken tristesse disguised as bonhomie. Only two months earlier France had disappeared into the Greater German Reich, and Paris was an occupied city. Democratic Denmark and Norway were memories only slightly more removed. And Beowulf battled Grendel in mortal combat while the birthplace of modern democracy was besieged in the Battle of Britain. In Asia, China was hemorrhaging.

As sophomore Bob LaCroix returned to Cornell for his third year in a double-major mechanical and electrical engineering degree, a certain amount of self-willed denial was understandable. Republican or Democrat (and the Boston LaCroixs were staunchly Republican), it was difficult to deny that Franklin Roosevelt was pulling the country inexorably from the prolonged purgatory of the Great Depression. While Republicans bemoaned the imminent demise of all things American, Roosevelt demonstrated that some things American, notably double-digit unemployment, could be dispensed with at little peril to the nation's essential fabric. Industrial recovery was underway; Social Security was in place; reflation, price stabilization, and financial institutional reform were taking root; infrastructure development, including rural electrification, was receiving huge dollops of cash. Conrad Black, in his weighty Roosevelt biography, provides a compact summary of the president's Depression-recovery achievements: "The New Deal was passing but not brilliant economics. As crisis management and preservation of a civil society, it was a masterly success."[6]

Arthur LaCroix, my grandfather, lost his wealth in the 1929 stock market crash and was in a driven rush to rebuild the family fortune, whatever the personal cost. He would die of a heart attack at the age of fifty-three. My father, the eldest of three sons and a daughter, was the first brother to enroll at Cornell, carrying on a tradition begun by my great-grandfather. In an era when an indigenous engineering degree and the ability to build things carried more cachet than a degree in managing paper flows for unconscionable recompense, two of the three sons took up engineering; the third entered medicine. The baby sister preferred the social fast-track, savoring mightily the post-Prohibition, Depression-emergent jubilation of Artie Shaw's Gramercy Five, the Harry James Boogie Woogie Trio, Lionel Hampton's All Stars, Muggsy Spanier, and Cab Calloway. Life was getting fun again.

In a Richard Henry Dana-style Grand Tour, my father had spent the previous year in the Canadian Pacific Northwest felling trees as an apprentice lumberjack. For an inflexibly pragmatic man, I have always suspected that along with enlisting as a fighter pilot and courting my mother, his lumberjack stint was a rare expression of a rigidly repressed romantic streak. Great-great-great-grandfather LaCroix (then DelaCroix), a recently arrived immigrant in Quebec, made his fortune in timber, starting as a lowly lumberjack, or "shantyman." Economic success fostered social aspiration. Like most newcomers-made-good, he emigrated as a Leveller, prospered in the free-for-all of a nascent capitalist democracy, and ended as an Anglicized aspirant to class distinction. He moved his family to the bastion of reinvented aristocracy, Boston, and the allure of legitimizing access to the ranks of a capitalist democracy's elite.

Emerson observed that "…a race yields nobility in some form, however we name the lords, as surely as it yields women."[7] Early nineteenth-century Boston had expelled a hereditary British aristocracy and substituted a homegrown commercial one. If the Norman noble was just the Norwegian pirate baptized, as Emerson said, the Boston aristocrat was the man-of-commerce transfigured to high-minded, public-spirited gentleman. But unlike the British system of titled primogeniture, whose signal merit according to Dr. Johnson was that "it makes but one fool in a family,"[8] the upper reaches of the American class structure were at least semi-permeably meritocratic. Emerson grasped the nub: "The doors, though ostentatiously guarded, are really open, and hence the power of the bribe. All the barriers to rank only whet the thirst and enhance the prize."[9] He was speaking of emerging Victorian England; he could as aptly have been describing the developing American mercantile elite.

My father was raised on the boiled, bleached, and burnished family mythography repackaging brutal, survival-dictated necessity as hard work ennobled by free choice. Where my remoter antecedents chopped wood because it was the only paying work available to unskilled immigrants, my father ingested fortifying tales, true enough, of the inherent nobility of man-without-means taming hostile nature by the strength of his will and the iron of his arm. It would not be surprising had he focused on just one stanza of "The Shantyman's Life"[10]:

> All you jolly fellows, come listen to my song;
> It's all about the pinery boys and how they got along.
> They're the jolliest lot of fellows, so merrily and fine,
> They will spend the pleasant winter months in cutting down the pine.

He most likely overlooked a more cautionary verse:

> The shantyman's life is a worrisome one,
> Though some call it free from care.
> It's the ringing of the ax from morning 'til night,
> In the middle of the forest fair.
> While life in the shanties, bleak and cold,
> While the wintry winds do blow,

As soon as the morning star does appear,
To the wild woods we must go.

Reality of life in the lumber camps fell something short of the family idealization. The camp comprised several single-room log cabins, each lined shoulder-to-shoulder with bunks encircling a stove, table, and chairs, serving alternately as kitchen, dining room, and entertainment center. Logging took place in the winter months, when logs could be more readily moved to the frozen rivers for marshalling before the spring "drive" downriver, so the shanties were kept closed tight. Most men smoked, cigarettes or pipes, and with a wood-burning stove the bunkhouse was atmospheric. Bathing took place on Sunday, the only day off, when axes were sharpened and equipment maintained, adding to the men's familial "closeness." Food was plebeian: baked beans, Boston crackers, pork, pea soup, lard, a vegetable now and again, sugar, molasses, and "a basin of reduced ice water, flavored with copperas, and called, by the low and uneducated, 'tea,'" as one experienced lumberjack described it.[11]

At night, the men competed in games of strength, read books, played cards, and sang. Particularly popular were the songs of "La Bolduc," the Queen of Canadian Folksingers and Quebec's first "*chansonnière*." A former housewife from impoverished origins, Mary Travers Bolduc spoke to lonely men with no pretensions and few prospects: "*Y'a longtemps que je couche par terre*" ("I've been sleeping on the floor a long time") and "*La Cuisiniere*" (The Cook").[12] Choppers, sawyers, swampers, teamsters, and loaders, unsentimental men one and all, grew wistful when a fiddle, harmonica, accordion, or "jaw harp" launched into one of La Bolduc's ballads. My father grew fit felling trees by day and worldly in the company of rough men by night. And he read hungrily.

Later in life, transposing coincidence and catalyst, he was fond of quoting Louis L'Amour (née Louis LaMoore) to explain his own intellectual wanderlust: "Books are the building blocks of civilization, for without the written word, a man knows nothing beyond what occurs during his own brief years and, perhaps, in a few tales his parents tell him."[13] Perhaps it was an unacknowledged tribute to a fellow wanderer: L'Amour, a French-Canadian, had too once been an initiate lumberjack.

7

3,000 Slaps

The essence of discipline in the Imperial Army lies in the lofty spirit of complete obedience to His Majesty...It is essential that each man...should be determined always to sacrifice himself for the whole...by reposing every confidence in his comrades, and without giving even the slightest thought to personal interest and to life or death.

—Japanese Field Service Code (War Department, January 8, 1941)[14]

It has been said that the Japanese Imperial Army of World War II was the last primitive infantry army of modern times. Where the U.S. military vigorously embraced the heterodoxy of novel tactics and technologies, the Imperial Army, despite an overlay of Western-instilled technique, organization, and materiel, remained the direct spiritual expression of a samurai tradition running back as far as the twelfth century. The essence of this tradition is well-expressed in the Meiji emperor's 1882 Imperial Rescript to Soldiers and Sailors: "The soldier and the sailor should esteem valor...cultivate self-possession, form their plans with deliberation...make simplicity their aim...and bear in mind that duty is weightier than a mountain, while death is lighter than a feather."[15] "Japan's 'blood-and-guts' generals," recorded the *Asahi Shimbun*, "emphasized fighting spirit and devotion to the Emperor over technological mastery. They lost a war in the process."[16]

Military and civilian socialization in pre-war Japan did not, as in the West, flow in parallel channels bridged exclusively by a subordination

20

of military to civilian authority. As early as the mid-seventeenth century, the famed swordsman Miyamoto Musashi, in his *Book of the Five Spheres*, drawing on the philosophical underpinnings of warriorhood in classical China, advocated a symbiotic pursuit of practical learning in both cultural and martial arts. Just as *Bushido*, the code of the warrior, stressed moral and cultural training and values, so scholars were schooled in martial arts. When the Meiji emperor abolished the samurai class and the feudal order it dominated in the second half of the nineteenth century, his Imperial Rescript retained the code of Bushido as the basis of the modern Imperial Army. By the early twentieth century, in a socio-cultural melding of Confucian paternalism, Zen discipline, Buddhist self-abnegation, and Shinto state loyalty, Japan achieved a model of civil militarism unrivalled since classical Sparta.[17]

From the age of eight—the equivalent of third grade—all boys were given semi-military training by teachers, most of whom were former military men or reservists. As they advanced to middle school, high school, and on to university, they received more formal military training under the tutelage of regular army officers, generally two or more hours per week and four to six days per year for maneuvers. The training centered on the seven "military virtues": loyalty, valor, patriotism, obedience, humility, morality, and honor. Those students who left school after the compulsory six years of primary school took one of two alternative paths. Special government Youth Schools were established to further military training received in primary school, bridging the period until a teenager reached legal conscription age. For youths identified as possessing leadership and technical aptitude, the Army established a system of army apprentice schools in five disciplines: aviation, artillery, signals, tanks, and ordnance. The apprentices, called Army Youth Soldiers, entered "youth training centers" immediately after primary school, at age fourteen to fifteen years, were given basic military training, and then inducted into the Army as the equivalent of an American private first class. Following a six months' probationary period, they were promoted to corporal. The apprentice courses lasted for two years, except for the three-year aviation course. By 1934, fully a third of Japan's suitably aged young men were trained at these centers. Transition to military life for most Japanese men was less rite-of-passage than intensification of long-accustomed routine.

In the decades following the Meiji Restoration, Japan enthusiastically absorbed Western military methods and means. The universal conscription system in place at the outset of the Second World War was introduced by German advisors during the Meiji period. It permitted all eligible males between the ages of seventeen and forty to be called up, although in practice the average age of Japanese conscripts was twenty years old. Class-A conscripts, the fittest, served initially for two years and later, as manpower demands increased, for three years. It was not uncommon for conscripts to be called up for two and three tours of duty. Yasuyuki Ishizuka was initially called up for two years. Following examination, he was qualified "Class A"—in good physical condition, not less than five feet in height, and thus "Available for active service." His first year of basic infantry training was an exercise in institutionalized brutality.

"The world's roughest corps of noncommissioned officers literally slapped and beat and kicked their charges into submission."[18] Noncoms struck junior soldiers, senior officers struck junior officers. Physical abuse was not random, it was systematic. While any effective military training aims to achieve the reflexive subordination of self-interest to the welfare of the unit, Japan achieved this through premeditated personal degradation. "You are nothing but wretched one-cent men!" recruits were lectured by noncoms, quoting the price of the stamp on the conscription notice.[19] Where American training valued adaptive initiative in combat situations, Japanese training assured the repetitive response of the automaton, animated by unquestioning, ingrained impulse. The massed banzai attacks with small arms and swords against heavily defended Allied positions in the latter part of the war were the most nihilistic expression of this acculturation. The training was meant to toughen recruits, inure them to pain and suffering. It did. It also inured them to the pain and suffering of others—the prey become predator. By the time a Japanese soldier entered combat, he was "an emotional pressure cooker." Joseph Stalin could as easily have been speaking of the Japanese as the Soviet Army when he off-handedly remarked, "It takes a brave man not to be a hero in the Red Army."

A contemporary of Ishizuka, writing in a letter to the editor of the *Asahi Shimbun* after the war, recalled his swimming instruction as a recruit. A rope was tied around his body—"like a cormorant in cormorant fishing"—and he was thrown overboard. When he lost consciousness from gulping too much river water, he was pulled in, resuscitated, and thrown back. His uniform froze. When not "swimming," his head was beaten with a green bamboo pole and his face slapped with leather slippers so persistently that his physiognomy altered. He commented without irony that he "understood why Japanese soldiers were strong."[20] A recruit in Ishizuka's future Fifth Division counted more than three thousand slaps administered by his corporal during the first ninety days of basic training.[21] Another recruit suffered forty-five years after the war from ringing in his ears, a by-product of beatings by higher-ranking privates. Whether from sadism or guilt compensation, many recruits recounted the crazed excitement that invigorated and prolonged beatings.

One of the clearest explanations of the perverse psychological dynamic bonding beater and beaten is furnished by the eponymous narrator, a one-time mob enforcer, in Salman Rushdie's *The Moor's Last Sigh*:

> A man who is beaten seriously...will be irreversibly changed. His relationship to his own body, to his mind, to the world beyond himself alters in ways both subtle and overt. A certain confidence, a certain idea of liberty is beaten out for good; always provided the beater knows his job. Often, what is beaten in is detachment. The victim...detaches himself from the event, and sends his consciousness to float in the air above. He seems to look down upon himself, on his own body as it convulses and perhaps breaks. Afterwards he will never fully re-enter himself...
>
> As for the beater: he, too, is changed. To beat a man is a kind of exaltation, a revelatory act, opening strange gates in the universe. Time and space come away from their moorings, their hinges. Chasms yawn. There are glimpses of amazing things... the past and the future too. It was hard to cling to these memories. At the end of the [beating], they faded. But I remembered that something had happened. That there were visions. This was enriching news.[22]

Perhaps the least enviable position was that of the recruit tarred, rightly or wrongly, with the epithet "pacifist." While many Japanese soldiers after the war expressed their abhorrence of the Imperial Army's treatment of its own soldiers, as well as captured enemy combatants and civilians of conquered territories, it is not surprising that little dissent was heard during the war. The case of an antiwar primary school teacher was typical. Early in the war, the teacher, considered an intellectual, resisted militarist education and was openly pacifist. He was arrested for violating the Peace Preservation Law and denied the "privilege" of active military service. Several years later he was conscripted to active duty. Viewed as a traitor by his superiors and compatriots alike, he was given "lessons" in the form of beatings with clenched fists, hobnailed military boots, clubs, and rifle butts. The beatings caused his back teeth to crumble.[23] Although the teacher survived the war to write about it, many in similar positions committed suicide or deserted, an act tantamount to suicide but compounding folly with disgrace to the family.

Ishizuka's recruit training phase, running from January through May 1938, focused on general military instruction including drill, bayonet fighting, target practice, and small unit (i.e., squad) training. During February, recruits underwent a five-day endurance march, bivouacking at night, calculated to toughen and teach endurance in cold weather (presaging Ishizuka's eventual deployment to Manchuria). Second-stage training in June and July concentrated on target practice, more bayonet fighting, larger unit (platoon and company) tactics, and daily twenty-mile marches with full packs. The third stage of training in August involved field works (e.g., construction), combat shooting, swimming, more bayonet fighting, larger unit (company and battalion) tactics, and daily twenty-five-mile marches with full equipment. The final stage of basic training, October and November, culminated in battalion and regimental training and full-scale autumn maneuvers. Live ammunition was used throughout, not without casualties. Night operations, a particular aptitude of the Japanese military in the Pacific War, were emphasized.

Musketry, forced marching, and bayonet training made up the central triad of recruit basic training. Of these, bayonet training was considered the most important. Forced marches were grueling exercises in endurance; the pace, however difficult, never varied once set. Falling out of a march was considered a disgrace and punished. Ritual suicides in atonement for being unable to keep up were not unheard of. Musketry focused on moving targets and achieving coolness under fire. Training was encapsulated in the maxim:

> Pull the trigger as carefully and gently
> As the frost falls in the cold night[24]

Bayonet training started as early as high school. Until the end of the Pacific War, Japan's national identity was expressed in terms of the Three Sacred Treasures of the emperor: the mirror (brightness and honesty), the jewel (compassion), and the sword (strength, resolution, and wisdom). The sword represented the spirit of the warrior; the spirit of the warrior was the spirit of the offensive, and the bayonet was the ultimate weapon of the offensive. Only by aggressive, competent use of the bayonet—nurturing the "spirit of the bayonet" as the field manual described it—could an enemy be forced to give ground. Bayonet instructors were frequently sword fencing masters.[25] Japanese recruits were taught to aim for the abdomen and the throat in long thrusts. If the thrust failed, they were taught to drop their rifles and resort to hand-to-hand combat. Night exercises were conducted with unsheathed bayonets. The skills honed in bayonet training proved ultimately more relevant to civilian massacres than to combat. The spirit of the bayonet in offence encountered the spirit of massed artillery, machine gun and rifle fire with close air support in fortified defense. The trench warfare with massed frontal attacks of World War I and the Russo-Japanese War was displaced by the mobility of technology and tactics in the Second World War. Japan did not adapt and paid heavily.

Following completion of his first year of training, corporal Ishizuka was posted to Manchuria. His physical stature and martial arts aptitude, combined with native leadership skills, resulted in his being singled out for noncommissioned officer training some months after posting to Manchuria. Following a period of "on-the-job" training with troops, he was assigned to a one-year training program at the NCO academy at Kungchuling, Manchuria. Ishizuka emerged a sergeant and resumed combat duty in the nightmarish conditions of the war for China. By now he was a honed example of *yamato-damashii*, the invincible spirit that led one inter-war Western observer to comment that the secret of Japan's unbroken record of success in war was "the men behind the guns."[26] Ishizuka, in turn, drilled his men in the fundamental precepts of Japanese warfare: "Aggressiveness should constantly prevail in combat...When attacking, be determined...always taking the initiative... vowing not to cease until the enemy is crushed. In defense, always retain the spirit of attack...never give up a position but rather die."[27] Japanese soldiers were "human bullets."[28]

A Japanese officer, writing in *Human Bullets* of his experiences in the Russo-Japanese War, cited, by way of contrasting the Japanese approach to warfare, the example of a captured Russian soldier pleading: "I have a dear wife; she must be extremely anxious about me...Rather than fight and be killed, I must save my life for my wife. If I die she will grieve and go mad. I am no match for the Japanese. It is silly to fight on, knowing that we shall surely be killed by the Japanese Army." The officer remarked that there "is an impassable gulf between this and the Japanese ideal and determination to die in honor but never live in shame." He noted the Russians were tough fighters but at the same time were "extremely careful of their lives." He concluded that these two characteristics are contradictory to each other. The Russians, he wrote, would "rather live as a tile than be broken as a jewel." The Japanese would "rather die beautifully than live in ignominy."[29]

On the morning of his departure for China, Ishizuka, like his father a generation earlier, cleansed himself with pure water, donned his best uniform, bowed to the east where the emperor resides, and offered his prayers to the family shrine of his ancestors. Taking his sword from the niche where it rested, he drank a farewell cup of sake with his family and to the accompaniment of a raucous procession through town, dedications at the local shrine, and grandiloquent farewell speeches by the town mayor and assorted dignitaries, left to join the Kwantung Army in Manchuria. His fervor was palpable. He would join the vehicle of Japan's ascendancy in the glorious effort "to regain the Asia Pacific; to reclaim what Japan ceded to the colonialists in the seventeenth century." By 1942, with the war in full gear, a Japanese infantryman's training was reduced to three months. But when Ishizuka completed his training, he was one of the most highly trained, determinedly aggressive fighting machines on the globe.

As he marched through Tokyo to the harbor and the waiting troop transports, martial bands played, flags and banners snapped, and massed onlookers, Ishizuka's family included, waved, laughed, and shouted "Banzai! Long live the emperor!" Within a few months, troop departures amid the galloping pace of war preparations turned highly secret; public farewells were a thing of the past. For now, the festive air lulled whatever apprehensions Ishizuka and his family may have felt over his first steps beyond his native land. None anticipated the world of Dantean malignity to which they would lead.

8

THE DEVIL AND THE BUDDHA

Man's inhumanity to man
Makes countless thousands to mourn.

—Robert Burns, *Man Was Made to Mourn*

The maelstrom of destruction visited on China by the Japanese Army in WWII was borne of biblical antipathy. In Japanese, the Imperial Army was called *kogun*; the Chinese referred to it as *hungjun*—a play on words with the same sound but different ideograms meaning "army of locusts."[30] Japanese soldiers were called *Dongjang kuizi*—"fearful Eastern devils." A people descended from the Chinese were trained to view the Chinese as subhuman. A Japanese officer wrote: "They are ignorant and greedy survivors of a decayed people; they know only the value of gold and silver and do not think of national or international interests.[31] They are a race of men who would risk even their lives to make money, and would live in a pig pen with ten thousand pieces of gold in pocket!"[32] Field operations were guided by the "three all" principle: "Kill all, burn all, destroy all."[33]

By the time Ishizuka arrived in Manchuria, the conquest of China was well underway. In July of 1937, the ever-busy Kwantung Army orchestrated the "Marco Polo Bridge Incident," a confrontation with Chinese troops bringing to a boil already simmering Japanese nationalism. With comparable motivations and long-term consequences to Hitler's Reichstag fire in Berlin, the trumped-up incident furnished the pretext Tokyo needed for a full-scale invasion of China. The Kwantung Army, long threatening the confining levees of international opinion and sanction, now burst with apocalyptic ferocity on a country already bleeding from a decade of internecine warfare between Chiang Kai-shek's Kuomintang and Mao Tse-tung's Communist Party. Before the conflict ended in 1945, more than ten million Chinese civilians died as Japan committed one and a half million troops to subjugate its "natural hinterland."[34]

Nothing in his family upbringing, schooling, or military training had prepared Ishizuka for the primal savagery of the China front's no-quarter-asked, no-quarter-given warfare. Landing initially in Dalian, the major port of Manchuria, it appears Ishizuka's unit eventually made its way to Shanghai, although his records from this period are incomplete. The new arrivals were integrated with veterans and moved south in an ongoing effort to suppress Chinese guerilla activities. In a reluctant truce, Mao and Chiang grudgingly suspended their fratricide to avert looming genocide. Combining harrying behind-the-lines tactics with more conventional warfare, retreating to China's interior and refusing to surrender, the Chinese created increasing frustration within the Japanese Army command.

In December 1937, in the notorious Rape of Nanjing, a six-week orgy of killing and looting unrivalled in modern history, the Japanese killed 300,000 Chinese and raped some 20,000 women, including the aged and pregnant.[35] A Tokyo Times reporter wrote "I have never been to hell, but there is a hell, it was in this city."[36] An Asahi Shimbun correspondent witnessed in a single incident 30,000 Chinese, mostly women, children, and the elderly, driven to the foot of the city wall. Machine guns raked the crowd and hand grenades were tossed from atop the wall; none survived. Chinese civilians were burned and buried alive, bayoneted, vivisected, used as target practice, decapitated, disemboweled, drowned, and dismembered. An enlisted man recalled bayonet drill with Chinese prisoners blindfolded and tied to stakes, a red circle drawn around the heart of each. The instructor explained that the red circle was the one place they were prohibited to stab. The prisoners were to be made to last as long as possible.[37] Photographic records of the massacre are indescribably horrible.

As with the European Holocaust and the Ottoman Turk slaughter of Armenians, there are those who deny that the Rape of Nanjing ever took place. And as with the Holocaust and Armenia, there is incontrovertible evidence that it did, not least from survivors, participants, and outside observers. But the massacre in Nanjing was simply the crudest, and cruelest, expression of a systematic policy of national coercion that had long-since abandoned any pretence of humanity—on either side. As the Asahi Shimbun put it, "Atrocity begat counteratrocity. Japanese commanders, provoked by unexpected Chinese resistance, grew ever crueler in the revenge they took on prisoners and civilians who fell into their hands."[38] An infantryman serving at the same time and in the same theater as Ishizuka wrote that three points were constantly drilled into the common soldier's head: "(1) if we don't kill, we will be killed; (2) the lives we have today we may not have tomorrow; (3) even if we can eat today we may starve tomorrow."[39]

Letters from Japanese soldiers serving in China make clear the extent of revulsion felt by many at their duties. But Japanese intolerance of dissent could as readily be turned inward as outward. Public dissent, especially in the military, was dealt with summarily and brutally. Few were brave enough to protest. Besides, the emperor had instructed his subjects to "Consider your superiors' orders as Our orders." An order by a superior officer was an order from the emperor. The oracle of the founding emperor of the Japanese Empire, Emperor Jimmu, had declared the emperor to be divine; it followed that his orders were commands from a god. The Imperial Army could do no wrong. An officer in the China campaign wrote: "I was ready and determined to die, that though my body be lost...my spirit would not forget loyalty to the Emperor 'for seven lives.'"[40] While there is no record of Ishizuka having participated in large-scale atrocities, there is no reason to assume he was exempt from the general dehumanization of a campaign whose only contemporary equivalent was the German-Soviet conflict on the Eastern Front. The scars of the conquest have outlived its participants.

Amid the abundance of literature analyzing Japanese behavior in China in the period 1937–45, the simplest explanation is perhaps the most compelling: a Japanese noncommissioned officer, a participant in several atrocities, wrote "Both the Devil and the Buddha exist in war. The Devil enters into people's souls, but human beings must find the Buddha for themselves."[41] In the *Harp of Burma*, through self-revelation akin to that of Erich Maria Remarque in *All Quiet on the Western Front*, a Japanese soldier discovered his own Buddha: "As I look back on what has happened, I feel keenly that we have been too unthinking…Many innocent people were sacrificed to a senseless cause…Our country has waged a war, lost it, and is now suffering. That is because we were greedy, because we were so arrogant that we forgot human values, because we had only a superficial ideal of civilization…We must work to bring what little relief we can to this pain-ridden world…Is that not essential—for the Japanese and for all humanity?"[42]

9

A LIFE ORDAINED

From the gates of feudal Edo, the eastern capital later known as Tokyo, the serpentine road to Nikko, ancestral home of the Ishizuka family, was lined with 14,000 giant cryptomeria, their ordered symmetry evoking Confucian virtue. Past sulfur-belching hot springs and quilt-work brown and green rice paddies, over pine-scented mountain passes, crystalline air scoring winded lungs, the hissing exhalation of volcanic Mount Chausudake signaled arrival in the mountain village whose beauty inspired the maxim "Never say *kekko* ("contentment"), until you've seen Nikko." At road's end, natural wonder yielded to man-made wonderment as the parting forest disclosed the magnificent Toshogu Shrine. Intricate painted wood carvings, shifting hues in optically hypnotizing empathy with pilgrims' prayers, evinced craftsmanship of an ethereal order. The daunting interplay of art and authority conveyed the granite immutability of a divinely ordained social hierarchy.

Within its hallowed precincts lay the apotheosized remains of the great samurai shogun Ieyasu Tokugawa, unifier of Japan, founder of the dynasty that ruled Japan for 265 years and the loosely portrayed namesake of James Clavell's *Shogun*. Originally intended as the locus of a political cult of the warrior, the shrine had morphed into a popular pilgrimage for commoners. Built in 1636 by Tokugawa's grandson, Iemitsu, the shrine cost an extraordinary $200 million in today's terms and employed 4.5 million workers, a measure of the totality of political control exercised by the shogunate. Today the Toshogu Shrine, like

32

the Roman Arch of Septimius Severus, survives as mute sentinel of a vanished ethos of order, discipline, and fidelity to authority. It mimes an authoritarianism that stemmed a destructive flood of civil discord but grew brittle without the renewing current of dissent.

Benjamin Disraeli quipped that "Great countries are those that produce great people." At the root of all states that transcended fractiousness to become unified hegemonic powers lay the iron will and encompassing vision of one leader: Germany's Bismarck, Russia's Peter, China's Qin Shi Huang, Italy's Garibaldi, and Japan's Tokugawa. Riven by centuries of internecine warfare, lacking an integrated economy, and with political control diffused among scheming, fiercely independent feudal fiefdoms, Japanese insularity was jarred by the advent of early Portuguese and Dutch traders and missionaries. The contrast between static Japanese feudalism and the progressive dynamism of the West—Reformation, Counter-Reformation, Renaissance, exploration, growth of a mercantile class—stunned a Japanese elite nothing if not adept at self-preservation. With political genius and military ruthlessness, the first of fifteen Tokugawa shoguns parried the threat of foreign intrusion and in 1603 unified the country under a single dynasty, abruptly closing the country to direct outside contact for most of the next three centuries.

In the Japanese equivalent of "all roads lead to Rome," the shogun established an interlinking system of five highways, the *gokaido*, emanating from the new capital at Edo. Through the *gokaido*, centralized political control was exercised and a national market economy stimulated.[43] The most famous of the roads, the Tokaido, extended from the eastern capital, Edo, the seat of the shogunate, to the western capital, Kyoto, seat of the Chrysanthemum Throne and the now-marginalized emperor. Traditional Japanese authority had revolved around the triangle of the imperial household, Kyoto, and the imperial shrine at Ise, home of the Sun Goddess, Amaterasu, mythological ancestor of the imperial family. The shoguns set up a competing triangle with the Tokugawa dynasty, its capital at Edo, and the Toshugu Shrine at Nikko. In a telling illustration of the relative power of the two triangles, an imperial envoy was dispatched to ceremonies held at the Toshogu Shrine for 222 years, from 1646 up to the modernizing Meiji Restoration and the end of the shogunate.[44] The Tokugawas sent no comparable mission to Ise.

The road in the eighteenth century was a harmony of theater and function. White-robed pilgrims on their way to Nikko vied with crippled beggars chanting *sutras* for alms from passing merchants. Pairs of taut-muscled *kago* bearers shouldered their passengers in shallow, circular baskets suspended from a long pole borne at either end, the most cost-effective taxi service on the *gokaido* since the shogun banned wheeled vehicles to prevent the arming and feeding of rebel armies. Farmers' wives collecting horse manure to fertilize the fields worked by their husbands bantered with itinerant pot-polishers offering personal contributions. Bald-headed nuns proffered entertainment in exchange for donations to their temple. Wealthy merchants ambled on rented horses in a contented somnolent haze. Musicians strummed on stringed *samisens*, roadside stalls offered sweet dumplings and tea, grilled bream, herring, sweet potato, and dried bonito. At every post station or roadside stop, government notices admonished the populace to lead lives of singular virtue, moderation, and obedience. And with the insolence of impregnable social ascendancy, topknotted, sword-wielding samurai swaggered through the deferentially parting sea of humanity.[45]

The most imposing sight on the road was undoubtedly the processions of daimyos, or great feudal samurai landowners, to and from Edo. The daimyos exercised near absolute control in their fiefs but on a national level were strictly regulated by the shogun. Thirteen articles of law issued by the Tokugawa shogunate regulated matters from castle and road repair to marriage, prescribing clothing to be worn, vehicles to be used, and protocol to be observed by each class. Samurai were instructed to study the arts and literature, refrain from debauchery and conspiracy, live frugally, and promote their retainers on the basis of merit.

Leaving nothing to chance, the shogun instituted the alternate-year residence system.[46] Daimyos were required to spend alternate years in Edo, leaving their wives and children behind as virtual hostages when they returned to the provinces. The resultant flow of retinues to and from Edo, vying for road space, lodging, horses, and carriers, produced feudal-era traffic jams. Daimyo trains of a thousand retainers each, melding security and ostentation, trailed for miles in a moving theater of flag bearers, bowmen, and pikemen, caparisoned horses bearing swordsmen in matching *hakama* (divided skirt), kimono, and *kamishimo* (wide-winged vests) bearing the heraldic symbol of allegiance, followed by clerks, grooms, armor polishers, footmen, sandal bearers, and servant-guards eagerly anticipating perceived offence. The trips, by shogunate design, were ruinously expensive, depriving conspiracy-prone daimyos of the financial resources needed to foment rebellion.

The shogun, his clan, and the 200–300 daimyos throughout Japan constituted the apex of the country's social pyramid. Beneath them in the caste order were the samurai. The *heimin*, next in the order, were the backbone of the Japanese economy: farmers, artisans, and merchants, including the feared *yakuza* and their *oyabun*, or godfather. The lowest caste was the *eta*, those whose livelihoods were considered unclean: butchers, undertakers, gravediggers, and entertainers. Buddhist clerics, physicians, and scholars were casteless but respected; ronin, or masterless samurai, were casteless but feared. Lieutenant Ishizuka's ancestors from Nikko were jizamurai, ranking below "true" samurai but landholders in their own right, like European country squires and poor landed knights. As a distinct caste, the jizamurai virtually disappeared during the shogunate, when they were given the choice of being true samurai or becoming peasants and losing their swords.[47] The Ishizuka family elected the honorable but ultimately impoverishing route of retaining their swords and their oath of selfless fealty to their daimyo, joining the cyclical trek between Nikko and Edo.

10

THE SOLITUDE OF SERVICE

Umberto Eco, in his polymathic *Travels in Hyperreality*, recounts an anecdote of Thomas Aquinas, a physically sluggish, insular, and self-content introvert, being made an object of ridicule by the other friars in the monastery. The playful monks shouted to Thomas that there was an ass flying outside the cloister. As he rushed to the window to see the phenomenon, the amusement-starved monks laughed uproariously. Thomas turned calmly to the mockers and remarked that to him a flying ass had seemed more likely than a monk who would tell a falsehood.[48] In 1940, when Roosevelt won a third term promising not to "send American boys to any foreign wars," it seemed a safer bet that asses would fly than monks would lie or America would emerge from its isolationist cocoon to resplendent world engagement.

Within a year, with adroitness bordering on legerdemain, Roosevelt had maneuvered the American public into mental, if not military, preparedness for the inevitable fight to come. And the American public was readier than it might have thought. In his frank memoir of Marine combat service in the South Pacific, *Goodbye, Darkness*, William Manchester remarks that "to fight WWII you had to have been tempered and strengthened in the 1930s Depression by a struggle for survival—in 1940 two out of every five draftees had been rejected, most of them victims of malnutrition."[49] With only 50 percent of today's population, the country was at once more homogeneous (partly at the expense of racial equality), socially consensual, and tightly disciplined. The integrity of the family was moral keystone. The country's latent

36

potential seemed—and was—as limitless as the vastness of its unoccupied space.

One cannot help being struck, in written accounts of the period or interviews with its participants, by the feeling of a club in which all the members knew one another, at least metaphorically, and while agreeing at times to disagree, even virulently, nonetheless shared behavioral norms and an implicit acceptance of the "rules of the club." It is the same sense of shared destiny and mutual self-sacrifice one finds in accounts of Victorian England. No doubt nostalgia filters retrospection. But near-Herculean feats of endurance and self-abnegation would not have been possible in the absence of societal cohesion, and acquiescence, undreamt of today. Tom Brokaw, in *The Greatest Generation*, captured the essence of the time: "Looking back, I can recall that the grown-ups all seemed to have a sense of purpose that was evident even to someone as young as four, five, or six. Whatever else was happening in our family or neighborhood, there was something greater connecting all of us, in large ways and small...The young Americans of this time constituted a generation birth-marked for greatness...It is a generation of towering achievement and modest demeanor..."[50]

It is remarkable, too, how readily, even anxiously members of all classes accepted combat duty once the country's course was determined. Manchester observed that most members of his Marine squad had been isolationists prior to Pearl Harbor. Unlike the Civil War and Vietnam generations, few availed themselves of wealth, position, connections, or university enrollment to avoid active duty. In a draft with 10 million inductions, serving scions of wealthy families, like alumni of elite Eastern universities, were the rule, not the exception. Two Kennedy brothers, one killed in action, Bush, and many others from the commercial elite; four Roosevelt brothers and the sons of Harry Hopkins, FDR's closest adviser, and Leverett Saltonstall, governor of Massachusetts and later one of the most powerful Republicans in the Senate, all served (Hopkins and Saltonstall were also killed in action). None sought or was given exemption from service.

The expectation of service was strong in most families, including the LaCroixs. My great-great-grandfather served as a Massachusetts volunteer with the Union forces in the Civil War. My grandfather served in France as a combat engineer during the First World War. My future mother's family, the Follmer and Voris clans of Pennsylvania, had begun a tradition of volunteer military service with America's Revolutionary War. That my father and uncles would serve with honor in their conflict was never questioned, even if endorsed less than enthusiastically by my grandmother. Patriotism was not brandished as a badge of distinction; it was simply a state of being, felt rather than articulated. The gut-felt belief in the rectitude of American democracy and institutions provided the bedrock of underlying purpose. And when these same men and women completed their service and won the war, they celebrated briefly and moved on with building lives to all external appearances unaffected by their experiences. They bore in solitude the recollection of events that must have changed them as much as the world they inhabited.

1 1

THE WEFT OF THE FAITHFUL

If the Confucian paternalism of the shogun was the warp binding the layers of the Japanese caste system, religion was the weft. Japan's twentieth-century imperialism was built on the spiritual foundation of state religion.[51] From 701, when the law of the land was first codified, until the end of World War II, religion was managed by successive Japanese governments as a tool of state authority.[52] The shogunate, ever pragmatic, tolerated religious diversity as long as it posed no threat to social stability, defined as the preeminence of Tokugawa authority. Christian converts, always suspect for their foreign alliances, were at first discouraged and then brutally suppressed following an uprising of 30,000 Christians in the early seventeenth century. Various Buddhist sects were also suppressed for exhibiting an unhealthy independence. But where America's founders eschewed from the outset any church-state nexus, the builders of modern Japan adopted a flexibly utilitarian approach. Like Karl Marx centuries later, the shoguns knew well the socially sedating value of mainstream religion.

It is a popular misconception that the Tokugawa shogunate stagnated during centuries of hermitic isolation. Japan's early isolation was imposed by the Dutch, whose control of East Asian waters permitted them to monopolize the growing Japanese trade, not by Japanese policy. And though, in the late stage of the regime, the shoguns did implement a formal policy of isolation (*sakoku*), for long they embraced Western technological advances—with the notable exception of un-samurai-like firearms. Through their familiarity with the Dutch language, the Japanese studied and emulated Western science and medicine. The shogun's edicts restricting Japanese trade to the Dutch and the Chinese in Nagasaki were designed less to restrict trade than to limit the unwelcome influence of Spanish and Portuguese missionaries. Religion then in Japan, as now in China, was subordinate to the dictates of social order. The shogun monitored potentially aberrant behavior by requiring every household to register with a Buddhist temple. Buddhism's passivity was less threatening than the proselytizing aggression of foreign Christianity.[53] As draconian as the controls were, the resulting social stability and economic growth permitted the development of mercantile capitalism, agriculture, and trade, accelerated urbanization, and produced literacy levels above those in Western countries of the period.

Asia in the nineteenth century was a dangerous neighborhood for an insular, less-developed country. By the time the Tokugawa shogunate collapsed in 1868, the new Meiji government was facing the twin threat of expansionist Western powers and internal civil unrest. Much like Thailand's fabled King Mongkut, nominally portrayed in *The King and I*, and his reforming son Chulalongkorn, the Meiji regime attempted to deflect the threats through a combination of reform, modernization (meaning Western emulation), and national cohesion galvanized by a strengthened cultural identity. In Japan's case, the instrument of that reinvigorated identity would be religion. Buddhism, an international religion, was considered insufficiently pliable for the purpose. Homegrown emperor-centered Shinto, however, was well-suited to the purpose, providing the natural symbolic vehicle for consolidating and mobilizing the nation.

In 1868, Shinto and Buddhism were officially separated; the complete removal of Buddhist influence from Shinto shrines was decreed. Shinto priests and institutions were given privileged status and financial support, thereby integrating emperor-centered Shinto beliefs into the power structure. A Department of Shinto Affairs was created, replete with propaganda officials. Ultimately Shinto was identified as a government institution, its priests as government officials, and its value system classified as moral instruction, rather than religious teaching.[54] Conflict with the freedom of religion article in the Meiji constitution was avoided by claiming that state Shinto was not a religion; the fiction of religious tolerance was preserved. Nonetheless, all other religions were either persecuted or subordinated to the cult of emperor worship. In a neat syllogism, all sovereignty and divinity were vested in the emperor; emperor-centered state Shinto was the only true religion; therefore all loyal Japanese followed unquestioningly the edicts of the emperor. Once the ultranationalists co-opted the emperor's authority, the circle closed.

Families like the Ishizukas, however, continued to draw eclectically on the tenets of both Buddhism and Shinto. Long after mandatory registration at a temple was discontinued, the Ishizukas, like many Japanese, maintained links with the original family Buddhist temple. After all, their ancestors' ashes were interred there. During the war, Asian adaptability and the avoidance of direct confrontation permitted Buddhist and even muted Christian worship to persist. Direct challenges to the state religion were dealt with summarily and brutally. Today, Lieutenant Ishizuka's family disclaims any particular religious affiliation but still visits the temple on Buddhist holy days and follows Shinto rituals in everyday observance. Perhaps, to borrow Monique Truong's comment on her fictional Vietnamese family in *The Book of Salt*, being pragmatically Asian, they hedge their bets.[55] The lieutenant's picture, and now his flag, rests in a well-tended Shinto home shrine. The emperor is notable in his absence.

12

THE DIMINISHING LIGHT

In the January 1942 edition of the British humor magazine, *Punch*, a satiric cartoon underlined with a quotation from Kipling's *Jungle Book* pictured Japanese soldiers as small, helmeted monkeys swinging from tree to tree down the Malayan peninsula. Reminiscent of the long-limbed Gauls 2,000 years earlier, who mocked the diminutive Romans from atop supposedly unassailable fixed battlements, the Western Powers indulged the opiating racialist fantasy that height and skin color somehow endowed their possessors with martial invincibility. The lethargy of long-accustomed imperial dominance was lulled by a practiced disdain for the ruled. Still-raw memories of the slaughter and Cadmean victory in the First World War produced pacifist recoil at the prospect of renewed conflict. Hitler had personally penned a detailed roadmap of future German expansion; Japan was no less forthright in its published demands for *Lebensraum*. Yet the blacker the impending eclipse loomed, the more desperately the West clung to an ever-shrinking penumbra of light.

Ishizuka and his comrades fought not simply as well-rehearsed, cult-intoxicated automatons. They battled with the conscious and zealous indignation of aggrieved national honor. Commodore Perry's Black Fleet had forced an opening of Japan in 1853, culminating in the fall of the Tokugawa shogunate and the restoration of the Meiji Emperor fifteen years later. The ensuing wholesale adoption of Western customs and institutions, imported in the spirit of "catching up" with modernity, included aspiration to colonial power status. The 1931 invasion of Manchuria was a marker call at a gaming table to which Japan considered itself an invited player. When the United States and the Western-dominated League of Nations condemned the invasion, Japan walked out of the League, fuming over the perceived double standard of established Western colonialists censuring an aspiring Asian one. Until world war broke out a decade later, the Japanese nursed from incipient resentment to full-blown psychosis their belief in a racially motivated conspiracy to deprive Japan of her deserved significance on the world stage.

Japanese perceptions of Western racism were not without foundation and resonated, at least initially, with many in Asia. In 1919, at the Paris Peace Conference ending World War I, Western countries rejected the simple Japanese request to have a racial equality clause included in the League of Nations Covenant. At the Washington Naval Conference three years later, the United States and Britain imposed on Japan's navy a cap of 60 percent of the shipping tonnage allowed the two Western powers. In 1930, the London Naval Treaty, concluded following Japan's piqued withdrawal, had the practical effect of denying Japan hegemony in its own waters. The affronts to Japanese pride fueled the militaristic and imperialist sentiments of Japanese government leaders and ultranationalists.

The United States was especially culpable in its anti-Asian, and particularly anti-Japanese, behavior. In 1905, the Asiatic Exclusion League was formed in California and lobbied for anti-Asian legislation. In the following year, the school board in San Francisco ordered the segregation of Japanese American students. In 1922, the U.S. Supreme Court declared Japanese immigrants ineligible for naturalized U.S. citizenship. In 1923, the justices upheld Washington and California rulings denying to any Japanese ineligible for citizenship the right to own property. In 1924, the Immigration Exclusion Act (also known as the Oriental Exclusion Act) virtually prohibited further Asian immigration. It also denied further European immigration, but the statute's most prohibitive provisions were directed at Japanese immigrants. If Western racism provided tinder to Japanese militant nationalism, the notion of "ABCD" encirclement provided the match.

The paranoia of "ABCD" encirclement was part pretext and part reality. Western Sturm und Drang over Japan's annexation of Manchuria in 1931, largely ignored by Japan, assumed unavoidably dire economic consequences once Japan launched its full-scale invasion of China in

1937. The "American, British, Chinese, and Dutch" ratcheted up sanctions of increasing severity to force a Japanese withdrawal from China. Abrogating in 1939 a twenty-eight-year-old commercial treaty with Japan to remove the last obstacle to a trade embargo, the United States in July 1940 prohibited the export of oil, aviation fuel, and most machine tools to countries outside the Americas and the British Empire. Following Japan's signing of the Tripartite Pact with Germany and Italy in October 1940, a total embargo was placed on scrap iron and steel. By the winter of 1940–41, one year before Pearl Harbor, shipments of strategic materiel and commodities essential to Japan's war effort had all but ceased: arms, ammunition, aviation fuel, and other petroleum products, machine tools, scrap iron, pig iron, iron and steel manufactures, copper, lead, zinc, aluminum, and other commodities.

The Japanese prevaricated, blustered, but refused to cede ground in China, ignoring the absence of a genuine casus belli. Instead, under "cover" of Germany's invasion of Holland, France, and Belgium in mid-1940, Japan invaded northern Vietnam. By mid-1941, coincident with Germany's invasion of the Soviet Union, Japan occupied all of Indochina. The United States and Britain froze Japanese assets and closed the Panama Canal to Japanese shipping. Oil was totally embargoed, and oil contracts, including those with the Dutch East Indies, were cancelled. By now, Japan had lost 75 percent of its foreign trade and 90 percent of its oil supplies.[56] Even its remaining textile exports were subject to heavy tariffs imposed by the British, Dutch, and Americans.

Iron and oil were matters of life and death; Japan knew it was going to war. It had for years been planning a "southern strategy" to secure resources. Events accelerated during the latter half of 1941. Late in the year, Ishizuka, who had been in action on the Chinese coast and later further inland, returned to Shanghai as part of a general massing of troops for an as-yet unspecified objective. The records do not indicate his unit of deployment at this period, but since his embarkation and destination points are known, it is reasonable to assume that he was deployed with an infantry regiment of the Fifth Division when it sailed south in early December 1941. Less than a month earlier, Lieutenant-General Tomoyuki Yamashita, commander of the Kwantung Army, had been designated commander in chief of the Twenty-fifth Army and placed in charge of all forces assigned to take Malaya and Singapore, the Gibraltar of the East. He would take on the British Empire with the cream of the Imperial Japanese Army: the blooded Fifth Division moving from Shanghai, the Imperial Guards Division from Saigon, and the Eighteenth Division from Canton.[57] As the troops marshaled at Samah Harbor on southern Hainan Island, awaiting Yamashita's orders, speculation was rife: were they headed for the Philippines, Thailand, Borneo—Singapore? The flood approached full surge.

PART III

THE SKY RAINED HEROES

13

UNKNOWABLE FEAR, UNREALIZABLE HOPE

The cause of this war is fundamentally economic. Fifty years ago Japan was more or less self-sufficient—the people could live off the land. Since then the population has almost doubled, so that Japan had to rely on outside sources for food supply and other economic requirements. In order to buy or import her commodities she had to pay ultimately in commodities. This effort on her part was prevented for one reason or another by other countries. Japan made attempts to solve the misunderstandings through peaceful methods, but when all her efforts were thwarted or negated she felt it necessary to engage in open warfare.

—General Tomoyuki Yamashita, The "Tiger of Malaya"[1]

From the crest of Bukit Timah Hill, overlooking the gash of the old granite quarry, across undulating waves of rubber and palm plantations to the red-roofed heart of the colonial city, the impregnable island fortress of Singapore lay open, expectant. Isolated plumes of smoke, the aftermath of aerial bombardment, rose like votive offerings, beseeching the intervention of an indifferent deity. As his men cut the line on the flagpole, sending the huge Union Jack cascading to the ground, Sergeant Ishizuka raised his sword in the air, his men following suit with their bayoneted rifles; in unison, facing east to the emperor, they thundered "Banzai, Banzai, Banzai" and launched into "Kimigayo," the dirge-like national anthem. Their exhilaration was palpable, their momentum unstoppable, their capacities infinite, and Japan's glory limitless. As in China, Hong Kong, Malaya, and now in Singapore, the divine wind of the Imperial Japanese Army would scour the stain of colonial dominance from Asia, the Greater East Asian Co-Prosperity Sphere flowering under the Rising Sun.

It was February 15, 1942, and Ishizuka and his men had spent two months battling down the Malayan peninsula and across the causeway to Singapore. General Yamashita, soon to be the famed Tiger of Malaya, was allotted one hundred days and three divisions to seize a military target exceeded in importance only by Pearl Harbor. Hermann Goering told Yamashita he would need eighteen months and five divisions to do the job. In the event, his Twenty-fifth Army took seventy days with three divisions. Landing in Thailand and Malaysia in perfectly timed concert with the attack on Pearl Harbor, they were to seize the eastern anchor of the British Empire, preempting British reinforcements. Expelling the Western powers from Southeast Asia, Japan would leverage access to the region's oil and other strategic raw materials to secure lasting hegemony over China. Self-sufficiency and Great Power status would erase the humiliating memory of Western economic diktat.

Carrying an average of ninety pounds of gear, excluding weapons, each man in Ishizuka's company was highly trained in the jungle use of bicycles. These bicycle units, with names like "Silver Wheel Unit," captured the imagination of the homefront media. They were the poor man's jungle equivalent of the German armored blitzkrieg—mobile, flexible, and fast. Unlike Thailand, British Malaya had a well-paved road system which Ishizuka and his men used to speed south from their landing point at Kota Bahru in northeastern Malaya toward Singapore. Like Churchill marching with Kitchner down the Nile to Omdurman, the Japanese wore helmets with back flaps to prevent sunstroke. Each company was supported by two mechanics to repair tires blown by the heat of the roads. Spare parts were requisitioned along the way, Japanese bicycles having been a popular local import before the war. In 90 percent humidity and ninety-degree heat, Ishizuka and his men would each lose an average of twenty-two pounds by the time they reached the Causeway.[2]

Racing through Malaya, the three divisions competed for the prestige of entering Singapore first. Duty and historical imperative fed their martial fervor. Bukit Timah (Tin Hill), controlling the key western approaches to the city, was taken on Kigensetsu, the 2,602nd anniversary in an unbroken line of emperors descending from the near-mythical Jimmu.[3] And as the saying went, "who controlled Bukit Timah, controlled Singapore."[4] But Singapore did not fall as readily or as cravenly as popular accounts would have it. British guns were not pointing in the wrong direction, although they were munitioned with high-explosive shells useful only against ships. Despite being poorly led and often equally poorly trained and equipped, Australian, Indian, Chinese, Malay, and British soldiers inflicted heavy losses on the invading Japanese. Yamashita himself later wrote "My attack on Singapore was a bluff—a bluff that worked."[5] Outnumbered three to one, his greatest fear was that he would be drawn into disastrous street fighting.

Japanese hubris and British confusion obscured the fact that neither side at this stage of the war really knew what to expect from the other. Japanese relentlessness partook of the superhuman. An Australian soldier described his first sight of an attacking soldier of Ishizuka's division: "squat, compact figures with coarse puttees, canvas, rubber-soled, web-toed boots, smooth brown hands, heavy black eyebrows across broad foreheads, and ugly battle helmets. Each man wore two belts—one to keep his pants up and one to hold his grenades, his identity disc and his religious charm—and when they removed their helmets, they wore caps, and when they took off their caps, their heads had been shaved until only a harsh black stubble remained. They handled their weapons as if they had been born with them. They were the complete fighting animal."[6] A contemporary historian captured the perceived essence of Japanese military élan, describing Japanese soldiers "as possessing hereditary bravery, having retained the virtues of the barbarian without the defects of civilization."[7]

Allied failure bred similarly exaggerated disdain among the Japanese. A Japanese officer asked rhetorically whether Japanese success was the result of "a mere 'Wild-boar' courage, not to know how to retreat? 'Backrowing' (Sakaro) was ridiculed by the old warriors of Japan...It may be a mistake, but 'to show one's back to the enemy' was always considered the greatest disgrace a samurai could bring upon himself—this idea is the central military principle of the people of Japan."[8] He comments sarcastically of European commanders boasting of "masterly retreats": "[They] do not seem to have gained many victories by their skill in falling back."[9]

The civilian population was transfixed by the twin specters of unknowable fear and unrealizable hope. The Americans were reported to have landed in southern Malaysia. Twenty thousand Chinese soldiers were seen disembarking at the Singapore wharves. One rumor, though, was easily verified: food, fuel, and water grew scarcer as Japanese bombing and strafing intensified. Refugees fled helter-skelter, seeking the illusion of security in the city's concrete public buildings. During surrender negotiations, Yamashita promised to keep regular army units out of the city; maintenance of order would be the responsibility of the Military Police, the feared Kempetai, supported by specially assigned units from his three divisions. Part of Ishizuka's division was assigned garrison duty in the eastern part of the island, guarding more than 50,000 prisoners of war in the soon-to-be notorious Changi Prison, depicted in James Clavell's *King Rat*.[10] The balance of the division was sent north to Kuala Lumpur. It is not known to which sector the sergeant was assigned. Shortly after the surrender of Singapore on February 15, 1942, Ishizuka completed his military term of service and returned to Tokyo. But it is a virtual certainty that prior to his departure he would have participated in the tragedy that played out within days of the British surrender.

14

A Thousand Ghostly Fears

Ghosts, real and imagined, haunt much of Singapore. In 1983 I completed my studies in England and came east to establish a corporate law curriculum at the rapidly expanding National University of Singapore. The university was situated on the crest of Kent Ridge, the site of particularly intense fighting between the attacking Japanese and the famed British Malay Regiment. Following the British capitulation, Japanese troops indulged their singular brand of nation-building, slaughtering en masse thousands of the local populace. Ethnic Chinese supporters of the displaced colonial regime were particularly favored targets. Many of these were interred in mass graves on Kent Ridge and only recently discovered during construction of the new university. The site was now believed to be haunted, inducing a local staff exodus from the premises before dark.

With wanderlust fueled by fortifying dosages of Maugham, Theroux, Orwell, Kipling, Burgess, and Clavell, I had zigzagged my way from London to Cairo, Bombay to Madras, Colombo to Singapore. I emerged from Singapore's Changi Airport into a country emblematic of a region: a roiling, still-in-suspension admixture of pre-war colonial legacy and accretive self-confidence resolving itself into crystalline commercial purpose. My taxi exited the airport onto a manicured palm, frangipani, and bougainvillea-lined six-lane highway with a median strip of massed blooming planters. The kilometers-long hash marks running down the center of the highway on either side of the moveable planters betrayed its secondary purpose: an emergency landing strip designed to accommodate heavy military aircraft. I passed the pre-war colonial bungalow of the Singapore Chinese Millionaires' Club, vestige of an era when Singapore could fit all its Chinese millionaires in a single building. In a few years, the building and its pastoral enclave would be leveled in a deluge of luxury high-rise condominiums as the fronting beach area moved steadily further out to sea in consecutive land reclamations.

Leaving the highway and crossing Beach Road, I traversed street upon street of Chinese, Malay, Indian, and Arab shop houses. Temples, mosques, and churches happily coexisted amidst organized mercantile chaos and its ageless Asian panoply of sights, smells, and sounds: cinnamon, clove, saffron, and nutmeg, rainbows of saris and batik, gaudy 24K gold jewelry, hand-beaten brass and luminous Thai silk, cured leather, woven cane and rattan, street-side solicitors, sides of pork, skewered snake, and charcoal sizzling satay. I emerged from Rochor Road at the Cathay Building, its bilious yellow bulk squatting opposite the new YMCA. The old YMCA, a rusticated Edwardian façade in alternate bands of red brickwork and white plaster, recently razed in an effort to exorcise the ghosts of the past, was the wartime headquarters and torture center of the brutal Japanese secret police, the Kempetai. Next to the Cathay Building, the 100 Steps ascend to Mount Sophia and the Methodist Girls' School. During the war, the Japanese placed severed heads on pikes all along the stairs to deter "aberrant" behavior. The victims' ghosts linger today.

The university provided housing in former British Army officers' quarters in one of several nearby ex-military cantonments. I selected a pre-war bungalow off Alexandra Road, very near the infamous Alexandra Road Hospital. On February 15, 1942, the day the British surrendered Singapore, Japanese troops, infuriated over the unexpectedly stiff resistance, entered the hospital and systematically massacred more than 200 doctors, nurses, patients, and attendants, bayoneting bedridden wounded and the anesthetized on the operating table. For perhaps the most disciplined military force in modern times, the Imperial Army's recurring homicidal spasms remain something of a mystery. Wholesale genocidal atrocities like the rapes of Nanjing and Manila were undoubtedly systematic punishment condoned on-high (precisely how high remains a matter of contention). But the ad hoc psychotic outbursts of individual units and soldiers appear as catharsis, venting the combined stresses of battle, draconian and systematically degrading martial discipline, and the racial vitriol embittering both sides of the Pacific War. Whatever the explanation, there is no justification. It remains an ineffable stain on Japanese history.

My house, it transpired, had belonged to a British officer and his family who were brutally murdered by marauding Japanese troops at the time of the Alexandra Hospital massacre. I was only beginning to sense what Wordsworth had understood so well: "From the body of one guilty deed a thousand ghostly fears and haunting thoughts proceed." But it was not until ten years later, when I married a talented and beautiful Singaporean lawyer whose family had more than its fair share of haunting memories, that I began fully to appreciate the crosscurrents drawing my life closer and closer to that of Sergeant Ishizuka.

15

THE UNBEARABLE LIGHTNESS OF FELICITY

Even by the standards of the diaspora-prone Chinese, the Hakka are singularly peripatetic. Originating in northern China around the Yellow River and making their nomadic way southward in bimillennial migration, the Hakka have been called the Chinese Jews. Fleeing flooding, drought, locust plagues, famines, and wars, the Hakka migrated to survive and preserve intact their defiantly unique cultural heritage. Translated roughly as "guest families," Hakka, like most guests, discovered the warmth of the welcome dissipated in proportion to the length of the stay. Among China's insular, dialect-dominated provinces, the Hakka found temporary respite but not home. Newcomers to territories already occupied, the Hakka were forced to subsist on less-desirable, less-arable land.

Typical of wandering peoples, ostracism and impermanence tempered a durable survival instinct to resilient toughness. Cultural conservatism cohabits in happy paradox with high risk tolerance in the Hakka. It is not by accident that they have produced a disproportionate number of visionary and pragmatic, as well as authoritarian, Chinese leaders, both at home and overseas: Sun Yat-Sen, founder of the Chinese Republic in 1905; Deng Xiaoping, paramount Chinese leader following Mao's death; Lee Kuan Yew, independence leader of Singapore; Lee Teng-hui, former president of Taiwan; and Li Peng, prime minister and prime mover of the Tiananmen Square massacre in 1989. Today, Hakka Chinese claim the widest geographic dispersion of any people in the world.

In 1879, Singapore, a prospering trading center celebrating its sixtieth anniversary as a British crown colony, offered those most precious and, to a Hakka, most elusive enticements: social stability, economic opportunity, and cultural openness—in short, a home. Mirroring the diluvial emigration in the Western world, ethnic Hakka, Fujian, Cantonese, Teochew, and Hainanese flowed in portentous exodus to the relative security and promise of prosperity in Europe's Southeast Asian colonies. My wife's great-grandfather, a Hakka named Loh Choon Leng, was no exception. Like Americans reared during the Great Depression, his formative life experiences had fired him with a dominating passion: a life without the enervating fear of financial want. He sold the family's heirlooms, booked uncertain passage on a tottery vessel through pirate-infested seas, and sailed from southern Fujian province, leaving behind a thousand years of ancestors.

A fellow Chinese émigré to Singapore described philosophically the ingrained Chinese yearning for security and the safe harbor offered in colonial Singapore:

> We Chinese are obsessed by a painful sense of the instability of life, of the fickleness of fortune. The gods are envious of human felicity. 'If a man has blessings, let him not enjoy all; if he has power, let him not use all' expresses this sense of man's insecurity in the world. This sense may give poignancy to our sojourn on earth; it may be the stuff of poetry. But, perverse men that we are, we long for firm ground beneath our feet so that we can stride along confidently and unafraid. To British law we... owed the inestimable blessing of having some firm ground in the quagmire of life. Within the confines of the law...the incalculable did not play so devastatingly with our peace of mind.[11]

The mystical Chinese classic, *I Ching*, or *Book of Changes*, perhaps the world's most ancient book at five thousand years old, advises that "Before the beginning of great brilliance and beauty there first must be a period of complete chaos." The Chinese, dreaming of the former, have endured more of the latter. It is estimated that in the six hundred years after the great Emperor Zhu Yuanzhang founded the effervescent Ming Dynasty in 1368, China endured famine of varying severity in nine out of every ten years. Two thousand years ago, the founding emperor of the Han Dynasty, at wit's end to feed a starving, restive people, issued an edict permitting people to sell or eat their children if necessary.[12]

If life on a physical plane was precarious, political life oscillated from despotic to anarchic. Chinese dynastic politics was based on the mandate of Heaven (*Tianming*). The emperor was the conduit and enforcer of Heaven's commands, being him/herself divine. Heaven manifested approval of an emperor with social order and bountiful harvests, displeasure with famine, drought, plague, and political upheaval. Heavenly displeasure to heavenly abandonment was a short leap. Loss of Heaven's mandate legitimized revolution and the transfer of the mandate to a new ruling house. Yet despite the abundance of interceders with an inside track to the divine, portent divination tended to the subjective. One believer's truth was another's heresy. The foreseeable result was civil strife in perpetuity. Demagogy tends to serve least those whom it espouses most.

The energies of the Chinese, though, are a volcanic force. Political tectonics may for a time repress, channel, or vent the force with artifice, but erupt it will. As in China today, nineteenth-century Southeast Asia ethnic Chinese immigrants, given egress, swept with feature-altering force over the economic landscape of Europe's new colonies. The emergence of a "bamboo network" of family and personal relationships (the touted *quanxi* connections), a shared if clannishly insular culture, and the immigrants' near-religious devotion to material success laid the groundwork of an eventual "greater China co-prosperity sphere,"[13] as Samuel Huntington has termed it. In contrast with the martially inspired and imposed Japanese version, the Chinese co-prosperity sphere's organic growth and extended root structure assure its longevity. The full extent of its contemporary economic and geopolitical significance is even now only faintly discernible.

With the astonishing linguistic and commercial agility characteristic of the overseas Chinese, Loh quickly learned English, navigating adroitly the new waters of colonial Singapore to establish a successful business as a tailor. Despite a racially stratified colonial administration and the squeeze of racketeering Chinese gangsters, the integrity of the bureaucracy and police, the accessibility of a transactional infrastructure, and the rule of law were remarkable departures from the warlord- and corruption-ridden world he had recently departed. As a measure of the distance traveled, his two grandsons entered banking and the colonial administration. The family grew, their endeavors prospered, and their fate became one with Singapore's. And the gods envied their felicity.

16

PAX BRITANNICA, PAX JAPONICA

The extended Loh family, two brothers, their wives and children, and several in-laws, were clustered in the eldest brother's house on Upper Serangoon Road, just above Singapore's Little India. The Lohs viewed the Japanese advance with particular trepidation. The eldest brother, a senior civil servant in the British administration and father of Fook Choon, my future father-in-law, had contributed to the "China Relief Fund," a conduit for funds to China's war effort. By no means rich, the families were sufficiently prosperous to attract notice in the grudge-settling free-for-all invariably attending the collapse of social order. The families' strained effort at Sunday morning normalcy—rice congee, heavily sweetened coffee, pork floss *baos*, and a studied avoidance of the war as conversation topic—was cut short by the urgent whine of the air raid siren. As adults and children rushed for cover under the large staircase next to the dining room, the ornate colonial building across the street exploded. A favorite uncle, herding the children to safety, was crushed to death as the shock wave pancaked a portion of the heavily timbered second floor.

For the previous week, the family had watched their world collapse amid mounting disorder. At the nearby KK Women's and Children's Hospital, teenage Loh Fook Choon and his elder brother Loh Tong Seng saw mounds of corpses—soldiers, civilians, women, children—through the open doors, a novelty to which they became quickly inured. They watched beturbaned Sikh soldiers throwing their uniforms and arms into the massive monsoon drains along Bukit Timah Road and demoralized Tommies straggling exhausted into the Cathay Building, a frightening acknowledgment of looming defeat. They peered from bolt-holes carved out of bomb rubble as air raid wardens, patrolling the cleared streets, looted abandoned homes before sounding the "All Clear" siren. Malay neighbors with whom the Lohs had lived in harmony all their lives were rumored to be spying for the Japanese. Most terrifying of all were the stories, whispered by recent Chinese émigrés to the boys' parents, of appalling massacres by Japanese occupation armies in China.

The occupation's beginnings were inauspicious for Singapore's ethnic Chinese. Representatives of each of the city-state's ethnic communities were sent to Bukit Timah to greet the conquerors. The Chinese were not represented; their leaders, known to have supported the China Relief Fund, were viewed as anti-Japanese and opted for a low profile. It was to be of little avail. Although all suffered in the immediate aftermath of the surrender, the Chinese were singled out for particular attention. Requisitioning of cars and bicycles and the looting to be expected from an occupying army certainly took place. Raping varied in intensity, depending on the character of the commanding officer. The area of the city occupied by the Loh family was fortunate in this regard. Slapping, beatings, and ingenious forms of humiliation were visited on the Chinese; the Indians and Malays, whose support the Japanese hoped for, were treated relatively better. Chinese girls and women were rounded up throughout the island, each marked with a tag in Chinese: "For Military Use."

Word of the surrender spread quickly. On Monday morning the brothers hiked to the colonial heart of the city, the large grassy Padang fronting the Cricket Club between the ocean and the imposing edifice of the Supreme Court Building. Anyone who has lived under a martial law regime will attest to the chilling, disembodied sound of rhythmically tramping massed troops and metallically clanking mechanized armor. With fear and wonder, the boys watched the column of Japanese troops round the bend near Victoria Hall, their bayonets still fixed on shouldered rifles, here and there a soldier's broad smile contrasting with the surrounding sea of impassivity. Many of the spectators, adapting to the new tide of affairs, waved small Japanese flags sewn for the occasion. The boys marveled that grown men not much larger than they were had defeated the tall white men whom they had always considered inviolable.

On February 18, 1942, three days after the British surrender of Singapore, General Yamashita's Twenty-fifth Army Headquarters issued orders to purge anti-Japanese Overseas Chinese in Peninsular Malaya and Singapore. The orders made no distinction between Straits-born Chinese (i.e., those born in Singapore, Malacca, and Penang) and recently emigrated native-born Chinese. Rather, they targeted identifiable groups of Chinese:[14]

- Any involved with the China Relief Fund,
- Rich men, who were *ipso facto* contributors to the Relief Fund,
- Journalists, school masters, and high school students,
- All natives of Hainan Island, categorized by the Japanese as without exception Communists,
- All volunteers to the British forces,
- Government servants and Justices of the Peace,
- Any Chinese of less than five years residence (who were assumed to have left China from anti-Japanese sentiment).

Singapore's 700,000 Chinese were herded into makeshift concentration camps where the haphazard process of selection took place over a period of days. Japanese officers standing in staff cars and holding long bamboo poles would signal a selection with a whack on the head of the unfortunate victim. Japanese suspicions were fueled to paranoia by local informers, in particular the ethnic Chinese Formosans (later Taiwanese), most saving their own skin at the expense of their neighbors. The detained, generally between the ages of twelve and twenty-eight, were segregated, trucked to beaches where Changi Airport stands today, tied together in groups of eight or ten with disused telephone wire, machine gunned and bayoneted, and buried in shallow trenches or consigned to the currents with the other flotsam of war. For weeks after, residents and refugees on Singapore's outer islands found clusters of mutilated bodies washed ashore.

Bad news wrought worse for the Loh family. Shortly after the death of the uncle in the Serangoon bombing, the family received word that another uncle had been killed in the intense fighting at Kent Ridge. Professionals and volunteers alike fought bravely but they were no match for the battle-hardened men of Ishizuka's army. Then, on Thursday, came the notice: "Those Overseas Chinese residing on [Singapore] between the ages of 18 and 50, must assemble on 21 February at [locations listed]… Those who violate this order will be punished severely. You should prepare your own provisions and drinks."[15] The announcement was signed by "The Military Commander of Great Japan." With apprehension, the family assembled at their designated location. After sweltering for four days under the tropical sun, the boys' father, following a brief, brusque interview, received the dreaded whack of the bamboo pole. His administrative skills saved him, after a fashion. Rather than board a truck for the terminal trip to Changi, he was herded onto a train headed for Thailand. For the next three years he would work on the Siam-Burma railroad, the infamous "Bridge on the River Kwai," and survive to tell the tale.[16]

The family was bereft of breadwinners. One brother found a job at the central city Cold Storage food market. Fook Choon joined a manual laborers' crew at the Harbor Board. Their mother took a part-time job in a gambling stall. All learned quickly the tenor of the New Order. On his first day at work, Fook Choon, passing through the front gate, was hauled up short by a Japanese corporal and slapped four times for failing to bow to the proper depth. He considered himself lucky; earlier that morning a similarly negligent malefactor was tied to a tree and beaten senseless with a sergeant's sword scabbard. The elder brother, later the same week, was summoned by management to an employee meeting where a friend and co-worker was paraded in front of the assemblage by three Japanese guards and then forced to his knees and beheaded. He had stolen rice to feed his family. The Lohs subsisted on palm oil bread and tapioca and most soon suffered from beriberi.

———————

The Japanese now committed the second great blunder of their new occupation, close on the heels of the Chinese massacres. Japanese fury over the unquenchable resistance in China, kept alive by a steady flow of funds and arms from the overseas Chinese community, as well as from Americans sympathetic to the eloquent, impassioned pleas of Madame

Chiang Kai-Shek, shifted emphasis from murder to extortion. As an act of repentance and retribution for their anti-Japanese activities, the Chinese were instructed to make a gesture of goodwill to the new military authority. Against a backdrop of ongoing executions and all-too audible torture at the central YMCA, the Chinese community was cowed into issuing the following public statement:

> In the past we were running-dogs of British imperialism. We wronged the Japanese and helped Chiang Kai-Shek in his criminal resistance to Japan. We now see the error of our ways and heartily repent. We pledge our support to the Military Administration. Of our own free will we offer the sum of 50 million dollars as token of sincerity.[17]

Every Chinese property owner was "assessed" 8 percent of the accepted value of his/her property. With their primary breadwinners either dead or in prison, the Lohs were in the unenviable position of having to sell property to make the assessment. The Formosans, working in tandem with the Japanese, acquired the land with newly issued Japanese currency at well under fair market value. By the time the war ended, the Lohs and many families like them had exchanged scarce land for now-worthless currency.

The Japanese understood well the deterrent value of fear and were unstinting martinets. Because of the father's established links to the China Relief Fund, the family was closely watched throughout the years of the occupation. Twice, Fook Choon's elder brother, Tong Seng, was arrested by the Kempetai and taken to the notorious YMCA. Understandably terrified, his questioning during his first arrest involved nothing more brutal than continuous slapping, a favorite Japanese technique of humiliation. Throughout the interrogation, he could hear the screams of torture victims in the back rooms. His second arrest, on suspicion of participating in a rice smuggling ring, resulted in a visit to the back rooms. For two days, he was subjected at varying intervals to the infamous water torture. He was eventually released, a remarkable piece of good luck. Today he laughs off the incident but admits that at the time he expected his head to end up on the 100 Steps.

The Japanese penchant for slapping was matched by a predilection for beheading, normally in public with the heads left on display as a deterrent to non-conformity. The simple savagery of the tactic, effective as far as it went, was ultimately counterproductive. Although crime in Singapore virtually disappeared during the Japanese occupation, initial pride in the remarkable successes of an Asian power was quickly displaced by disgust, embarrassment, and soon thereafter, unalloyed hatred. One Singaporean, writing of his "fellow-Asiatics'…failure to display generosity, magnanimity, and chivalry in the day of their triumph," quotes Montaigne's comment on the Germans: "Cursed be these men: for they know neither pity nor honour."[18] The enduring legacy is such that when my future wife attended the Methodist Girls' School on Mount Sophia, at the top of the 100 Steps, in the 1980s, students refused to use the most direct means down the hill, as ghosts, however imaginary, gave rise to very real terror.

As humorless as were the occupiers, the very gravity of the times gave rise on occasion to perverse levity. Passing a restaurant in Chinatown, Fook Choon was startled to see patrons leaping helter-skelter from the first-floor windows. A Japanese officer, drunk on mao-tai jiu, a strong sorghum-based distilled liquor, had taken exception to his dinner companions, drawn his long sword, and waded into the assembled patrons. Miraculously no one was injured, other than some sprains from the jump. The Kempetai materialized and charged the building while the enraged officer continued to lay waste to the now-empty restaurant. The crowd watched incredulously as the Kempetai emerged with a heavily beaten officer meekly in tow. Apparently what was good for the goose was good for the gander.

The genuinely admirable honesty of the Japanese in relation to personal property, at least in peacetime, was humorously reflected in a published account of a series of light bulb thefts in an occupation-period government office. The employees were mustered and lectured by their Japanese overseer in English, the authorities having despaired of enforcing a Japanese language-only regime: "You know how serious is stolen to the Japanese. Five electrical globular objects lost in two consecutive nights in succession. We must now finger-print your five fingers in both hands. Very sorry to do this. But in Japan no stolen. We open doors at night."[19]

While some 50,000 overseas Chinese were being massacred in Singapore and Malaya, General Yamashita delivered a speech to the representatives of the Overseas Chinese Association. Discoursing at length on the causes of the war, he extolled the moral and spiritual ascendancy of the Japanese race, virtues reflecting their lineage as descendants of the gods. The Europeans, in contrast, were monkeys, a fact demonstrated conclusively by Darwin. It required no great intelligence to postulate the winner in a war between gods and monkeys.[20] Whatever the objective historical and economic roots of the Pacific War, the ease with which all participants fell into racial caricature compounded the "gall of bitterness" with the "bond of iniquity."[21] Only the Nazi treatment of *Untermenschen* in Germany and its occupied territories could rival the resulting dehumanization of man-made conflict.

The self-perpetuating force of the war's racism was thrust on me early in my stay in Singapore. Walking arm-in-arm down Armenian Street with Eiko, a tall, light-complected Japanese flight attendant, we approached a group of Chinese men sitting on a low wall fronting the old colonial school. Dressed in sleeveless T-shirts, shorts, and zoris, the men's advanced age belied the early end the medical profession promises chain-smokers of filterless Indonesian clove cigarettes. They were gesturing, laughing, and arguing full throttle in Fujian. On seeing us, they abruptly grew silent. With a baleful look, one of the men half-spat, half-spoke an epithet clearly directed at Eiko. The imprecation dripped venom but before it fully registered another of the men throttled the appalling mucous-harvesting roll of the throat Paul Theroux has termed "the Call of the East" and spewed a huge glob at Eiko, which landed on her ankle.

The insult was a bolt from a sunny sky. Speaking no Chinese and immersed in conversation, Eiko was flummoxed. She would have been none the wiser fathoming motive. Very few of Japan's post-war generation have any inkling of their country's wartime misdeeds in occupied territories, school curricula offering up a watery gruel of sanitized, feel-good history. Even less could she have imagined that a half-century after the war a cadre of avuncular mahjong players held her responsible. I was apoplectic, but battering a bunch of bitter old racists, gratifying though it might be, was hardly the stuff of chivalry. I counter-attacked with my limited array of Cantonese curses, the dialect being well-suited for the purpose, and shuttled Eiko around the corner to a consoling bowl of noodle soup. We could explore later what manner of ghosts peopled a world of hate as enduring as this.

The irony in this instance was double. It is an observable fact that demographic variations in diet are reflected in contrasts of physique and disposition. The warrior Sikh and Rajput farmers of northwestern India, fed on a diet of whole meal chapattis, stand in marked contrast to their more diminutive, and less martial, southern rice-fed countrymen. The Han Chinese, rising in the temperate wheat-growing northern valley of the Yellow River, expanded south to conquer the sub-tropical rice-growing Yangtze River valley. Northern Chinese, the mainstay of elite units of the People's Liberation Army, are fed on a millet- and wheat-based diet and overhang their rice-consuming Cantonese and Fujian cousins from the south. The majority Japanese, ethnic Yayoi, are descended from Chinese-Mongolian stock and with a traditional diet of rice and fish tend toward the blunter features and shorter stature of Western stereotypes. Yet on the northern Japanese island of Hokkaido, indigenous Ainu, bred historically on a meat-dominant diet of bear, fox, wolf, ox, and horse, display contrastingly tall, light-complected, high nose-bridged features. Eiko was a particularly striking example of the racial intermixing of the Ainu and the Yayoi.

The Ainu are a Japanese irony. With their Caucasoid features and un-Japanese body hair, they have traditionally been an ostracized and marginalized minority in conformist-obsessed Japan. While their origins are a mystery, recent work by a respected University of Michigan anthropologist indicates that the Ainu, a warlike people, established such power and prestige in medieval Japan that they intermarried with Japanese nobility and royalty, passing Ainu blood and features to the upper classes, in particular the samurai. He believes this explains why features of the Japanese ruling class are so unlike those of typical modern Japanese.[22] Other anthropologists suspect the Japanese practice of "white-face" so common in, for example, Kabuki theater, originates from the medieval period as a way of emulating the "royals." The implications in race-conscious Japan are unsettling. As one Japanese anthropologist commented to his American colleague, "I hope you are wrong."[23] Predictably the findings have been hijacked by Aryan fringe groups in the West, seeking to find in commonality one more excuse for individuation.

Chinese, Malay, and Indian survivors of the occupation of Singapore, none Japanese sympathizers, often told me that the Japanese squandered fecklessly the moral, military, and political advantage they gained with many Asians by the conquest of Malaya and Singapore. A former Kempetai officer in Singapore, quoted in Henry Frie's *Guns of February*, admits as much in his memoirs: "We lost this war already [following the massacres] as far as morality was concerned."[24] N. I. Low, in his firsthand account of the occupation years, offers a rather more nuanced conclusion: "The Nip was as inscrutable as fate and as incalculable as a thunderclap. And yet he was surprised that he was not a great success in the winning of hearts…There were times, however, when I felt that I could forgive the Japanese a great deal if they…could only smile at their own posturing, if they showed any sign of realizing the ludicrous discrepancy between their pretensions and their actual performance— the mountain making so great a fuss to bring forth so small a mouse."[25]

Commenting on the massacres and the Japanese occupation in general, he noted that "hatred was generated in the hearts of many of us, not against the Nips only, but also against our own people."[26] Locals of all races displayed willingness, even eagerness, to enter into a Faustian bargain with the Japanese. Of a local Malay policeman cooperating with the Kempetai to torture a suspect, an Indian merchant trafficking with Japanese officers at the expense of starving neighbors, or a fellow Chinese pointing out homes of beautiful young girls to be impressed into military brothels, he first concludes that they were free agents, not simply men responding to orders. But on retrospection he finds "It is as easy to get up a rage…as it is to get up a thirst. But, placed in the same circumstances, are there any of us who would have behaved differently? The system was to blame, not the individuals caught in it."[27] And if he were to choose between systems, "The Pax Japonica, we realized, was far inferior to the Pax Britannica we had known in the days of plenitude and peace."[28] But not all suffered equally under the new Pax Japonica.

17

YIN AND YANG UNITED

Crossing the Singapore-Malaysia causeway before dawn, I arrived at my newly commissioned factory in the outskirts of Johor as the enveloping jungle mist fled before light's first advance. An apt metaphor for my investment, I mused. The factory security guards, normally hearty in their "*Salamat Pagi, Tuan*," nodded glumly. Approaching my office at the back of the large production floor, I saw through the glass-fronted reception area, slouched defiantly in my desk chair, a malevolent muffin: soulless raisin eyes glowering from the vascular dough of a voluptuary's face. I knew him to be a mid-level gangster, an enforcer with the local Chinese triad society, named Siew Yap Chuck or, to his constituents in his absence, "Fat Fuck" or "FF." We were locked in a battle of "face."

"Get your fat ass out of my chair," I said, playing to the watching audience of Malay, Chinese, Indian, and Thai workers. In the circumstances, conciliation would be perceived as terminal weakness.

"You pay or you no got chair, maybe you no got factory, *quai loh*," he sneered menacingly. The irony of an ethnic Chinese in Malaysia calling me a foreign devil grated, as FF no doubt knew.

"I told you before; I deal only with the Shan Chu (literally "Mountain Master"—the Boss). You wanna talk, you set up a meeting with the Dragon Head. Now get the hell out of here." I gambled on knowing the limit to my friend's patience—a foreigner would be excused transgressions fatal to a local, up to a point. Our sparring had up to now been verbal, or at least guttural, and I hoped to keep it that way.

The thug scanned me with the delicious disdain of one used to dispensing and withdrawing at will another's right to exist. If men are made in God's likeness, this specimen was evident proof that even the Almighty would benefit from periodic anger management. A purposeless slab of flesh he might seem, his being was my bane. His entire demeanor exuded the hovering, barely repressed violence that was the stock-in-trade of the triads. As an acknowledged Tai Chi master, he was a jackhammer in repose. I had witnessed him, standing flat-footed and face-to-face with a 200-pound cinderblock of a Chinese construction worker, thrust his open-palmed hand into the man's solar plexis, sending the crumpled victim sprawling, gasping for breath. Tai Chi had more lethal applications than the circulatory stimulation of octogenarians in the local park.

Nearly a year earlier I had left the law faculty at the National University of Singapore and bought out a small Australian manufacturer for which I had been consulting. The company had developed a proprietary production process for silica-coated roofing products used in low-cost housing of the Habitat for Humanity variety. Labor problems at the Adelaide factory, combined with prohibitive transport costs to Asia, were draining the company, and the Australian owners had had their fill. I negotiated with the Malaysian Industrial Development Authority for a special incentive zone site, essentially jungle and a promise of future infrastructure, closed the Australian factory, and moved the plant to Johor Bahru. Saul's conversion on the road to Damascus was nothing like as abrupt as my education.

Though they generally limit their extortion to the Chinese community, my Johor operation, with its predominantly Chinese management and isolated jungle site, had apparently attracted the local triads' attention. Their initial overtures were community-spirited enough: a regularized financial contribution scheme would ensure uninterrupted operations of an important local employer. My managers deferred to me, and I demurred to the triads. This created some displeasure. The threat behind the smile gave way simply to the threat. I arrived one morning to find vertical scorch marks running the length of the factory's front and back walls. FF's enforcers had tried to torch the place; the factory was made of asbestos. Shortly after, working through a graveyard shift, I emerged from the factory to find my car's tires slashed. FF oozed in the next day, commiserating over the deplorable xenophobic propensities of the Malay.

The Mr. Smith naiveté of my expressed resolve to my staff "not to deal with gangster scum" soon produced unintended fruits. I had presumed that cavalier dismissal, conveyed with a seeming indifference to consequences, would induce a hasty retreat to less obstinate targets. This was, as Dean Acheson has written of Gallic logic, "an erroneous conclusion deduced from an erroneous premise."[29] Failing to dislodge either the factory or my resistance, the triads shrewdly decided to waylay individual workers. The beatings were not excessively brutal, but they didn't need to be. By selecting a worker from each ethnic group—Chinese, Tamil, and Thai (the Malays were exempted to avoid attracting unwelcome official attention)—they created such terror that I couldn't lure a worker within shouting distance of the factory. My suicidal instincts were my own affair; my workers were in this for a paycheck and the ability to spend it, not the expression of some higher moral purpose. I could pack or parley. The question was with whom I would parley—the point on which FF and I had so far agreed to disagree.

My dilemma lay in the structure of a triad society. Unlike the Italian Mafia or Japanese Yakuza, both monolithic organizations with centralized authority and a rigid chain of command, the triads are loose-knit gangs with diffused power bases and a horizontal, modern, corporate organization. When a Mafia or Yakuza thug demands something, you may be fairly certain he speaks for "the" organization. When a triad demands something, it is useful to know where in the food chain the predator fits. Multiple gangs may be in competition for the same turf; a given enforcer, though generally autonomous, may have neglected his obeisance, prompting an aggrieved higher-up to hold the payer accountable for misdirected payments. Paying a predator too far down the pecking order is fattening the goat to attract the lion; you end up as collateral damage. I knew I would pay; my concerns were how much and to whom. My insistence on a more senior-level meeting was a serious affront to FF's face.

In biological terms, triads are highly evolved ectoparasites. They attach to and feed off, without killing, the host, at least until their own life cycle has been completed or a preferable host found, the latter defined as one permitting the parasite to feed through several generations. A cultural anthropologist—or an evolutionary biologist—would marvel at their adaptive mutability as they have spread, primarily from southern China, to host communities spanning the globe. The Red Queen hypothesis states that organisms struggle constantly to keep up in an evolutionary race between predator and prey, and the triads are perfect examples. They have perfected a Hobbesian social model of singular efficiency, internalizing the principle that order is founded on organized coercion—the same despotic dominance behavioralists have observed in communities of macaques.

The triads originated in the mid-seventeenth century as secret political societies formed to reinstate the "native" Han Chinese Ming Dynasty after its overthrow by the "foreign" Qing Dynasty, the Manchus, from Manchuria in northern China. The term "triad" was coined by the British to describe the sacred symbol of the secret societies, a triangle containing the Chinese character "Hung," representing the union of heaven, earth, and man. "Hung" is a homonym for the Chinese word for "brave" but was also the family name of the Ming emperors.[30] The Hung League, in its earliest incarnation, was a protector of the people against a repressive Manchu regime, but eventually exploited its secrecy and martial arts skills for criminal ends. Today, it is considered the original triad society on which modern-day gangs model themselves.

In China, the Hung societies worked actively to undermine the Qing Dynasty, playing pivotal roles in a number of bloody rebellions, including the nineteenth century Taiping and Boxer Rebellions, both crushed with the support of the Western colonial powers. The triads supported Sun Yat-sen in his successful republican revolution of 1911 and later fought the Communists with Chiang Kai-Shek, himself closely linked with Shanghai's secret society. In Southeast Asia the triads spread their tentacles from the tin mines of Malaya throughout the burgeoning commerce of the ethnic Chinese community. The early preeminence of the Cantonese in triad activity was, by the time Loh Choon Leng arrived in Singapore, largely supplanted by Hakka immigrants, although competition was frequently violent. Presaging their later structure in the United States and Canada, triad links with Chinese merchant associations, or "Tongs," meant that the lines between legal and illegal activities often blurred. In exchange for "fraternal" support, representation, and protection, legitimate businessmen such as Loh paid dues or "taxes." To a recent immigrant in an alien environment, the security purchased was money well-spent.[31]

The Second World War represented an evolutionary leap forward for the triads. With the indestructibility of a virus, they adapted to the Japanese occupation of Singapore, Kuala Lumpur, Hong Kong, and the cities of China by offering their unique skills to the new conquerors. Utilizing front companies, the Japanese organized criminal enterprises managed by the triads. Beyond their "traditional" functions—extortion, protection, prostitution, gambling, and the like—the triads policed the local population and suppressed anti-Japanese behavior, a catch-all category under whose heading crimes from grudge reprisals to simple opportunistic theft took place. The triads completed their transformation from protector of the prey to predatory cohort.

As my factory operations came to a virtual halt, still I held out. A craven collapse would only engender later, and greater, demands. I padlocked the factory gate, leaving word for FF that his unreasonable demands left me no choice but to close the plant and relocate it overseas. I calculated his embarrassment over losing a potential "client" would eclipse the chagrin of admitting to superior authority. Three days later my Chinese foreman called: FF "requested" my attendance at a dinner in Johor Bahru the following Friday. The dinner would be held at a sprawling Cantonese Chinese restaurant overlooking the Straits of Johor, within hailing distance of the Sultan's palace from which General Yamashita had watched Sergeant Ishizuka's division cross into Singapore. The restaurant was well-known to me—a popular, highly visible venue owned by five Chinese brothers and named, evocatively, "Jaws Five."

Chinese dinners are invariably group affairs, and I expected to have company. I was nonetheless taken aback when I arrived to find nine baleful-looking Chinese men seated in silence around a dining table in a private room at the back of the restaurant. I was motioned to a seat between FF and an older man to whom the others kowtowed but to whom, along with the rest of the table, I was never introduced. My salutation and proffered hand were reciprocated with an unsmiling grunt. The rest of the table stared opaquely. Tea and food came and were consumed in absolute silence: mobsters' cloaca in monkish cloister. The table cleared, it was down to business.

A bottle of Hennessy X.O., ten glasses, water, and a bucket of ice were placed in the center of the table. The Cantonese water their brandy but compensate by drinking their brandy like water. While pouring, FF launched the evening's first conversation with a genial overture. "You like brandy, Mr. Rick? We Chinese drink good brandy—X.O., best quality." The sound X.O. is similar to the Chinese word for "best quality," a fact the manufacturer uses in its advertising. Without waiting for a response, he pushed the water, ice, and three ounces of brandy at me, and in perfect synchronization the entire table, without a smile, shouted "*Gom bui*" and bottomed their glasses. Still, the enigmatic figure on my left said nothing, betrayed nothing. Reaching across me, FF refilled his glass, then mine, then his own, finally passing the bottle around the table. Another bottle arrived silently.

"You got good factory, Mr. Rick. Good product. You very smart: you put American and Chinese together. Chinese best to make money; Americans good organization. Yin and yang very, very good. You make lot of money."

"I'm not making any money right now." Pause, another "dry the cup." Another refill.

By now, eight of the nine Chinese were glowing red; only the Sphinx on my left retained his original color. The drinking was rhythmic, a pendular swing of glass to mouth, pause, gulp, back to table, never slackening, never quickening. Some of the men's expressions had softened from Siena marble to fired clay, but only FF spoke.

"You know, Mr. Rick, Asia not same as Europe." Europe was the generic land from which all white people came. "Asia have different customs, many different habits. We Chinese very old history. You know Middle Kingdom? For very long time Chinese people suffer—no food, wars, people lose everything. Europeans, Japanese, everyone take from Chinese. Chinese lose face. No one protect Chinese." Two or three of the men started to sag in their chairs, the rest slowly glazing. FF's soliloquy rolled on while I marveled at the rigid, unblinking, intimidating self-control of the boss on my left.

FF came to the point. "Chinese need protection against all enemies. We help Chinese families find security. Security very important to Chinese peoples. We must find monies to help all Chinese peoples."

Clearly I had missed the point. I was being asked to tithe to a benevolent philanthropic society. "I am already helping Chinese families by paying them to work at my factory. I don't have any extra money to pay for other support. If I have to pay extra money, I will not be able to pay these people to keep working. You don't want to jeopardize their security, do you?" My companion on the left fidgeted almost imperceptibly.

FF pointed to a miniature mandarin orange tree adjacent the small Buddhist shrine at the side of the restaurant. "Mr. Rick, you know lot about Chinese customs. We Chinese very superstitious. No person have good luck unless make offerings to ancestors. Lunar New Year most important time of offer to Chinese. In seventh month Chinese must make offer for hungry ghosts. No offer very bad luck." I took the opening; it wasn't likely to be offered again.

"We Americans also believe it is important to honor our ancestors. We visit the graveyard and place flowers at the grave. It is important to remember. Perhaps I could help to honor the ancestors of my employees at the New Year and during the Hungry Ghost Month. This would also be very good for the morale of my employees." FF broke into his version of a broad smile, essentially a fissure induced by unseen stresses. The Boss without more stood up to depart. His nearly comatose minions grunted and groaned to their feet to surround him as they poured out the door into two waiting raven-black Mercedes and roared off. FF nodded and followed them out. I was left alone. I had a drink.

For the next two years, until I sold the factory, FF appeared religiously on the eve of the agreed occasions to collect a small red envelope containing the fruits of our hard-fought truce. Each time, I recalled an account I had read of an inscription in a notorious triad meeting hall in Singapore: "Yin and Yang united produce everything by metamorphosis." Necessity, opportunity, adaptation, survival: it was not only the triads who found their evolutionary pace quickened by the exigencies of war.

18

SYMPHONIE IMPROVISATION

The century of aeroplanes has a right to its own music. As there are no precedents, I must create anew.

—Claude Debussy

Some predators are instinctive, some incipient awaiting a nudge, others deeply latent. For some the hunt is passion, for others a vocation, yet for others an avocation. U.S. military combat training at the outset of the Second World War, calibrated for peacetime inertia and years behind the perfected martial mills of Germany and Japan, catapulted from cottage industry to conquering juggernaut with astonishing speed. The somewhat ramshackle footpath connecting American foreign and military policy was transformed within a few years to spanning, metalled imperial boulevard. The avocation of killing acquired a professional pedigree, replete with the sophisticated training of any other serious vocation. And in all areas of the war effort, the laxity of form and precedent that served in peacetime was supplanted by rigorous adaptive improvisation.

If the Second World War was the apotheosis of age-old nation-state competition gone awry, the methods of its execution, particularly in the novel reliance on air power, were without precedent. The complexity and magnitude of a two-theater war created unprecedented demands on national systems of production, logistics, and training, all under the compressed, unforgiving conditions of total war. As in the emergence of a new musical form, minor tinkering with long-established rules of composition was inadequate to address the needs of a new era; demonstrated inadequacy yielded to wholesale reinvention. Only a maestro of the caliber of General George C. Marshall could have produced seamless textural unity from innovation amidst the disharmonies of early failure.

A man as remarkable for his integrity and humility as for his talent, Marshall was appointed Army chief of staff by Roosevelt in the autumn of 1939. Over the next six years until his resignation as General of the Army in late 1945, Marshall oversaw the expansion of the U.S. Army, including the Air Corps, from 200,000 to 8.5 million soldiers. No less remarkably, he oversaw the Herculean production and procurement effort required to support what one author has termed the first example of "technological warfare on a global scale."[32] Relying on a blueprint called the Army Supply Program, the Army Service Forces bought, stored, and distributed the Army's equipment and supplies in a program involving over 600,000 prime contractors, untold numbers of subcontractors, and a budget exceeding $68 billion.[33] As one West Point historian has written, "his character and accomplishments are so exceptional that he is regularly placed in the company of George Washington when parallels are sought."[34] Yet his humility was such that his 1943 summary of military operations was written without a single use of the first-person pronoun.

Serving after the war as Secretary of State and later as Secretary of Defense, Marshall is best remembered for his namesake plan to resurrect economically prostrate Europe, for which in part he became the only professional soldier to receive the Nobel Prize for Peace. However his most enduring American legacy must be his abiding devotion to the subordination of military to civilian authority. Marshall wrote that "[The American Armed Forces] have a great asset and that is that our people, our countrymen, do not distrust us and do not fear us. They don't harbor any ideas that we intend to alter the government of our country or the nature of this government in any way. This is a sacred trust...We are completely devoted, we are a member of a priesthood really, the sole purpose of which is to defend the republic...I don't want to do anything...to damage the high regard in which professional soldiers in the Army are held by our people..."[35] As *Time* magazine wrote in naming him "Man of the Year" in 1943, "American democracy is the stuff Marshall is made of...[he is] the *civis Americanus*."[36]

Marshall's orchestration of massed troop and aviator training in the midst of an unprepared-for two-theater war was one more example of adaptive genius surmounting near-impossible logistical hurdles.

THE FIRST MOVEMENT—ALLEGRO IN SONATA FORM

Exposition–The Rhythmic Theme

In June 1942, Cornell ROTC-trained Second Lieutenant Robert LaCroix enlisted in the Army and was assigned, in cadence with his Cornell engineering training, to the Material Center, Experimental Engineering Section, Aircraft Laboratory, Wright Field in Dayton, Ohio.

June 21, 1942
Wright Field

Dear Mother and Dad,

I reported for work on Friday morning and was assigned to the aerodynamics lab for work on performance of army planes. However, most of the men in that section were MIT men who had had four years training in just that line, whereas I had had only three short courses on that type of work. I therefore decided that was not the place for me and talked my way into something that...has a definite future: jet propulsion, more commonly known as rocket ships...I am very lucky to get into this...It is a subject that very little is known about, and it is a subject that has numerous applications—applications that are beyond the reach of present day devices...[T]he more I get into it, the more I...realize its possibilities, either in military or civil life. It is, however, a subject which is in the same stage that the automobile was in about 1905, or the airplane about 1911.

Bob

July 12, 1942
Wright Field

Dear Mother and Dad,

I am getting a lot of practical application of straight engineering design...I have been able to learn...about materials such as steel and alloys, about valves, test apparatus and correlating the work in the drawing room with the work in the shop...

The rocket unit is something that is very vitally needed at this time by our forces. The Germans have had a rocket unit for several years, but our country didn't discover that we needed it until we tried, under war conditions, to increase both the bomb load and the range of the flight. This can be accomplished only by increasing the length of take-off to impossible lengths, or by using some such unit as the rocket to speed up acceleration during take-off.

The rocketry research conducted by the U.S. military during World War II, although years behind Germany's, laid the foundation for future rocket and missile development programs. The emphasis during the war was on Jet-Assisted Take-Off (JATO) units and missile test articles. Fuel was a particularly thorny issue. Working with private contractors, the U.S. Army Air Corps evaluated a number of solid-fueled and liquid-fueled JATO concepts before developing an actual engine. Early solid propellants cracked while liquid oxygen had to be maintained at supercold temperatures and evaporated quickly. A reliable solid propellant was developed when one researcher mixed ordinary paving tar and asphalt with an oxygen-rich potassium compound and developed the first solid propellant that did not crack or explode. Gasoline and kerosene, both storable at room temperature, were mixed with red fuming nitric acid but caused the engines to chug and explode or shut down. Only when nitric acid was mixed with aniline, a colorless oily liquid derived from coal tar, did researchers finally achieve a liquid fuel rocket with storable propellant.[37]

Although the United States experimented with rocket-powered aircraft during the war, none was deployed. However, the budding technology found its way into a number of successful practical applications. The Wac Corporal, standing for "Without Any Control" and corporal being the next rank above private (its predecessor rocket), was developed by the Jet Propulsion Laboratory, an Army-sponsored research arm of the California Institute of Technology. It was twenty-one feet long, had a diameter of twelve inches, three tailfins, and could produce a liftoff thrust of fifty thousand pounds. Once the allies captured and merged the technology of German V-2 rockets with the Wac Corporal, the two-stage "Bumper-Wac" became the first rocket to carry an object into space (to an altitude of nearly four hundred kilometers) and the first rocket to be launched from Cape Canaveral.[38]

The military viewed neither surface-to-air nor air-to-air missiles as a wartime priority, the former since no one expected Japanese aircraft to penetrate U.S. air space and the latter because Allied air supremacy predated their commercial availability. Air-to-surface missiles were a different matter. The five-inch "Holy Moses," a High Velocity Aircraft Rocket (HVAR), effective against both land and ship-based anti-aircraft emplacements, was widely used with nearly a million produced during the war. The "Tiny Tim," another forward-firing rocket, weighed about 1,284 pounds and was primarily launched against fortified pillboxes and bunkers on the Japanese home islands.[39]

Of more immediate relevance to the war effort, the bazooka of popular fame was a rocket-powered grenade developed from early work by Dr. Robert Goddard (the "father" of modern rocketry) and introduced in 1940. The military relied heavily on barrage rockets to soften up enemy positions prior to land or sea-launched assaults. The M-8, for example, was fired from truck-mounted or tank-mounted eight-tube launchers called the "Xylophone" or sixty-tube launchers called the "Calliope." An air-launched version of the M-8 was fired against Japanese positions in Burma in the winter of 1943. This marked the first time that U.S. rockets were fired offensively from the air.[40] High-Velocity Spin-stabilized Rockets (HVSR) fired from ships and PT boats at the rate of up to five hundred per minute were used extensively at Iwo Jima and Okinawa.

Despite my father's intellectual fascination with the emerging field of rocket technology, the romantic allure of combat flying very quickly asserted itself.

Exposition–The Transitional Passage

July 26, 1942
Wright Field

Dear Mother and Dad,

I am beginning to understand what is meant by the impatience of youth…I like the work here very much…but the longer I stay here, the more I would like to fly…I have seen very little news of the Chinese-Japanese situation, but what I have seen hasn't been good. The Japanese seem to have got most of the good bases in the Pacific which means that a terrific carnage is brewing there…Being a 2nd Lieutenant is nice, but it has all the griefs, none of the experience, and few of the privileges of the other ranks of officers…I wish that they would [move me] in a hurry so that I [can get some combat] training.

Exposition–The Contrasting Lyric Theme

August 2, 1942
Wright Field

Dear Mother and Dad,

This letter may or may not surprise you…[but] if I can pass the physical exam…I am going to get my wings…The work here at the field is interesting, but I definitely don't like just sitting here and waiting…I really want to fly. Every time a ship takes off here I wish I were with it…Dad, you will understand more than mother…that if I ever want to have a crack at combat, it will have to be now. After all, did you go across in the last war only for patriotic reasons, or did you have at least a little desire to see a little action before you [were] tied down to an armchair? In other words, if I don't see combat, I probably will never be satisfied. If I do see it, I probably will wish I never had. So, which would you do? I think that you would take the course I am going to try.

August 10, 1942
Wright Field

Dear Mother and Dad,

Can a young engineer be of more value with a slide rule in his hand, or with a gun or plane? The main work here is distribution and red tape and testing to see that the government is not chiseled by private concerns...[E]ventually a lot of this will be turned back to private companies...[so] the work we young lieutenants do here is not as important as that which we could do in work [overseas in combat]...I want to fly, not sit in an airport office somewhere signing procurement blanks...In other words, once I get across, I want to be able to give a little hell rather than receive it all the time...

Exposition–The Closing Subject

And then there is the perennial American male fascination with "blowing shit up."

September 1, 1942
Wright Field

Dear Mother and Dad,

Today the mechanics were warming a large bomber up and a motor caught fire. The crew ran like all hell, got out of the ship just as one of the gas tanks exploded. This turned the middle of the ship into one of the prettiest infernos you have ever seen. Then another tank let go and split the ship in two, the wings falling sideways, the nose down, and the tail up. Then the last tank let go and there was a real explosion. What ammunition there was let go into the ground. It was really pretty. The exciting part about the whole thing was that there was a large transport near—Douglas C-56. The flames started to touch that and there was a mad scramble to clear it. However, we managed to clear it before it caught fire.

If you would like an idea of what a burning plane is like, set the plane in the yard. The wings would cover most of the side lawn. The inside of the plane will hold more men than our front room. The bomb bays will hold weights equivalent to three cars. And there is about or more gasoline in the plane than there is in 30 automobiles. It takes weeks to build, months of training to fly and seconds to destroy. You may be getting an idea of why I'd like to fly.

September 6, 1942
Wright Field

Dear George [younger brother in the medical corps],

I am…doing engineering work. It probably sounds funny to you, but I am working on rockets. It really is interesting, especially when one of them blows up. So, if one of my arms flies past you up there, mail it back to me…It is interesting, but I want to fly. I think you would if you hung around the planes for a while. The pursuit planes are very small, but they are very fast and deadly. Then there are the large bombers…You would like to see the B-19, the biggest ship in the world. It is bigger than you could possibly imagine. It always seems like a miracle that they can fly…What I would like to do is to get a permanent commission and get my wings. That way I could fly the rest of the war...learn a little about leading men...and then after the war...get sent here [to test pilot new ships]...

Exposition–The Codetta

October 4, 1942
Wright Field

Dear Mother and Dad,

Thursday I took the four hour physical exam and passed it. Therefore I am now on my way to getting my wings... The other day I went through four of the largest Army bombers, not counting the B-19. They are really huge inside. I would a lot rather fly a [fighter] plane...

Development

And so began the process of creating a fighter pilot. In successive stages running over the next twelve months—from pre-flight school, through primary, basic, advanced, advanced gunnery, and tactical training—a winnowing selection process produced a highly trained stock of bomber and fighter pilots, bombardiers, and navigators. An early emphasis on military discipline (marching, ceremonies, inspections, and military customs and courtesies) and vigorous physical conditioning was increasingly supplemented by training in academic subjects designed to prepare men for the increasingly technical nature of air combat: mathematics, physics, usage of aeronautical charts, and the very unpopular radio code instruction. The West Point code of cadet discipline and honor, including the traditional class system with hazing, was introduced as the model for the preflight schools. The system was abolished in 1943 as not being suitable for civilian soldiers. Morale, particularly among pilot and navigator trainees, was high.[41]

Trainees were either officers or cadets. An officer took a physical and was ordered to preflight school directly in whichever specialty he requested. My father requested "pilot" and was duly assigned. Officers took the same courses as cadets, only more of them. Assuming they passed the (then) nine-week preflight training course, officers were ordered to primary school, where flying commenced in earnest. Cadets followed a different path. A civilian or an enlisted man wishing to fly applied through channels and waited. He was eventually given an exam testing his general knowledge of aviation and simple engineering and physics. If he passed, he was sent to one of three classification centers in the United States and given several days of stiff mental, aptitude, and physical exams, mainly math, physics, and physical coordination tests. Candidates with the highest rating in these exams were sent to navigator school, those next in test rank to bombardier school, and those who tested best physically but lower mentally and who so desired were sent to pre-flight school. On graduation they moved with the officers to primary school.

At primary school, officers and cadets, who were segregated in pre-flight, were combined, roughly five officers to every two hundred or so cadets. Primary training lasted for nine weeks, followed by nine weeks of basic training, and nine more weeks of advanced training, successful completion of which earned a man his wings and his bars. Bombardiers and navigators got their wings in about six months, pilots in about eight. Additional periods of specialized instruction followed, including "transition" flying on obsolescent combat aircraft before being assigned to operational units, where they were given transition on current fighter types. Transition to the specific aircraft to be flown in combat was the last stage of a pilot's individual training. A newly minted pilot was then trained as a member of a combat unit. Crew and unit indoctrination normally required about twelve weeks, depending on the demands of the combat theaters and the availability of planes for training, after which the aerial teams were sent to staging areas to prepare for movement overseas. Thus, more than a year after he started flying instruction, a skilled pilot emerged "ready" for combat.[42]

Recapitulation

November 20, 1942
Kelly Field
Aviation Cadet Center
San Antonio, Texas

Dear Mother and Dad,

I am enjoying myself immensely. The fellows are a swell bunch—all officers (1ˢᵗ, 2ⁿᵈ lieutenants. And a few captains) and mostly college men…In each class here there are about 100 officers (students) while in the corresponding class of cadets, there are 2–3 thousand cadets…probably because of this [ratio], they really enjoy making the officers work…Oh well, it will all be worth it if I can get my wings…55% of cadets and 70% of student officers wash out…

We get up at 5:30, breakfast 6:20, close order drill at 8, calisthenics 9, commando course and track and games 10 until almost 12. Eat at 12:10. Classes start at 1, end at 5. Supper 5:30, bedcheck at 10…During the odd hours we make beds, scrub floors, wash the walls, stand inspections, etc.

There is only one cloud on the horizon. I passed the last physical, but only by the skin of my teeth. Evidently the eye infection I got caused trouble, for I just barely got 20-20 vision from my right eye. I only got that by memorizing the eye chart before the test…So, unless I can step it up, I won't pass the next exam…in 8 weeks. I'll worry about that when it comes.

December 4, 1942
Kelly Field, Texas

Dear Mother and Dad,

Just finished another full day of work and play. Started this morning 5:30, got up and scrubbed floors, walls, etc. And I mean scrub. On our hands and knees. Not even cadets or enlisted men do that. Then mess and more cleaning. Then to fill in our joyful young lives, we took a cross-country run of two miles over the roughest, toughest, and wildest course you have ever seen. This was the first time I have gone over it. I came in 5th of about 115 men, which isn't bad.

Classes all afternoon. Physics and math (I help other fellows with it), code (it's beginning to go fast, so that keeps me awake), plane and ship identification. It seems that a few of our own men were shot down by their buddies at the beginning of the war, so ever since the air corps has been given a very intensive course in identification of planes and ships of all countries. The last two hours…have been spent on trying to learn the difference between…ships of our navy and the Japanese navy.

You ought to see the rivalry around here regarding football. Quite a few Georgia boys. Several Texas A&M. Others from all over the country. Money floats all over the place afternoons of football games…I think this will do for now…The Civil War is starting again. Georgia boys vs. a couple of northerners. Marching through Georgia is not a popular refrain…I really like it here…getting in condition, plenty to do. This is more like the Army.

December 12, 1942
Kelly Field, Texas

Dear Mother and Dad,

Enclosed…please find latest report on progress of one Lt. LaCroix…Plenty of work…I really like [this life]…My average is about 98%…We signed up for primary schools. Three others and I want to go together (a Penn boy, a tall lanky Georgian and a Puerto Rican, Esteban)…This will have to suffice. General Arnold[43] is coming tomorrow…thus I must sleep tonight.

Enclosed find two pictures. One is of my first solo flight. The other is of a rather nice young lady, Skippy, I have gone out with lately. Pretty and with far above average personality and ability. Her father is Major General C____. Ever heard of him and if so, where and how and why? Met Mrs. Wainwright the other day at Skippy's. She is the wife of the general[44] who was captured early in the war when he replaced MacArthur. Quite a lady.

December 25, 1942
Christmas Morning
Kelly Field, Texas

Dear Mother and Dad,

A lovely, merry Christmas. Very.

My course here is about nine weeks…so I have about 2 ½ weeks left…I have been going out quite a bit with the general's daughter…I have never seen anyone who could handle a group of people…as well as she does. I am learning a lot from her…[But] the only things I am really interested in are my wings and a permanent commission...Plus the very important fact that I am going to get into combat somehow...A wife would be a definite hindrance.

We are getting a very intensive course in gas warfare...Walk into a gas chamber with mask—the tear gas is so thick it burns your skin. Take off your mask and walk across the room and out. Then stagger blindly for five minutes until you can see again. Then we detonated land mines of mustard gas, etc. We would stop near the gas to smell it...some of them such as mustard and phosgene are pretty damn potent.

The day all the pilots graduated, General Arnold talked to us...We stood formation three hours Sunday morning. He is a good speaker—short and to the point. (The long part was waiting for him.)

THE SECOND MOVEMENT—ANDANTE IN TERNARY FORM

Primary training marked the first rung in the pilot's steady ascension through increasingly complex, powerful aircraft to, in my father's case, the P-51 Mustang fighter plane. The tempo was slow, if taut, as the military sought to separate the wheat from the chaff at this most rudimentary stage of flight training. Flying a small, low-horsepower plane rugged enough to take the punishment inflicted by a novice, the student in the pre-solo phase mastered general operation of a light aircraft, achieving proficiency in forced landing techniques and in recovering from stalls and spins. Precision of control was developed in the intermediate phase by flying standard patterns, known as elementary 8s, lazy 8s, pylon 8s, and chandelles. The accuracy phase demanded high proficiency in various types of landing approaches and landings. The acrobatic phase required the ability to perform loops, Immelmann turns, slow rolls, half-rolls, and snap rolls. Each student in primary was required to make at least 175 landings. At least half of flight time was to be solo (as opposed to dual).[45]

The method of teaching men to fly military aircraft remained fundamentally the same from 1939 through 1945. The sequence encompassed an explanation by the instructor of each new maneuver followed by actual demonstration by the instructor, supervised student performance, correction of student errors, and then practice. The student, as far as practicable, was taught by the same instructor through all the lessons of a particular training stage. This "all-through" system enabled students and teachers to develop the mutual understanding essential to learning. Ground training, conducted in parallel with flight training, involved classroom lectures, demonstrations, and discussions, with aural or visual drills. Training films, slides, charts, and mock-ups were also used. The most important synthetic training device was the Link trainer, an early flight simulator permitting effective instrument training.[46]

Primary flying schools were operated by civilian companies under contract. Basic and advanced flying schools were operated by the Army Air Force. The civilian primary schools were started in 1939 by nine civilian contractors without contracts.[47] They responded at the outset to General Arnold's urgent plea for support and relied on his statement that he thought he could get the necessary funds from Congress the next year.

Theme and Initial Motive–Solo and the Landing

January 12, 1943
Stamford Flying School
Stamford, Texas

Dear People,

I have soloed...I have a little trouble with landings [though]. Once in the air, I have no trouble, but coming to the ground is tough. I was flying this morning and one of the famous Texas dust storms blew-up—in about 20 minutes this was a real hurricane, the worst we have had. It was really tough landing for you could hardly see the ground...In our class of 200 here, 55 have already been washed out.

January 17, 1943
Stamford Flying School
Stamford, Texas

Dear Family,

Now the flying begins…The next week and a half will tell whether I can fly. If I last that, I probably will last four weeks, at which time I will see whether I can fly the way the army wants…Anyway we start flying tomorrow. We will fly a two-cockpit, low-wing, 175 hp Fairchild. It is a beautiful little plane, its only trouble being that it is open and cold as the devil…We were given a leather flying jacket, helmet, gloves, goggles and a zoot suit. The latter is leather, fur-lined jacket, pants and boots. You feel like a teddy bear and are four times as warm.

The Second Motive–The Army Way

January 28, 1943
Stamford Flying School
Stamford, Texas

Dear Family,

I am beginning to understand why 75% of the cadets wash out…Flying itself is easy (relatively). The really tough job is to fly the Army way. That's the reason so few get through…Incidentally for your assurance, in the last year of flying, there has only been one fatal accident here—and that was the student's fault.

January 31, 1943
Stamford Flying School
Stamford, Texas

Dear Family

*I ought to solo towards the end of this week…This game is an
awful lot of work, but the further you get into it, the more you like
it. There is no thrill like going up to 6000 feet and spinning down.
You are looking straight down, the earth revolving around you. The
air-speed indicator climbing up, the air whistling. Then you kick
rudder and stick and the earth stops revolving. Then you pull back
on the stick and you seem to weigh four times as much, while the
earth fades away below. Or stalls. You pull the stick back until the
plane is headed up at about 45 degrees. Hold it until it loses flying
speed. The bottom suddenly seems to drop out of the plane and you
are just falling in air. When you see the earth in the windshield instead of the sky, pull back on the stick and go up and do it again.*

*While all this is going on, the instructor is talking through the
gosport. As a maneuver reaches a climax, he talks faster and faster.
And boy, can he swear…"The nose is low. Pull that left wing up,
Mr. Your motor is speeding up. You're too low. Get that nose up.
Look out for that other plane. Damn it, pull up that nose. More
right rudder. Your left wing is low. I said 80 miles per hour—not
82. Get that speed down…"—by the hour.*

*The first two or three times the cadet goes up in these planes,
he usually gets sick (although I never did). After that, nothing fazes
him—but those first days really are miserable. Especially when they
wheel the ship up to a hangar and the cadet has to wash the tail
surfaces while all the other cadets watch.*

*I can see why, once [flying], people never quit it. To a grounded
man, flying is dangerous, daring, etc. Once in it, it is not dangerous,*

daring or even frightening. You get up in the air and forget all that, for after all—the plane is safe. Besides, you always wear chutes. It is hard to describe. I may starve after the war, but I'll never be sorry I came here.

Can't think of anything I want for my birthday. So, I'd rather you would skip it…Maybe you could send me some candy or cookies. But for gosh sakes—pleuse, no more religious articles.

The Third Motive—The Washout

February 15, 1943
Stamford Flying School
Stamford, Texas

Dear Family

We are really flying now. One hour of dual and two solo every day. It is a lot of fun to be up there by yourself. That is one place where nobody can tell you what to do and where you really have to make up your own mind…You know, flying would make a really fertile field for psychologists. You see fellows go up day after day. Some drop out every day (35% of my class already). A very few just aren't flyers. Others are afraid of the plane. Straight and level flying is one thing. The first time you go up to do a spin solo really takes guts for some people (I got around that by climbing to 5000 feet and spinning it almost before I had time to worry about it). After the first time, it's easy. The beginning of acrobatics throws out a lot—both on the basis of fear and on the basis of lack of quick action.

Perhaps I am making this game sound tough and dangerous. It is neither. It is the hardest thing to learn and the easiest to do. But as for danger—there is none…only about two fatal accidents in the [last two years].

Finished up navigation this week. I have the highest average in several classes here—98%. All my other grades are well above 90%.

The process of winnowing a pilot from a washout was ultimately conducted in the unforgiving conditions of flight. And despite my father's filially sunny optimism, the toll was staggering. In his sweeping study, *Fire in the Sky: The Air War in the South Pacific*, Eric Bergerud remarks that:

> In the harsh world of military training, a washout was a psychological blow. However, the rigors of training were expected to prove the complex and subjective judgments of individuals by performance...Combat training of any type was hazardous, but none remotely approached the dreadful peril faced by airmen prior to entering combat...This meant that many cadets were killed in training. Some were simply in over their heads; others showed the poor judgment of a rookie...training was very much a matter of 'sink or swim.' Thousands sank and never resurfaced...The Allied air forces did not squander lives without thought, yet the needs of war necessitated an approach to men and machines that would be unthinkable today. Put simply life was cheap during World War II.[48]

As brutal as it was, the winnowing was not foolproof and men ill-suited to the demands of aerial combat received wings. The consequences could be disastrous for both pilot and squadron. Bergerud quotes a veteran carrier fighter pilot:

> Some guys would panic. They shouldn't have been in fighters. You could tell who they were. You could tell who wasn't going to survive. They filled a seat. It's sad, but they filled a seat. When I had squadrons I told some pilots, and this is God's truth, that you're filling a seat but you're not capable here and you better watch your ass...A symptom would be trying to be too smart. They think, but they don't develop habits of flying intuitively. [A fighter pilot] can't think. You have to prethink. It all has to be preplanned. If you're 'too smart' you think about the situation as it happens. That's too late. I had good friends lost in combat because they were trying to think how to fight a Zero. You don't think, you do it.[49]

Theme and Fourth Motive–Solo, the Loop, and the Roll

March 9, 1943
Stamford Flying School
Stamford, Texas

Dear People

We now have exactly 50% of our class left…Can handle this ship pretty well, am anxious to try higher-powered ships… Only have a week of flying left…have to get in a school check ride, an army check ride and a cross-country solo trip…The last check ride is interesting—we go into a spin, then directly into a loop, then around again directly into an Immelmann, recover with a snap roll, a slow roll, and then a half roll to leave you in inverted flight. Then they cut the throttle and you roll out and try a simulated forced landing. It keeps you moving and thinking.

Also received your card on "pick ups." Please don't worry so much about my moral life. It really is in pretty fair shape. Considering the army, I am still an angel.

THE THIRD MOVEMENT—SCHERZO

The tempo and intensity of training increased. Basic school had one overriding objective: to make military pilots out of primary graduates. A secondary objective was the selection of students for single- or two-engine advanced training. More pilots wanted fighter assignments than slots were available. Students in this phase learned to operate a plane of greater weight, power, and complexity than the plane mastered in primary. They were also introduced to new aspects of airmanship: learning to fly by instruments, at night, in formation, and cross-country. Military instructors emphasized precision and smoothness of airplane operation, and a large portion of flying time was devoted to repetition of maneuvers to develop proficiency. The first phase of basic was transitional, ensuring familiarization with the plane and fundamental operations. The second, diversified phase involved accuracy maneuvers, aerobatics, navigation, instruments, and night flying.[50]

Instrument training was doubtless the most important part of the basic curriculum. Combat experience had demonstrated the necessity of flying at night and under all weather conditions. Instrument training, like all other facets of the curriculum, evolved quickly in the first years of the war. Early instrument training emphasized needle (rate-of-turn indicator), ball (bank indicator), and airspeed indicator. Gyroscopic instruments were practically ignored. In 1942 the Navy developed an improved method of instrument flying relying chiefly, and for the first time, on the directional gyroscope and artificial horizon. The Army Air Corps adopted the training system in mid-1943.[51]

Experimentation and Innovation

March 21, 1943
Enid Army Flying School
Enid, Oklahoma

Dear Family,

Our basic classes seem to be experimental... This station... is being built up to take the place of Randolph [Air Field], the "West Point of the air"... By the way, my roommate and I got the highest possible recommendations for basic—based on our flying alone. At least that's what our instructor told us. As for ground school, I didn't actually figure it, but if I didn't have the highest average of officers and cadets, it was close to it. Hope I can repeat both here. Enough of the bragging.

March 28, 1943
Enid Army Flying School
Enid, Oklahoma

Dear Family,

We are starting flying all over again in many respects, for this ship is entirely different—fast and powerful. We step into the cockpit, pull the canopy over our heads, and we are completely surrounded with instruments. It took me several hours to memorize the position and use of each. Since we do blind and night flying a little later, this last is very important.

We also have quite a bit of Link trainer work. This Link train-er is something I've seen before but never used. It is an engineering miracle. You get into the cockpit and pull the hood down and it is just like being in an airplane. Complete cockpit instruments. You fly by these, simulating blind flying—climbs, stalls, spins—every-thing, and only three feet off the ground. As you do these maneu-vers by instruments alone ("seat of the pants" rules don't help here), they are recorded in every detail on a graph which an enlisted man watches. It is really clever. It is a lot tougher than flying an actual plane, though.

When, due to weather or darkness, a pilot cannot see outside the cockpit, the plane is operated under "Instrument Flight Rules" using instruments and the radio. In the early years of flight, long before the flight training simulators in universal use today, pilots learned instru-ment flight through a trial and error process—too often, the latter. In early 1934, the Army Air Corps was ordered to undertake delivery of airmail in the United States. Army pilots were ill-trained and inexpe-rienced in instrument flight, and five pilots were killed in the first few days of mail delivery.

Edward Link was a pilot from a family of organ builders. He dreamed of creating a "pilot trainer" that would permit pilots to learn instrument flying while remaining safely on the ground. He left his family firm and, with the experience gained building organs, constructed a prototype pilot trainer using air pump valves and bellows to make the trainer move in response to its controls. Although the military immediately saw the value of the trainer, they lacked funding in the pre-war years to initiate major production and procurement. It was only after Pearl Harbor that the armed forces received sufficient appropriations to permit them to contract for Link's entire production. Link's company built over ten thousand Link trainers during the course of the Second World War, in which virtually every pilot received instrument training. While a typical training airplane in 1945 cost more than ten dollars per hour to operate, the Link trainer cost just four cents per hour.[52] How many lives of pilots like my father were saved through improvisation and adaptation can only be guessed.

The Families Behind the Flyers

April 2, 1943
Enid Army Flying School
Enid, Oklahoma

Dear Dad,

I think I will write you more often. When I write to the family, I have to be careful for they...don't know just how much to worry. You have been through it and know how it is, so telling you of accidents, etc., shouldn't scare you as it might Mother.

The primary trainers were plenty safe...The Basic Trainer (BT) is another story, though...a larger ship (450 hp), radio equipment, different type flaps, changeable pitch propeller and a few other headaches we didn't have before...It is easier to stall and much faster. So naturally there are a few accidents. These are invariably due to a student's becoming frightened and freezing. There is only one secret to flying—keep your speed up. If you remember that, you will always be safe.

Remember in your war [WWI], they took a man and gave him a ship. He taxied for a few days and then took the plane up. If he came down alive—good pilot. The other case they didn't worry about. Now we fly dual until we have been trained in every possible dangerous attitude. Then we are soloed. I will probably solo late this week.

There are a lot of thrills in flying…One is to be 7000 feet up and look down…The world looks clean from up there…Another is to get the ship into an inverted spin or something it doesn't want to come out of. The few seconds you fight it before it recovers are a lot of fun…But this BT is [powerful] and can be dangerous. So I will stick to the schedule in it…There are two things I have stayed away from (most of the time): dog-fighting and hedge-hopping. They are two things that are not condoned under any conditions. Nothing washes a man as quickly as either of these. With acrobatics, you can always claim you did a legal maneuver improperly.

April 20, 1943
Enid Army Flying School
Enid, Oklahoma

Dear Family,

Night flying is a lot of fun, but a strain on you. When you are up in the sky…and know there are 40 or 50 other planes milling around that same place—at 130 mph—you don't go to sleep. We have been practicing landings both with and without lights. And without lights you have a tough time.

My Puerto Rican friend's father came up to see him. Esteban says he has aged 15 years in the last few months. I hope you don't worry that much about me, for it is senseless...All these accidents you hear about are a result of carelessness and stupidity—mainly the latter...You might be interested to know that we haven't had a single serious accident yet...The reason so many were washed was that they were dangerous flyers. I don't care if you lose weight for me—you can stand a little less—but I don't want to come home in a few months to find you white-haired—any more than you were when I left.

The Shape of Things to Come

May 9, 1943
Enid Army Flying School
Enid, Oklahoma

Dear Family,

The foreign news sounds pretty good. The internal news puts a garbage dump to shame. Normally the army leaves politics and labor alone. But I have never in my life seen a group as definitely opposed to anything as the army is to Lewis and the strikes. That includes officers, cadets and enlisted men. If they sent any of the troops I have talked to into the strike areas, there would be...bloodshed. I have never seen a group of men of all ages as completely mad in my life.

Passed my re-check without any trouble...Of all the officers who started with me in San Antonio, only about 48% are left. Also, of the 53 in my flight here (11 officers, 42 cadets), only 8 officers and 18 cadets are left...[I have] an instrument check and a couple of instrument cross-countries...follow that up with formation flying. Soon after that we will be sent to advanced.

David Brooks, in his perceptive "comedic sociology" *Bobos in Paradise*, comments that the generation of our parents, those entering adulthood at the time of World War II, appears in retrospect "weightier" than our generation.[53] The political, military, business, and cultural leaders of the period project a gravitas notable in its comparative absence today. John L. Lewis, president of the United Mine Workers for forty years up to 1960, was a case in point. The son of Welsh immigrant parents, Lewis dropped out of school after the seventh grade and entered the mines at age fifteen. His native loquacity in unflagging defense of the underdog powered his rapid move through the trade union hierarchy. A polarizing figure of volcanic temper, viscerally felt convictions, and ferocious demeanor, he founded what became the Congress of Industrial Organizations (CIO) in 1935 when the American Federation of Labor (AFL) refused to open its ranks to unskilled workers.

Lewis was a strong supporter of Roosevelt's New Deal policies and in a show of patriotic unity pledged a policy of "No Strikes" when the United States entered the war. In 1943, believing the government was taking the workers for granted, he initiated a series of immensely unpopular strikes. The strikes won significant concessions for the miners but estranged Lewis from the White House, the War Labor Board, the public, and fellow labor leaders. They were also largely responsible for the eventual enactment of the restrictive anti-strike Taft-Hartley Act. The military newspaper *Stars and Stripes* damned Lewis for his "coal-black soul."[54] Over the span of his career, he was variously described as a "labor statesman," an autocratic "per capita counter," and "a labor boss of the most conventional kind."[55] He was at the least an unapologetic realpolitician. Following a falling-out with Roosevelt and with a view to enhancing his power base, Lewis supported Wendell Willkie's presidential candidacy in 1940 and at one point even chaired the Republican Party's National Labor Committee.

In later years, following a series of economically devastating national coal strikes, Lewis won renewed esteem for his advocacy of "cooperative capitalism." While his more conciliatory approach to labor-management relations increased union power and improved worker pay in the short term, in the longer term it hastened the introduction of technology that rendered the human miner increasingly redundant. It was one more example of the law of unintended consequences operating on paradigm shifts with their origin in the iconoclasm of the Second World War. Nonetheless, Lewis's achievements on behalf of American coal miners are undeniable and deserving of recognition. Hardly less notable was the personal probity he demonstrated in voluntarily giving up his office and the power he had fought so long and so hard to acquire.

THE FOURTH MOVEMENT—RONDO

As a pilot's competence grew, so grew his confidence, so grew his joy of flight for its own sake—the spirited romp through the pure air the angels breathe, as Mark Twain described the space between the clouds. An increased tempo of learning mirrored a blossoming awareness of the unbreakable bond between training and survival. Advanced single-engine school prepared students in five phases (transition, instrument, navigation, formation, and acrobatics) for subsequent combat flying in fighter aircraft. The training planes were more powerful machines approximating the characteristics of combat aircraft. Adapting to the early lessons of combat, increasing emphasis was placed on formation flying, especially at high altitudes and using the close, three-plane V-formation.[56]

Advanced emphasized not just expert flying ability but also skill in fixed aerial gunnery. Most promising students—those who were to become combat fighter pilots—were assigned to a fighter-transition and gunnery stage. Fixed gunnery practice took place in the standard advanced training plane and in obsolescent combat types (e.g., P-40 or P-39). Great improvements in gunnery training came with synthetic trains and the gun sight-aiming-point camera introduced after 1942.[57]

Survival and Self–Reliance

May 26, 1943
Aloe Army Air Field
Victoria, Texas

Dear Family,

You probably wonder at my being at single engine advanced…
Fighter work will make a better pilot out of me…I have
found that the best pilots (regarding coordination, judgment,

flying ability) are pursuit pilots, for the heavy [bomber] is like flying a Link trainer. It will also teach a lot more self-reliance since a fighter is on his own—doesn't have a navigator, bombardier, radio man or gunners. As far as fighting goes, I would far rather have my own guns and plane to play with—I have far more confidence in myself than I have in other people…Bear in mind…Life expectancy in either case is about the same.

To Know the Clouds

June 4, 1943
Aloe Army Field
Victoria, Texas

Dear Family,

I have soloed the AT-6. It is really a beautiful ship. Ten years ago it would have been called a pursuit plane. 550 hp. Plenty of speed. Retractable wheels, constant speed prop, guns and lots of other good points.

We are left a lot more on our own here…We are allowed to play around the clouds here…You get up above a series of clouds and it is like a series of plains and mountains…You really can't appreciate the speed of a plane until you dive through and around clouds…

As a sort of pre-combat course, we get a lot of skeet shooting, the object being to teach lead and alignment necessary to hit a moving object. Aerial gunnery is a lot like skeet, for it is necessary to lead a flying plane by quite a distance…While we are here, we only use cameras [instead of live ammunition] in order to avoid danger to civilians…

Survival: Bomber versus Fighter

June 16, 1943
Aloe Army Field
Victoria, Texas

Dear Family,

[You asked me about the relative safety of bombers versus fighters.] When the invasion [of Europe] comes, the main part of the offensive will obviously be bomber work. And fighters for strafing, light bombing and bomber protection…The Germans will only have two effective defenses. One will be [concentrated] and effective antiaircraft fire. The other will be an immense concentration of fighters.

Bombers will fly through flak concentrations that will necessarily increase casualties. A bomber is effectively an almost stationary target—because of size and speed. Fighters, on the other hand, will not be concentrated upon to the same extent. They also have the great advantage of being able to move fast and in any direction.

…Looking at it coldly and impartially, my chances of getting through the war are 50-50 with leanings against it…From your viewpoint, bombers are the thing for me. You hear reports of their safety, etc. But if a bomber goes, the crew has no chance. If a fighter goes, 7 out of 10 chances are that the pilot can bail out. He hasn't got propellers, bombs and a crew in his way.

Fighters are no longer the dog-fighting sky knights of the last war. Fighters are probably the most specialized and highly skilled units in the war. A fully trained fighter knows more about flying, weather, radio and self-reliance than bombermen will ever know, simply because a bomber is a Link trainer with two or four of everything: navigator gives course, radioman receives orders, bombardier says do this, gunners do the fighting…Fighter work will also best prepare me for test-pilot work.

The Evolving Profession of Killing

June 23, 1943
Aloe Army Air Field
Victoria, Texas

Dear Family,

Killing is a painstaking game and the Army is really refining its technique. After nine months training for our wings, we are sent to tactical units for another five months—more or less—before we can go across. The way I have it figured, this will send me across either just after the invasion [of France] is well underway or about four months before it will begin. In either case, I won't be sent in untrained.

Survival, Training, and the Cool Head

July 5, 1943
Aloe Army Air Field
Victoria, Texas

Dear People,

Next week I will go to the gunnery [Matagorda] island...ranges, speeds, deflections all enter in...making it a lot of fun but a complicated subject...We are finished with night flying. We flew every day and every night last week. Bed at 3:30 AM, up at 9:30...I have passed the only checks we get—transition, acrobatics and instrument checks...

Queer thing happened. At night you can't see the ground, so you can't land a hot ship (forced landing). Therefore we had orders to bail out if anything happened. A cadet got lost, ran low *(he thought) on gas. Got rattled. Bailed out. It came out in the investigation that he had left the ship ten minutes' flight from the field—with 40 minutes gas in the tanks. In other words, he lost his head and lost a $40,000 ship. I've never heard anyone raked over the coals as he was for three days after that. He wasn't washed out, but he was lucky he wasn't...*

Incidentally, I have already applied for the European front as first choice...Pacific second...I think the really rough going will be when we get to the northern part of Italy...The mountains and passes...will be the hard nut to crack...I hope I will be over there by that time.

July 19, 1943
Gunnery School
Matagorda Island, Texas

Dear People,

Greetings...from the end of the world. One full week of gunnery gone and it seems as though we just got here—a year ago...We are about a mile from the alert room. It is a quarter of a mile to the parachute room. A quarter of a mile more to the ammunition building. Three quarters of a mile more to the planes. We walk that about four times a day. When you have on flying clothes, a Mae-west, a parachute and your ammunition belts, you aren't in the best costume for a long hike.

The island's some 70 miles long, two or three miles wide. Plain, ordinary, flea-bitten, hot, blowing unadulterated sand. Miles on miles of it. All exactly five feet above sea-level. Not a single green thing—except some seaweed on the mossy shores. On top of it all, the officers here have decided this is the last chance to make it tough on the remainder of [my] class—all 20% left—so they're doing their damnedest… This place was supposed to be gunnery and a life of ease. We fly two days and have one "off." On that day off we just load and unload cases of ammunition (110 lbs. each), paint and supply ammo, harmonize guns and sights and a few other odd jobs.

I guess the reason we are all so peeved and upset is that we are so close to our wings. It has been a long pull. Anything that might upset it now would be hard to take. Now I have all that off my mind, I am happy again. Well, almost… Shot some darn good aerial gunnery scores today. The secret seems to be to get so close you can't miss. The latter keeps you on your toes.

Headline, *The Boston Daily Globe*, August 3, 1943:

Headed For Aerial Battlefronts—
These Greater Boston boys have been awarded their silver wings following consolidated graduation exercises at airfields in Texas:

List of names with pictures, including:

"Lieutenant Robert E. LaCroix, 970 Center Street, Newton Center."

19

"THANKS TO THE SOLDIERS, THANKS TO THE SOLDIERS"

Soon after the conquest of Singapore, when the Greater East Asia Co-Prosperity Sphere appeared a coalescing reality, Sergeant Ishizuka was mustered out of the army. Returning to Japan, he moved in with his elder sister, a self-sufficient rice shop operator in central Tokyo. Putting behind, or at least aside, the memories of the past three years, Ishizuka attempted to pick up the thread of domestic tranquility he had dreamed of during years of brutal training and combat. He resumed his studies in Tokyo and a year later received his teaching license. He also resumed his judo training, entering competition bouts and in 1943 triumphing as Japan national judo champion. He secured a teaching position at Rawa High School in present-day Saitama Prefecture, just outside Tokyo, and embarked with chastened optimism on his life's dream. Normalcy, though, was not easily come by in wartime Japan.

The Great Depression of 1929 was a tolling bell for both German and Japanese democracy. Just as the economic breakdown of the early 1930s terminally undermined Germany's Weimar Constitution, so in trade-dependent Japan the tsunami unleashed by Western economic upheaval ultimately overwhelmed the reforming Meiji Constitution. The "militarist thirties,"[58] as the fateful decade before Pearl Harbor has been termed, were marked by the push-me-pull-me of emboldening military adventurism abroad and reactionary conservatism at home. The Kwantung Army's Manchurian and Marco Polo Bridge Incidents were simply the outward symptoms of a malaise raging deep within Japan's domestic body politic. Vocal proponents of a liberal parliamentary democracy led by a constitutional monarch's benign guidance were soon drowned in the growing din of bellicose nationalism.

Any society in transition from feudal authoritarianism to liberal democracy will produce fissures between the threatened status quo and the aspiring new order. Poorly managed, the fissures will expand to faults and the resulting displacement will threaten social order. Pre-war Japan was a predominantly agricultural population, conservative and accustomed over centuries not to discourse but to direction. Urban intellectuals, the primary movers of Japan's nascent liberalization, frequently espoused a Marxist-influenced leftism. With trade unions and the alien concepts of universal suffrage, participatory democracy, and freethinking social mores, they shocked what the *Asahi Shimbun* has called the "moral majority" of the time.[59] As the depression worsened rural poverty, an already docile population was only too willing to seek guidance and security from familiar icons. The rift in society intersected with a comparable, and incomparably more dangerous, rift in the military. Flaws in the Meiji Constitution furnished motive with means and opportunity.

The revolution culminating in the Meiji Restoration was led by talented young samurai disturbed by Japan's feudal backwardness and the realistic possibility of Western domination. Modernists and nationalists, they were also, by and large, social conservatives with authoritarian instincts. Their "acquired" desire to emulate Western liberal democracies was tempered by the "intuitive" Confucian paternalism of the ruling class. The Meiji Constitution they produced internalized this conservatism, first and foremost in its insistence that the constitution was "given" to the people by the emperor. Public officials consequently viewed themselves as accountable to the emperor, not to the people or their elected representatives. Presaging the ministerial domination of Japan's post-war economic miracle, they blocked democratic reform efforts on the grounds that only they knew what was best for the public.[60] The inherent conservatism of the bureaucracy and the reactionary suspicion of the "moral majority" dovetailed neatly with conservative capitalists anxious to suppress assertive trade unions and to secure access to raw materials for Japan's industrial machine. But the driving force of emergent Japanese authoritarianism was the officer corps of the Japanese navy and army.

Drawing eclectically on Western precedents, the framers of the Meiji Constitution found much to emulate in the limited democracy of Bismarck's Germany, where the Kaiser occupied the center of the German polity with power to replace prime ministers.[61] Rejecting the marginalization of the emperor during the shogunate, the Meiji Constitution restored the emperor to his former glory at the center of the Japanese polity.[62] In what was to prove a fatal miscalculation, the heads of the army and navy were placed in direct subordination to the emperor, not to civilian authority. Practically, this meant that no government cabinet could be formed without an active-duty general and admiral serving as ministers of the army and navy.[63] The implications were ominous: disputes within the military hierarchy quickly infected government policy and, with their ability to influence civilian authority, military policy soon became government policy. Between mid-1932 and August 1945, nine of eleven prime ministers were either generals or admirals.[64]

In an interesting parallel with both pre-Mao and contemporary China, albeit with different outcomes, the liberalization of Japan brought increasing prosperity to an urban elite but left the agrarian majority in a stagnating backwash. The resulting rural resentment, in Japan's case, was not limited to the peasantry. Much of the young officer corps in the Imperial Army was drawn from impoverished farm families not unlike Ishizuka's.[65] Already opposed to democratization and its alien spawn, the resentment of these young officers was readily co-opted by leaders of the Army's two main factions, the "Control" and the "Imperial Way." Both anti-democratic, both expansionist, the Control faction advocated a policy of expansion into China only while the Imperial Way faction believed that Japan should dominate all of eastern Asia.[66] The depth of the differences created a state of near-civil war, each side employing tactics of assassination and propaganda. However promising early democratic liberalization had appeared, bloody military revolts by young officers in 1932 and 1936, in which a number of senior government ministers were murdered, effectively silenced antimilitarist opposition. Under the legitimizing cloak of Japanese tradition and reverence for the emperor, the country willingly marched in lockstep.

Yasuyuki Ishizuka took up his teaching duties in an educational system thoroughly infiltrated by militarist thinking. Students bowed to a photograph of the emperor at the school's entrance, were drilled on the nobility of the "samurai spirit," received as gospel Shinto religious theories affirming Japan's divinely ordained destiny, and read from texts instructing them on their role as masters of the Greater East Asia Co-Prosperity Sphere. The moral teachings of Japanese Shinto were super-structure constructed on the unshakable social foundations of Confucianism. The military simply co-opted and refocused what was received wisdom of the ages and what the Meiji Emperor had articulated in the Imperial Rescript on Education of 1890:

> Our Imperial Ancestors have founded Our Empire on a basis [of] …loyalty and filial piety…This is the glory of the fundamental character of Our Empire, and herein also lies the source of Our education…
>
> Our subjects, be filial to your parents…bear yourselves in modesty and moderation…develop intellectual faculties and perfect moral powers…advance public good and promote common interests; always respect the Constitution and observe the laws…
>
> So shall ye not only be Our good and faithful subjects, but render illustrious the best traditions of your forefathers. The Way here set forth is indeed the teaching bequeathed by Our Imperial Ancestors, to be observed alike by Their Descendants and the subjects, infallible for all ages and true in all places.[67]

When the incendiary bombing raids toward the end of the war were exacting a terrible toll of life and property, students were trained to open the school shrine housing the deity and to protect the Imperial portrait and the Imperial Rescript on Education, even at the cost of student lives.

School instruction and teacher and student behavior were monitored by a vast police network. Proscribed books fell into three categories: Group A included works critical of fascism by liberal writers, Group B included works of socialist and communist orientation, and Group C comprised classified or secret documents issued by the various ministries—War, Education and Home Affairs—relating to student affairs and the surveillance of student ideological tendencies.[68] Among the latter category was a volume entitled "Tactics to Stamp out Antiwar Feelings." Its strategies of mob psychology were so effective that a post-war religious sect (coincidentally headed by a former member of the military police) used them in its recruiting efforts. The Special Higher Police published a *Monthly Review* that catalogued "cases of irreverent speech and conduct toward the Emperor, communist movements, anti-military and antiwar movements, professions of faith and criticisms of the Yasukuni Shrine by Christians and anti-Japanese actions by Koreans," explained one former teacher.[69] The Special Higher Police monitored readership of the *Review*.

Morning teaching staff meetings for Ishizuka commenced with the clapping of hands in prayer in front of the emperor's shrine in the principal's office. Late in the war, after Ishizuka's re-conscription and deployment to the Philippines, the morning staff meeting might include bamboo-spear and stone throwing drill in preparation for the expected American invasion. Students policed themselves in conformity-driving, fault-finding sessions called "review meetings." Patriotic sentiment was reinforced during morning assemblies, when students were lined up at attention for lecturing and drills. In one instance recounted by a former pupil, the principal asked an assemblage of 1,500 seven-year olds, "Let's say that an American flag is placed here. You are all walking toward it. What would you do?" In unison, the children shouted, "Trample on it as we pass by." Only one young girl, the daughter of a doctor, replied confidently, "Bow deeply as I pass by." The year was 1941. Denounced with a thunderous roar by her classmates, the child's parents were immediately summoned to the principal's office and lectured severely on the proper moral instruction to be dispensed at home.[70]

After the war, a former middle school principal wrote:

> The prewar education system suppressed freedom of thought and conscience, ignored basic human rights, and intently pressured the entire country toward war. But it did not spring up suddenly one morning. Rather, it was the result of change piled upon change, a little at a time, in an effort to reach a goal. I did not know what I could do concerning these gradual steps toward war and so just looked on. I have nothing but feelings of remorse and shame for my vacillation and inconstancy—as an

educator—in support of this militaristic education...I want us
to face up to the fact that when we overlook [minute infringe-
ments on the Constitution], we are in danger of repeating the
errors of the past...

We must stand up with a strong will against anything that
infringes...the conscience and thought of the people and tram-
ples on their basic human rights.[71]

One wonders how many young students shared the principal's view
as in concert, marching in imitation of their country's leaders, they
sang:

Shoulder to shoulder with elder brother, I go to school today,
Thanks to the soldiers, thanks to the soldiers
Who fought for our country, for our country.[72]

20

SYMPHONIE IMPROVISATION–
REPRISE

August 31, 1943
57th Fighter Squadron
54th Fighter Group
Bartow Army Air Field
Bartow, Florida

Dear Family,

Right now I am so nervous that I can hardly write. I was checked out in the AT-6 yesterday, so today I probably will take up the P-51—alone, of course, since it is a single place fighter. Anyway, the jump from 550 hp to better than 1500 hp is quite a jump, so I am a little nervous. There is no real reason to be nervous, but I am.

The ship itself is a beautiful job. Naturally I can't tell you the details, but it is one of the easiest to fly, yet probably the hottest and best ship that has come out in the war to date—on either side. This field is a pretty good one—all new ships, good crews. The instructors are all men who have just come back from combat, so are all up on the latest combat maneuvers… The course outlined for us is entirely practical and very interesting.

Once a pilot had his wings, he was assigned to transition on specific combat airplanes. These were complex, high-performance aircraft, and emphasis was placed on the acquisition of flying techniques preliminary to combat operational unit training. Pilots continued to receive ground instruction in equipment and practical maintenance and intensive training in armament and fixed gunnery.

The penultimate stage to combat deployment was combat crew and unit training—a system termed "OTU-RTU"—Operational Training Unit/Replacement Training Unit. The objective at this stage was to provide efficient combat units through operational training on the plane a pilot would use in combat. Maximum individual proficiency was now paired with precise coordination among the pilots of each squadron and group—the teamwork so critical to the success of combat operations.[73]

Training emphasized high-altitude operations and the development of combat vigilance and aggressiveness. Pilots focused also on take-off and assembly procedures, precision landings in quick succession, formation flying under varying conditions, and the execution of offensive and defensive tactics against air and surface forces. They were instructed as well on how to maintain aircraft in the field, on procedures for movement to a new base, and on necessary administrative and housekeeping activities.[74] Training continued in advanced acrobatics, aerial bombing, and gunnery exercises and in simulated individual combat and instrument and night flying. Pilots were to participate in at least one supervised interception and three attacks on bomber formations at an altitude of 20,000 feet or above.[75] Special attention was given to offensive actions against surface targets, such as strafing, rocket firing, and skip bombing.[76]

September 5, 1943
Bartow Army Air Field
Bartow, Florida

Dear Family,

This P-51 is a real plane. As long as you fly it, everything is OK. If you relax and let it fly you, that causes trouble. You know, I have been higher in it and gone faster in it than most people now alive will ever go or have gone...I still feel that a fighter is the only thing to be in when the fighting starts. When you are moving better than 500 mph, there isn't very much that can stop you.

This game requires the ultimate in physical perfection. Along with high speeds go great forces...So, it looks as though I shall have to give up my drinking, or at least limit it to very occasional bouts. I'll have to sleep more...Women aren't any trouble—there aren't any here.

When we finish here, we will be able to take care of ourselves. However, I think one thing should be stressed more: self defense on the ground. Forced landings are common and 85% of those who land behind enemy lines get back. The other reason is that when we are short of planes, the air corps is occasionally used as a ground force.

I got over my case of nerves OK. I went back to the line and played around the ship until I lost the nerves. It is the second time I have even had them. Most people get them when they solo first. I didn't. I got them first time in basic just after I had a very minor accident. That, combined with a few other factors, gave me a case of nerves which lasted a few hours. It is a funny thing. Most flyers get them once in a while—usually when you least expect them. I think it was due to a ride I had yesterday. While I was landing, the instructor tried to fight my controls and as a result we had what might be called a rough landing. I took the plane right up again, shot three perfect landings. There is nothing that makes me as mad as an instructor or pilot who is on the controls when I am trying to fly. It is dangerous. However, from now on I fly solo ships, so I am happy again.

In Steven Spielberg's *Empire of the Sun*, the central character, Jim, a young English boy incarcerated in a Japanese prison camp in China, is singing a salute to departing Japanese kamikaze pilots when a flight of P-51 fighters suddenly swoops in on the unprepared Japanese. The audience's spirits soar with the boy's as he shouts triumphantly "P-51! Cadillac of the sky!" As he watches, rapt, from a rooftop of the prison camp, a P-51 roars by at eye level and the pilot, with casual bravura, salutes the boy. The pilot's unaffected camaraderie, his heedless aplomb, and the throbbing strength of his sleek silver plane capture in a subliminal flash all that a liberating America represented in the Second World War. It is a brilliant, powerful scene.

The P-51 was a single-engine, low-wing monoplane, lighter than the P-38 Lightning or P-47 Thunderbolt. The P-51H, my father's plane, had a range of 1,800 miles, a top speed of 487 mph, and a service ceiling of more than 40,000 feet. It was armed with six .50 caliber machine guns and could take rockets or bombs up to 2,000 pounds. Sixty years after the war, surviving German and Japanese soldiers recall the hopelessness and fear inspired by the ferocity of P-51 assaults. "When I saw those Mustangs over Berlin, I knew that the war was lost," remarked Herman Goering at the Nuremberg Trials. When, courting my future mother after the war, my father buzzed her town in central Pennsylvania in his P-51, the entire town turned out to cheer rapturously. The panache of fighter pilot and fighter plane alike made them the hussars of their day.

October 5, 1943
Bartow Army Air Field
Bartow, Florida

Dear Family,

We are in the midst of aerial gunnery, strafing, skip bombing and dive bombing. It is a lot of fun, but by no means as simple as it sounds. The complicating factor in combat flying is that everything must be thought of in terms of formations, rather than of the individual...Had a very sudden awakening today...It was about something I had known but not fully appreciated, namely, constant and increasing visual alertness.

A group of instructors and a few of us trainees—all in P-51s—were to escort a group of bombers on a mission. Everything went well: we met the bombers, started to escort them. Then some P-47s attacked us—designated as enemy for this problem. [B]y the time those responsible had seen them, they had already attacked and would have shot down a good number of the bombers...I happened to see them, so I felt good...We escorted the bombers and they did their bombing. At that time we were again attacked and this time practically none of us saw them. It really wakes you up when you think of what would have happened if they had used 50s [.50 caliber machine guns] instead of cameras. It turned out fairly well, though, since it was our first mission of this type, since the formation was one we had never used and since visibility was nil. We learned a lot from it.

One amusing thing happened, though. The bomber pilots saw the attacking planes, spoke on the radio in the most scornful voice you can imagine: "Here come those [censored] pea shooters." About 30 seconds elapsed. "Cripes, but they are fast." They aren't going to live that down for a while.

October 13, 1943
Bartow Army Air Field
Bartow, Florida

Dear Family,

I have some news for you. Bad from my viewpoint. Good from yours...I [have been appointed] gunnery instructor. Out of the 60 of us here in my class, two of us were chosen to stay here as instructors. This was determined by our flight commander [based on] our flying ability and our gunnery scores. (The two of us had the highest record fire of any trainees to-date.)

Now, although I am none too keen on the idea, I will get a lot of good experience here. There is still the probability of foreign service—after a few months as instructor. And I will be flying the newest P-51... But it still would have been nice to have stayed with the same fellows, for I have a couple of darn good friends here. It also would have been nice to be going across in a couple months instead of some six months or longer. This way, though, I will eventually go across in a fighter group, rather than an unprotected, stripped down reconnaissance group...

You asked about my schedule. I am flying A-36, P-51A and P-51B. We fly any ship on the field. Our schedule has been ground school half a day and flying the other half—with skeet, hangar work, maintenance, armament, intelligence report reading, aerial gunnery, film analysis—and night flying. I have flown the famous P-47—the Thunderbolt. The more I fly it, the less I like it. It doesn't compare with the P-51 in any way. It is safe enough. Trouble is that it is too much work to fly. Like driving a truck versus a roadster. After flying the P-47, it is like taking a vacation to fly the P-51. I guess my only true love...is the P-51.

October 23, 1943
Bartow Army Air Field
Bartow, Florida

Dear Family,

Being instructor gives a lot of privileges and leeway. All the dog-fighting, acrobatics, low altitude buzzing that I want. Gives responsibilities, too. When you take up a few green train-

ees on a flight, you can't get lost, disobey regulations, do any sloppy formations, etc. (Do I sound like a dignified, serious instructor?)

The first time I was up in the P-47, one tank ran dry and the motor quit before I could shift tanks. Those few seconds it took to get it going again seemed like eternity. It is amazing how much you can think of in so short a time. I've run through the entire gamut of emotions [recently]. I really had a case of nerves last week. Went into a dive in a P-47…Controls froze. Going too fast to bail out. Pulled out by luck at 800 feet going almost 600 mph—or roughly 880 feet/second. Lady luck gave me about .9 of a second leeway.

[Been thinking of marrying Tillie but] I'm not willing to assume the responsibility of a wife…As you hinted Dad, in this game you must be careful, but you can be too careful. Combat tactical flying requires split-second decisions. If you try to take time to reckon your life's chances—as you would if a wife and kid were home—you might…lose your split-second timing, which is fatal.

Writing in *Fire in the Sky*, Bergerud observes "that what the civilian world considered maturity could in fact be a danger in combat."[77] He quotes a B-25 crewman:

I found that a lot of the married men didn't come back. They were a little older or had more responsibility. There might have been a little hesitation. It wasn't good to think if you were a pilot. There were a lot of young war widows. That was my observation. Being cautious wasn't always safe. Their mind was at home with their wife or baby and not where they were. They'd get to daydream, and one split second and you're gone. Trouble comes fast because you're moving so fast.[78]

December 21, 1943
Bartow Army Air Field
Bartow, Florida

Hello,

We (and all the training schools) are so tied down by regulations—so-called "safety rules"—that we can almost only fly straight and level. Over a period of time accidents are bound to happen. Naturally these are played up in papers. A bunch of fool women, old men and editorial writers starts drives with the result that the army is forced to put out regulations. To a certain extent, it is right, but when a fighter pilot of my class (P-51s, etc.) goes across, a good share of his work is strafing. The rest is along the line of dog-fighting and attacks on bombers.

A few months ago, a P-51 crashed into a bomber on simulated attack. Now all our passes are made at a target flying straight and level. Dog-fighting—once in a while there is an air collision, so—no dog-fighting. Strafing—nope. Some farmer complained because his cows ran across a pasture. Some war-worker complained because he couldn't sleep all afternoon, so now we can't do any low altitude work...It is getting so that we are graduating kids from here who have never buzzed or been in a dog-fight...Perhaps all these rules do save pilots and planes. I don't believe it though. It may decrease accidents here (but not much), but when a pilot gets across, he doesn't have more than one chance and...if that one chance is the first time he has tried [a maneuver]...he is the first one shot down.

But we don't even dare break a regulation anymore. I haven't dog-fighted or buzzed in quite a spell. Anyone caught breaking regulations is discharged and drafted as a private. The risk isn't worth it.

William Manchester, explaining how young Marines mustered the near-suicidal courage required to wade ashore under heavy enfilading fire from entrenched Japanese emplacements, said that "none of us thought we would be the one to get it; it would always be the other guy." Bergerud quotes a fighter pilot on the aircraft carrier *Enterprise*: "Younger men thought less—that was good. Young people just have no doubts, no reflections. They don't think, they do it. You can't dwell on things. If someone was lost, he was lost. You didn't talk it over. You just get up and take off again."[79]

My father made similar observations. However much the psychological defense mechanism underpinned almost incomprehensible courage, the statistics showed how often the "other guy" actually "got it," both in training and in combat. According to the *Army Air Forces Statistical Digest, World War II*, between December 1941 and August 1945, there were 15,000 fatalities involving 14,000 wrecked military aircraft in the continental United States *alone*.[80] Pilots generally viewed these losses as an unfortunate but necessary cost of combat preparation. Civilians viewed the situation differently. The smart money would have been on the pilots.

February 24, 1944

Dear Family,

By now you have received my telegram telling you I am a 1ˢᵗ Lieutenant.

June 4, 1944
3ʳᵈ Air Commando Group
4ᵗʰ Fighter Recon. Squadron
Lakeland Army Air Field
Lakeland, Florida

Above you see my new address. I received my orders last Friday, moved over here…I will be on my way to the Pacific [in about two months]…I want to go across…All the fellows with whom I should have gone across are almost ready to come back. Then they can relax for the duration. I still have to sweat it out...

I will be in the 3ʳᵈ Air Commando Group...If you read the comic strip "Terry and the Pirates" you will learn as much as I will be able to tell you. I'm going to have to work harder to stay in this outfit. It is all hand-picked and a darn good, tough outfit....Saw the famous Col. Phil Cochran the other day—the Flip Corkin of the papers. He was over at our field.

I have lost count of my [war] bonds. I have been buying them every month. If I am killed, don't forget that in addition to my property, you are also able to collect my insurance, pension, and six months gratuity pay.

A 1981 biography of Milton Caniff, the creator of the long-running *Terry and the Pirates* and *Steve Canyon* comic strips, called him the "Rembrandt of the Comic Strip."[81] When war broke out in 1941, Caniff put his hero in the uniform of the Army Air Forces. When Terry received his wings as a fighter pilot, in a famous Sunday strip entitled "Let's Take a Walk, Terry," the pilot listened to a speech by his commanding officer, admonishing him to show proper respect to the inventors of powered flight, his aircraft's designers, his support crew, and to the military bureaucracy. The strip was read into the *Congressional Record*.[82]

The cast of the strip was largely based on real-life characters, including Maj. Gen. Claire Chennault and Gen. Joseph Stilwell, as themselves, Lt. Peter Pipper (John F. Kennedy), Miss Mizzou (Marilyn Monroe), Lt. Upton Bucket (Bill Mauldin, the infantryman's counterpart to Caniff), and several from the Air Commandos, most notably Col. Flip Corkin (Col. Philip Cochran). Cochran, the prototypical modest-but-dashing hero that Americans needed early in the war, was a founding officer of the Air Commandos. An ROTC graduate of Ohio State, where he met Caniff, Cochran began a remarkable wartime flying career as a P-40 fighter pilot in North Africa. After six months of combat, he had downed several German planes and won the Distinguished Flying Cross with two clusters, a Silver Star, the Soldier's Medal, the Air Medal with three clusters, and the Croix de Guerre with Star and Palm.[83] His exploits in Burma as co-commander of the First Air Commandos, and those of his fellow air commandos, provided a constant stream of color for Caniff's popular strip.

Caniff once wrote that "These scrappy American [pilots] make better copy and are better models than can be hired from an agency. The only trouble is that their real life adventures are so spectacular I must [work continuously] to keep up with…them…"[84] The official history of the Air Commandos records that "No other artist ever came close to Caniff in his ability to capture the look, feel and flavor of the Air Force. He made a point of knowing what he was talking—and drawing—about. If his characters seemed real, it's because they often were."[85]

June 6, 1944
3rd Air Command Gp.
4th Ft. Rec. Sq.
LAAF
Lakeland, Fla

Dear Family,

The end of another long and hot day. Flew P-51 and P-40 to-day—4 ½ hours—and I'm really tired. Hmmmm—couple nurses just came in (I'm at the club)—maybe I'm not so tired.

We are really training intensively now. Seven day week—start at 6:45am (at the flight line), finish 6pm +. Makes a long day. However, if I can stay in this outfit, it will be worth it…They are all good pilots and good fellows.

Well, the invasion [of Europe] has finally started. Guess I can't make that pleasant little party. Chances are that I'll be in another just as interesting, though. The closer it comes the more anxious I get. Also, a little scared at times when I think of the consequences of the "for keeps" contest. It's pretty natural, I guess, for most of the others seem to feel the same way about it.

How would "Captain LaCroix" sound? I was given the job of sq. gunnery officer. Things are a mess and I'm having one h—l of a time getting them straightened…To be perfectly frank, the job is a little big for me. It is an awful lot of responsibility—it depends on me whether our bunch will get one [Japanese] zero or 100 zeros. But I'm working like the devil to keep the job…I think I can do it.

September 8, 1944
4th Fighter Squadron
Alachua Army Air Field
Gainesville, Florida

Dear Family,

We have finally finished our maneuvers. We are all finished with all training…with the exception of a cross-country…Things have progressed nicely.

As for my crash [during a training exercise]—you should know enough not to worry about it. After all, I wrote you half a dozen letters without even having brought it up. For your information, though…after the crash landing, I got clear of the ship and patched myself up as best I could. Planes found me half an hour later, but they couldn't get to me until four hours had elapsed. I had an inch and a half gash in my head, injuring my vanity more than anything else, for they had to shave my head for a 2" circle. It is almost all grown out now though. The gash wasn't even serious enough to take stitches in. I flew the next day. Happy now?

RECAPITULATION

October 7, 1944
Officer's Club—Drew Field
Tampa, Florida

Dear Family,

It seems funny to be all finished with flying. The next time I fire my guns and drop bombs, it won't be for fun. Wonder where it will be. We all have our own ideas, but I guess we won't actually know until we are on the way... The time is drawing close.

Between July 1, 1939 and August 31, 1945, a total of 193,440 pilots (including 35,000 fighter pilots) graduated from Army Air Force advanced flying schools. During the same period, more than 124,000 students failed to complete the primary, basic, or advanced stage of pilot instruction. This figure, including fatalities, amounted to about 40 percent of the number that entered the flying course.[86] During the course of the war, more U.S. servicemen died in the Air Corps than in the Marine Corps. Improvisation was not a free ride.

21

SHIPPING OUT

12 November 1944
West Coast

Dear Dad

Still enjoying a life of ease and luxury. The fattening before—?

Have gone into San Francisco a couple or so times, on pass. It is really quite a town. Lots of bars, liquor, and women. What more can a man want? California women, if San Francisco is a sample, are plentiful, beautiful, and tough. A nice combination as long as one has no serious intent. You may remember a Colliers article on the penthouse bar on top of the Mark Hotel. Anyway, it is the most beautiful set-up I've ever seen. The room itself is semi-circular with large plate-glass windows. You can look out at night all over the town of San Francisco. The lights, etc. are really beautiful. The room itself is air-conditioned, painted a nice, cobalt gray-blue color. It is quiet and nice in there. I was thinking about our penthouse trips, Dad. I wish you could have been there with me.

"From the river the low cry of dark shapes and winking lights that were ships echoed and re-echoed through the canyons of the avenues."[87]

Tough women, always-save-once smart; tough men, always-save-once gullible: "No, Charlotte, I'm the jury now, and the judge, and I have a promise to keep. Beautiful as you are, as much as I almost loved you, I sentence you to death." "How could you," she says. "It was easy."[88] Fog-muted gunshots and languorous blonds billowing smoky cynicism; moral ambiguity secreted in swirling gray-black shadows. Film Noir is 1940s' San Francisco; 1940s' San Francisco is Mickey Spillane. To atmospheric fatal encounter was added the leavening churn of 1.7 million troops on their way to war, washing over a city of a third as many inhabitants.

By November 1944, San Franciscans could be forgiven for thinking the war was winding down. Earlier that year, all coastal watch stations and the aircraft warning center in City Hall, as well as the Pacific Coast Warning Service in the stock exchange, were closed. The Western Defense Command eased blackout restrictions, allowing interior lighting in stores and bars as long as the light was six feet from the windows. This included jukeboxes and pinball machines. A conference was held at the Fairmont Hotel to coordinate victory garden activities. Stockpiled civilian defense supplies were auctioned off, and the state of public order was such that the deputy police chief was at leisure to propose a resolution of the Irish problem: The United States would act as "guardian" of all of Ireland for the duration of the war, after which the people would vote to choose their own form of government. There is no recorded response from Messrs. Churchill and De Valera.[89]

7 November 1944
West Coast

Election day. Don't know yet how it will come out, but here is hoping.

Things have been running along as usual—enjoying life with little work. Had a dance at the officer's club last night. Went stag, had a pretty good time. The USO put on one of the best stage shows I've ever seen. It was really good—women, jokes, dancing, singing.

*After it, we saw the show "For Whom the Bell Tolls." You should
see it, if you haven't already. It is a fair study of the more elemental
emotions of life.*

*Just heard the election returns—I'm afraid we will have four
more years of inefficiency, decay, and politics. Well, now that the
election is over, we'll have to do our best. How long do you think
utilities can keep away from government ownership? I don't imagine these next four years will be too easy, to say the least. The first
and most important thing—on my end—is the winning of the war.
Civilians will have to straighten out the other end.*

Barely a month after the 1944 general election and anticipating an
unfavorable ruling by the Supreme Court, the War Department announced the revocation of the West Coast mass exclusion order of people of Japanese descent. In the frenzied months following Pearl Harbor,
Americans of all stripes, from columnist Walter Lippman to California
Attorney General (and future Chief Justice of the U.S. Supreme Court)
Earl Warren, demanded federal action against Japanese-Americans.
In early 1942, President Roosevelt signed two executive orders and a
law passed unanimously by Congress creating the legal framework for
the evacuation and internment of 120,000 Japanese-Americans in ten
guarded, barbed wire–enclosed camps. Many Americans were appalled
by the treatment of people innocent of any wrongdoing except their
racial origin. U.S. Attorney General Francis Biddle was adamant: the
Justice Department would not support evacuation or relocation of any
citizen not charged with a crime. But the prevalent view was expressed
by Assistant Secretary of War John J. McCloy: "[I]f it is a question of
the safety of the country and the constitution…why the constitution is
just a scrap of paper to me."

The camps compounded legal disenfranchisement and cultural humiliation with the economic loss of dispossession. Repeated challenges
to the legal buttresses of the internment regime were rejected by the
Supreme Court, citing the exigencies of war. In the camps themselves,
leadership positions were offered to the *Nisei*, or American-born Japanese, while the older generation, the *Issei*, normally venerated in tradi-

tional Asian culture, was ignored. Those sent to the camps were forced to abandon all but a few of their personal possessions, sell their homes, farms, and businesses at desperation values, or board them up against better days. Vandals and thieves often left them with less than the legally sanctioned vultures to whom they were alternately prey. By the time the 1948 Japanese-American Evacuation Claims Act paid out 37 million dollars in reparations, the Federal Reserve Bank estimated Japanese-American internees had lost 400 million dollars in property, excluding losses from business interruption and denial of constitutional rights.[90]

It is an easy, and perhaps a necessary, thing to condemn the Japanese-American internments on grounds of racism pure and simple. But many otherwise fair-minded men and women appear genuinely to have been persuaded that Americans of Japanese descent posed a serious security risk on the West Coast. Justice Hugo Black, speaking for the majority in upholding the exclusion order, wrote that "Our task would be simple, our duty clear, were this a case involving the imprisonment of a loyal citizen in a concentration camp because of racial prejudice...[The petitioner] was not excluded from the [West Coast] because of hostility to...his race. He was excluded because we are at war with the Japanese Empire, because the properly constituted military authorities feared an invasion of our West Coast and...military urgency demanded all citizens of Japanese ancestry be segregated..." In a later case, Chief Justice William O. Douglass wrote that the exclusion orders had one aim alone: the "protection of the war effort against espionage and sabotage."

It was not until hearings convened in the 1980s to consider additional restitution to the families of internees that the full extent of the factual misrepresentations on which many had relied became apparent. The FBI, the Justice Department, and the Office of Naval Intelligence had all vigorously opposed internment, arguing that Japanese-Americans were by and large loyal and innocent of charges of espionage and sabotage. The 442nd Regimental Combat Team, made up of Hawaiian and mainland Nisei, was the most decorated unit for its size and length of service in the history of the U.S. military. Its 14,000 fighters earned 9,486 Purple Hearts, 20 Medals of Honor, and 7 Presidential Unit Citations.[91] Justice Frank Murphy, writing for the dissent in the same case in which Justice Black had defended against accusations of racism, made the obvious point: Japanese-Americans should have been treated "on an individual basis" through "investigations and hearings to separate the loyal from the disloyal, as was done in the case of persons of German and Italian ancestry."[92] However rationalized, the internments were a "legalization of racism."

As comforting as it might have been, the re-emergent normalcy at home was deceptive. The invasion of the Philippines was barely underway. Okinawa and Iwo Jima were months in the future. The Battle of the Bulge had yet to erupt. The Frauenkirche's Baroque grandeur still dominated an unblemished Dresden skyline. The death camps at Auschwitz, Bergen-Belsen, Buchenwald, Dachau, Jasenovac, and Sachsenhausen were with maleficent energy "belching outrageous flame."[93] In the months of November, December 1944 and January 1945, American killed, wounded, and missing totaled 72,000, 88,000, and 79,000.[94] The end of the war was lifetimes away.

22

DAMN FOOLS AND THEIR FLYING MACHINES

On an ultramarine blue disc, the Southern Cross consisting of five stars in white between a flaming comet, the head consisting of a white five pointed star, charged with a red roundel, within a blue disc outlined in white, its tail consisting of three white streamers; all surmounted by an Arabic numeral "5," golden orange.

—Insignia of the Fifth Air Force (Including Third Air Commando Group)[95]

The military historian B.H. Liddell Hart noted wryly that "The only thing harder than getting a new idea into the military mind is getting an old one out." The American Revolution was won in large part because the Americans adopted guerilla warfare tactics to defeat a far superior British force unable to break from the traditional tactics in which they were well-practiced. At the outset of the Pacific War against the Japanese, the Americans found themselves in the reverse situation: schooled and skilled in the traditional Europe-centric warfare of massed armies and aircraft, they faced an elusive, dispersed enemy in terrain and climate entirely unforgiving. The war became a daily battle for communications and supply lines, often requiring Special Forces operating deep in enemy territory to shut off the flow of food, ammunition, and equipment—literally to starve the enemy.[96]

The U.S. Army Air Force Air Commandos were an early attempt to overcome the inertia of tradition. The mercurial British General

Orde Wingate, a Churchill protégé, conceived the unorthodox antecedent of our present-day Special Forces, the British Long Range Penetration operations in Burma. The legendary Merrill's Marauders was the American counterpart. Wingate requested American air support for his behind-the-lines operations and received the approval of Churchill and Roosevelt at the 1943 Quebec Conference. General Arnold was charged with implementation of the support plan. In consultation with Wingate and Lord Mountbatten (overall commander of allied forces in the China-Burma-India theater), Arnold selected two American fighter pilots, Colonels Philip Cochran and John Alison, to head the project. Arnold's thinking, as he explained it at the time, was that "Fighter pilots were selected as they are damn fools enough to try anything that isn't orthodox."[97]

Arnold's conception of the Air Commandos was a highly mobile fighting unit complete with its own transportation and services. It would be "an experiment looking toward future air warfare."[98] The Air Commandos were intended to operate as airborne special forces: seizing and holding enemy airfields, providing close air support for ground troops behind enemy lines, acting as an independent striking force, and furnishing supply and evacuation support. The experiment was launched successfully in Burma with the First Air Commando Group. Success bred emulation, and the Second and Third Air Commando Groups, with handpicked fighter pilots including my father, were formed. The Second went to the Burma theater; the Third was sent to New Guinea, arriving in November 1944.

25 November 1944
Dutch East Indies

At this point I am in a transport plane, flying over New Guinea. Have spent a couple of days at Biak, waiting around. A group of us spent the time exploring the Jap fortifications. They really had this place tunneled and fortified. The island is coral, so they just had to do a little more tunneling and they had perfect impregnable fortifications—fortifications that you can't see until you are on them.

I'll never understand how in the devil we ever captured the island. Even Guadalcanal didn't compare with this. When you realize that this was just a small island and that there are hundreds more like it, you begin to realize the proportions and difficulties of the Jap war.

We've seen some beautiful country. I've never seen water as blue in all my life. And it is almost always sunny weather. A week here and you begin to look like a native. Slightly yellow and black. The Atabrine[99] we take dyes your skin yellow as long as you take it. It fades back to normal about two months after you quit taking it.

Don't worry so much about me. When my time comes, it will come and it wouldn't matter much whether I was here or there. Besides, we won't start our fighting for a while yet.

The battle for Biak, William Manchester wrote, resulted in the most murderous discovery of the Pacific War. Until then, the Japanese had defended each island at the beach. When the beach was lost, the island was lost. The surviving Japanese troops would re-form for a massed banzai attack, often quaffing sake and beer to bolster courage, and rush straight into a wall of American artillery, tank, and small-arms fire. American casualties were as minimal as Japanese were horrendous. After Biak, the enemy retreated into interior caves. Rooting them out fundamentally altered the cost of American victory.[100] Douglas MacArthur's island-hopping strategy was an attempt to recalibrate the cost equation.

Island jungle fighting involved perils beyond the omnipresent threat of Japanese ambush, sniping, and assault. Malaria, dengue fever, scrub typhus, dysentery, jungle rot: the physical counterpart of psychological combat stress, producing fatigue and the "bulkhead stare" of looming mental breakdown. The neuropsychiatric incidence rate for American soldiers was highest in this theater. Bottomless swamps gulping tractors, tanks, and men without a trace; slicing kunai grass; leeches and crocodiles—freshwater and saltwater; "Wait-a-Minute Vines" with razor sharp thorns. In the Solomons, an entire squad of U.S. infantrymen was crushed by falling giant trees during monsoon rains. In New Guinea, a top Japanese general and his aides drowned when their canoe capsized attempting a crossing of a monsoon-swollen stream during a retreat from Port Moresby. While natives, particularly those who had prior experience with the Japanese, often assisted the Allies, tribes in New Guinea's interior were intensely warlike and loathed outsiders. Downed fliers disappeared in the jungles of New Guinea.

29 November 1944
New Guinea

Had one of the most useful and interesting lectures today I've had since college. We spent the day out in the jungle learning about the few poisonous or dangerous insects and reptiles, how to get water out of vines and trees, how to get food and what is edible, etc. If I ever bail out over the jungle, I'll be able to get back to my own men, although it would take months. We have the natives on our side, which is a big help. (It seems the Japs took a few too many women to make the blacks happy). You would be surprised at how much edible stuff there is in a jungle. At any rate, as long as I keep out of the Japs' way, I'm pretty confident that I could live for months on either jungle or ocean. You might remember that.

Found something else you can send me, any and all the Tabasco sauce or other hot sauces would be more than welcome. You see, Dad, spam in this war corresponds to salmon in the last war. Luckily, though, in the last week I've only had it about 14 times. However, can't complain too much, while we were in the jungle we got some fresh jungle cucumbers (look like green oranges) and some pau-paus.

These pau-paus look somewhat like a yellow cantaloupe, except the outside is smooth and a little bit poisonous to the extent of causing a rash if held against the body. However, the inside is almost orange and just as soft and nice as an over-ripe melon. It tastes…like cantaloupe, pineapple and peaches put together. Most delicious thing I've found in years. Anyway, we got several of them and brought them back to camp for fresh fruit.

Outside of the heat, it is pretty nice here. The territory looks like a combination of Florida, New Hampshire and the bare mountains of California. The only incongruous features are driving on the left side of the road and the Aussies. They talk pretty much like Englishmen except they don't have quite as much of a mush sound. They are a tall, lean, tough tribe. We like them a lot better than Englishmen.

No one who has not served in the military, lived on a Pacific island, or been British can truly appreciate the dark humor of Monty Python's SPAM sketch:

Restaurant customer: "Well, what've you got?"

Waitress: "Well, there's egg and bacon; egg sausage and bacon; egg and spam; egg, bacon and spam; egg bacon sausage and spam; spam bacon sausage and spam; spam egg spam spam bacon and spam; spam sausage spam spam bacon spam tomato and spam."

SPAM (capitalization is obligatory) was launched by Hormel in 1937 as "the Miracle Meat."[101] In 1940 it was the subject of perhaps the first singing commercial, a jingle to the tune of the chorus of "My Bonny Lies Over the Ocean":

SPAM SPAM SPAM SPAM
Hormel's new miracle meat in a can
Tastes fine, saves time.
If you want something grand,
Ask for SPAM.

Requiring no refrigeration and exempt from the wartime rationing of beef (SPAM consists of chopped pork shoulder and ham), the military and the public, both at home and abroad, quickly took to the Miracle Meat. Nikita Khrushchev, in advertising you couldn't pay for, credited SPAM with the survival of the Russian Red Army during the Second World War. SPAM persisted after the war as the keystone of the British dietary pyramid, a particular point of grievance with Monty

Python. SPAM went on to sponsor George Burns's and Gracie Allen's network radio show, including the porcine celebrity "Spammy the Pig." A little-known religion called "Spammism" even worships the meat.

SPAM has also been a remarkably effective tool of cultural, or at least culinary, imperialism. Prior to World War II, Pacific islanders in Micronesia, Melanesia, and the Marshalls lived a relatively healthy life consuming locally caught fish and homegrown chicken, okra, and taro. When the American military departed, or retired into segregated local base installations, it left behind literally mountains of SPAM. Conversion of the local populace was a foregone conclusion, as was, coincidentally, the steady and unabated rise in cases of circulatory diabetes and gout, not to mention gargantuan weight gain.

Today, Guam, Saipan, and Samoa, all affiliated territories of the United States, consume at least 50 percent more SPAM than Hawaii, which leads the fifty states in SPAM consumption. At a Denny's restaurant in Guam, one can satisfy a SPAM-attack with a "Five-Meat Omelet," each meat a SPAM derivative, served with "two selections of starch." The largest floor display in the Guam K-Mart is the small Annapurna of SPAM cans crying out for panfried companionship with some fried rice, fried bananas, and fried eggs topped with, of course, SPAM. Mickey Mouse and Ronald McDonald may be the feted icons of American cultural influence, but Spammy the Pig is its unsung hero.

---

6 December 1944
New Guinea

Enclosed please find ten photographs of natives. These pictures were taken at a native village near Lae—a short ways from here… Notice the bones in their noses. Only about half of the natives have them now, but they are still pretty common. Most of the bones are human bones, for these natives only recently ceased head-hunting. Mother, please don't be shocked, as you may, at picture No. 1 [native women with breasts exposed]. Put it in my album with the rest, for it is part of my experiences here. If you tend to be shocked, look through National Geographic.

This afternoon I saw something I'll remember quite a spell. Went to a native "sing-sing." This, evidently, is an annual ceremony, 5 or 6 tribes gathering to celebrate. These natives in separate groups of tribes are all painted up, have elaborate beaded dresses and other body ornaments. Some of these look like inverted bows with birdlike objects fastened to the bowstring so that, as the weaver dances, the object moves up and down. Some had very beautiful beak dresses made of rare jungle-bird feathers. Others had some bamboo monstrosities. A few natives lucky enough to have them wore mirrors on their hats. Quite a few of the natives had G.I. shorts or belts, apparently these objects being considered rare possessions. Most of them, however, wore the usual bright shirts of brilliantly shaded cloth—the louder the better. The village inhabitants not dancing—only the warrior class dances—were camped all around. Incidentally, the local chaplains had made a little "suggestion," for all the young women wore covering of sorts over their breasts. This is very unusual. The older women, however, paraded in their usual lack of clothes, their either pregnant or malaria-bloated stomachs hanging ludicrously in front. You know, nudism may be healthy, but an old woman is definitely not an object of beauty.

Anyway, to continue, the dancers are usually in a circle, somewhat as in the movie versions. The dances consist of mainly beating their gourd-drums. Strangely enough, the music and the dances seem to be in pretty much of a set pattern, although it takes quite a while to discover it. Their singing—although it lacks anything resembling a tune—is really quite harmonious—that is, all the singers are vocally complementary. At any rate, this dance goes on for two days steadily, the dancers sort of running a marathon. As soon as one falls out, another takes his place. Each of the five tribes seeks to outdo the other. Incidentally, although there is quite a variety of bead dresses in each tribe, each tribe has a distinctive trend of painting and headgear which is basically uniform in theme.

These natives run around all the time, trying to get rides in jeeps, etc. One came into our tent one afternoon carrying a two-foot machete. It turned out he wanted to barter sea-shells for goods of various kinds. At first glimpse, though, we all reached for our .45's. Some of them are still plenty wild, as some Japs can testify.

A week by longboat and another on foot out of Samarinda in East Kalimantan on the island of Borneo, adequately plumbed urbanism had devolved to a preadamite Eden. Nature exploded in a riot of fertility: carrion-scented, trampoline-sized carnivorous rafflesia blooms, red and white hydrophilic nose-apes, omen-laden rhinoceros birds, beamy wings conjuring an unsettling deep-forest steam engine, razor-tusked foraging boar, 200-foot iron, ebony and tapang trees bestriding like Norse titans a mist-embraced Valhalla. I had set out to sample firsthand the dense, steaming, other-world into which men like my father were so abruptly thrust. It was a walk into the world before memory: a journey to breathe "a virgin atmosphere,"[102] to see that which, as Edmund White has said of Paris, can be seen by the walker alone.[103]

At seventy-three, my Dayak chief guide, Majid, aged but ageless, withered yet annealed, was a kindred spirit with those stolid Masai hunters whose energetic "saunter" had me wheezing in their dusty track during perambulations through the Rift Valley. Being outpaced and outlasted by a septuagenarian is not the stuff on which an explorer's self-image is nourished. Only my two younger Dayak companions, carriers and apprentice guides, had the tact (assuredly feigned) to appear intermittently winded during daily ten to fifteen mile treks.

Majid lived and fought through the Japanese occupation of Borneo, the western colonial regimes and independence struggles that preceded and succeeded it. And now he was battling to retain the evaporating memory of an ancestral forest. He recounted the tale of a battle lost before it was fought. Collapsing social order, economic privation, and a post-Suharto political vacuum had stimulated corruption and accelerated illegal logging. Indonesia bans riparian logging, fearing the domino effect of erosion, silting, and flooding, and stations customs agents at intervals along key rivers to interdict illegal loggers. Working in tandem with offshore Japanese timber processing ships, local gangs bribe officials, whose legal wage is less than one hundred U.S. dollars per month, to turn a blind eye. The gangs then move up the river at night with motorboats and chainsaws to denude huge sections of the banks, using the river's natural road to float log rafts to the waiting Japanese ships. Voracious hardwood demand in Asia and the West ensures large profit at little risk.

The Borneo rainforest, like much of its counterpart in New Guinea, is unlike the entwining, entrapping quagmire of popular imagination. The arching canopy, a verdurous and nearly impermeable mantle some 150 feet above the forest floor, greedily intercepts the sun's rays, consigning the vaulted cathedral below to light-speckled gloaming. Monopolizing a phototropic world, the roof of the rainforest is home to 80 percent of rainforest life. In feudal emulation, the canopy furnishes its tenants with home and sustenance in exchange for their fructifying labors. Life in profusion is concentrated in the trees: toucans, orangutans, macaws, cuckoos, hornbills, hair-raising howler monkeys, mosses, lichens and orchids, flying squirrels and Flying Dragon lizards, lemurs, geckos, parachuting Paradise tree snakes, parasitic wasps, fox bats with six-foot wingspans, Red Leaf monkeys, Asian Fair Bluebirds, Whitehead's Spider Hunters, Gold-Whiskered Barbets, huntsman spiders the size of a human hand, tailless whip scorpions, six-inch centipedes, Bornean Bristleheads, long-tailed parakeets, man-thick liana vines, armored pangolins. Entomologists "fogging" a single tree with insecticide can easily recover five thousand distinct species of insect life in the collecting trays placed at the base of the tree.

But this benevolent Antaeus has feet of clay. Like the mythical Greek giant, the rainforest draws its strength from the earth, in this case only about four inches of fertile topsoil. Below this thin layer of life lies a coagulant of clay incapable of sustaining the massively intricate ecosystem of the rainforest. As Hercules strangled Antaeus by lifting him off the earth, logging of the canopy spawns erosion in monsoon rains, removing forever the vivifying link between earth and forest. Semi-tropical forests logged in Tasmania to fuel coke ovens in the nineteenth century remain barren moonscapes more than a century later, not a sprig of green to be seen. When I stood on the seashore of Sarawak, on the western side of Borneo, in 1983, the rainforest bordered the beach; twelve years later it was not visible from the beach. Mile-upon-mile of eroded, unarable, unoccupied wasteland is the only remnant of a 70-million year legacy. Incapable of regeneration, the most prolific and durable life system known to man capitulates to a memory measured in generations.

With the anger of remediless injustice, Majid swelled with indignation at "those who whored on his virgin Amazonia,"[104] as Luis Sepulveda has described the loss of another legacy in *The Old Man Who Read Love Stories*. His black-brown eyes sparked, his jaw set, and his muscular brown arms pulsed with the surge of his fury. Misreading my dismay as reaction to his uncharacteristic eruption, he exhaled and grimaced in semi-apology. Still, knowing he had once been an active headhunter, I could not help shuddering at each tenebrous glare. I wondered whether one foreswore headhunting as one might cigarettes or carbohydrates. Were there patches, designer diets, and support groups to ease decollation dependency? Were there relapses?

The logistical complexities of jungle fighting, combined with the relatively uncharted nature of much of the terrain, made native guides and porters indispensable. Native culture is tightly knit; an offense, even inadvertent, against one villager could have repercussions that rippled through an entire clan, village, or tribe. Small numbers of Japanese military police and personnel abused local native women, something for which they were never forgiven. They compounded their foolhardiness during retreats by murdering dozens of native laborers whom they were concerned might reveal sensitive troop movement intelligence to the Allies. In contrast, the Allies made financial restitution whenever bombing or strafing runs accidentally destroyed native fishing boats or village property. So the Allies benefited not just from cooperative native labor but from intelligence on Japanese dispositions they would otherwise have lacked.

In his revealing book on the land war in the South Pacific, *Touched With Fire*, Eric Bergerud points out that Japanese soldiers paid the price for their callousness: small units that became lost or were forced into the bush simply disappeared. Native guides with Allied troops would periodically strip off their uniforms and slip into the jungle barefoot, wiping out Japanese patrols without a sound.[105] Recovered diaries of Japanese soldiers retreating to the interiors of both New Guinea and Borneo attest to the lethal unseen efficiency of native hunters. It was a real-life reenactment of a Grade-B African explorer movie: a throbbing jungle cacophony of insect and animal profusion lulls, a sudden deafening cessation of sound, a premonitory rustle of nearby trees, the jarring emptiness of vacated humanity. In the 1970s, the Singapore government, confronting a menacing proliferation of kleptomaniacal monkeys in the public botanical gardens, brought in rifle-bearing hunters to quell and cull the Simian troublemakers. The hunters made no headway, each shot dispersing the remaining troop into the concealing flora. Dayak tribesmen with blow-pipes, imported as "remedial consultants," soundlessly eradicated the sociopaths.

The cable-sinewed Dayak guide, a body-length blowpipe in one hand, a *mandau* in the other, gestured to catch my attention and jabbed the machete-like knife at the forest canopy some two hundred feet above. Suspended in time as in space were the remains of an American World War II fighter plane, its wing insignia clearly visible through the enshrouding flora. Shaking his head and shuddering, the Dayak murmured "No tiwan" and hurried on.

The canopy-filtered light glinting on Majid's raised *mandau* sundered my reveries. I understood the gravity with which the Dayaks regard the land of the dead. In their cosmology, the human body possesses two souls. One remains with the corpse until the flesh has decomposed; the other remains in the vicinity of the death awaiting the performance of prescribed rituals to ease the soul on its dangerous journey to the afterlife.

In preparation for the secondary burial or tiwan, the deceased's body is interred in a holed urn to permit egress of fluids. The receptacle is then stored in the home for several months until decomposition is complete. On an auspicious date, the bones are exhumed, cleaned, and placed in an ossuary, the process culminating in a village-wide feast to launch the soul on its way to the mountainous land of the dead. The absence of tiwan implies unrest, an unsettled spirit, a memory incomplete. The lost American aviator—unremarked, uncelebrated—wandered unsettled.

---

8 December 1944
New Guinea

Worked on my plane all day, finally got it fixed up. Some care-
less [censored] in the factory left a loose bolt in the back. That fell
down, shorted out some wires. Just because of one careless fool, we
almost wrecked a ship. I'd sure like to fix up a twin place fighter
and take some of those men up and scare hell out of them. And
believe me, I could give them a case of nerves they wouldn't forget
in a long time.

Beer tonight. Got our weekly 3 cans. We put it in a wet stock-
ing. After an hour or so the evaporating water cools the beer several
degrees. You know, it is surprising how quickly you learn to like
warm beer. In fact, I like anything and everything except spam. I'd
still rather eat anything rather than spam: cold, or cool, clammy,
greasy spam. When they have that, I cook up some extra rations we
have. Vegetable stew and hash, dehydrated beef and rice, canned
beans and beef—they all taste pretty darn good and do give us a
little variety. We can't complain. Besides, it doesn't do any good.

From the way I've talked, you probably think life is miserable.
It isn't. We kick mainly to keep happy. We have everything we need
and are comfortable. We work, but it is the type we like, so no one
objects. When a fellow gets his own plane, he doesn't mind work-
ing on it all the time. You sort of get to like a plane like you do a
woman—except you can't physically love a plane. So far I haven't
figured out a name for it.

Rosie the Riveter was both measure and metaphor of the American public's total wartime engagement. Her muscled forearm, bandan-
naed and coveralled figure projected an androgynous neutrality without
which America's prodigious munitions production effort would have
been impossible. She was as much a harbinger of the post-war industrial
New World as were changes in manufacturing processes and quality

control. As with all change, the abandoned status quo implicit in her newfound role was not received with universal enthusiasm.

Manufacturing quality control during WWII was a work in progress. American corporations before the war focused on perfecting manufacturing processes, with attention to product inspection and rudimentary statistical quality control. Total quality management did not evolve until after the War. Shortly after Pearl Harbor, the United States enacted legislation to place the civilian economy on a military production footing. Military contracts until then were typically awarded to manufacturers who submitted the lowest competitive bid. Products were inspected on delivery to ensure conformity with specifications. In wartime, where a lapse in quality consistency could easily cost lives, "quality control" took on the added significance of "safety assurance."

Conscious of its military personnel in the field, the armed forces attempted to inspect virtually every unit of product to ensure its operational suitability. This regimen required such huge inspection forces that problems developed recruiting and retaining competent inspection personnel. To overcome the bottlenecks without compromising product safety, the military began to utilize sampling inspection in lieu of unit-by-unit inspection. Private sector consultants, in particular Bell Laboratories, developed sampling tables to standardize sampling inspections and published them as a military standard, Mil-Std-105. The tables were incorporated into military contracts.[106]

In a classic spin-off benefit of increased war spending, civilian suppliers were tutored in statistical quality control techniques in military-sponsored training courses. While the training led to quality improvements in some organizations, most companies did little beyond pay lip service to the true integration of these techniques in their production processes. The pressing demands of a two-theater world war, driving all government procurement decisions, meant companies continued to treat production deadlines as their top priority. Most quality control programs were terminated once government contracts concluded. A lapse in quality control might remain hidden until the operation of Murphy's Law revealed it in the heat of combat.

11 December 1944
New Guinea

As you probably realize, our nerves are beginning to tighten up. This waiting is worse than combat, for the unknown is worse. Anyway, people are beginning to snap at each other. I went through it, have gotten my nerves back to slope by means of work and sleep. They probably will tighten again after we leave here, though.

We aren't flying much for the time being, which suits me fine. I don't want to put much time on my ship before actual combat. What we are doing now is rough, but naturally doesn't compare to the real thing. We will all be glad when we get moved up.

Talk is getting around to the usual subjects—wine, women, sex, and flying. Of course we throw in a lot of bitching about food, organization, and other complaints. However, the squadron is in pretty fair shape right now. There are a lot of what you might call "personality clashes" which may cause trouble. Some of the formerly "steady" men seem to be on the edge of hysteria. For the most part, though, we will end up pretty well, I think. We have all the advantages in our favor. However, the outstanding question at this point is whether to classify a platinum blonde as precious metal or common 'ore.

Wish we would get some mail. We had one mail delivery in Frisco, haven't had any since. Morale will jump 500% when we get it. There isn't one of us who wouldn't have given all our other things in exchange for a little mail.

We sit here by the hour—writing letters and talking stories. Two of the fellows here can tell them by the hour. Once in a while we get a really clean one. Sometimes our flight leader tells us horror stories, having gone through the battles of Guadalcanal and several others. However, we are too close to appreciate very many of them. Some things that are factual here are almost unbelievable, yet can and have been proved by photographs and other means. Before you are here long, you begin to look at a Jap like an animal—an animal that has to be respected for fighting ability, but hated and despised as a man. You can't call them human beings—they aren't. However, I'm beginning to sound like a propaganda booklet so I'd better stop. This type of thing is restricted—guess they are afraid of waking the American public out of its stupid complacency.

25 December 1944
New Guinea

Dear Family,

Another Christmas come and almost gone. Last year—Dallas. Year before—San Antonio. Next year—maybe home. Maybe China. Who knows…I flew a fuel consumption test on my plane yesterday afternoon. I was up over three hours and believe me, a rubber boat is the hardest and most uneven seat you could ever find. You get numb, sore, aching and all you can do is swear since undoing the safety belt isn't the best idea in the world. Anyway, I flew over some of these 7000 feet mountains. You can see numerous streams that start with a trickle at the top, end up in a rushing torrent cascading over 200 ft cliffs, sometimes larger. Surrounded by dark green jungle, it really makes an impressive sight.

Went to midnight mass in our thatched-roof chapel. Some of the boys made up a choir, did right well. It was a beautiful mass—all the more so, I guess, because it was set in such rough surroundings, but nevertheless was about our only link with home. Our outfit hasn't had mail for over two months now. Incidentally, guess the phrase "no atheists in foxholes" was correct—about 98% of the fellows received communion. Slept late this morning—about 8am. Had a wonderful turkey dinner.

I've gotten one good break. The old flight was broken up and I am now in a flight with two of the best possible pilots. The third is a good pilot, but is rather young and immature. The flight leader is fast, aggressive, but old enough (28) to have a little common sense—a perfect combination for a fighter pilot who wants to be a live hero—and that suits me fine. The others can be the dead heroes if they want. I believe in making the Japs die for their Emperor. Latest saying—Banzai—more blood for Roosevelt. Little incident that happened on Leyte. An American cornered a Jap in a cave, called in "Come out and surrender, you little yellow [censored]"; Jap answered back "Come in and get me, you dirty [censored]." It seems the Japs are cognizant of American tendencies.

Life here is quite pleasant—a lot more so than it will soon be. I've been trying to put on weight, but the almost continuous dysentery sort of tends in the opposite direction. So far, I've stayed almost the same. We have a lot of fun, though—fellows working for the same things, troubled with the same ailments, enjoying the same relaxations, swimming, combing the jungle for fruit, wild-pig hunting, bull sessions and occasionally a beer party. Last night, five tent mates polished off 44 quarts of Aussie beer. Only had three myself, though. Guess my stomach isn't big enough.

One of the most pleasant diversions here is buzzing—outlawed in the States. It is a lot of fun to go up and down a 7000 ft mountain like you go over a roll-a-coaster. It still pays to be careful, though. We lost one of our new replacements the other day—same reason—got careless, too low, hooked a wing. Not much of a Christmas present for his family. That is the trouble with new pilots—they overestimate their ability and judgment.

My father and the Third Air Commando Group were with MacArthur as he leap-frogged west from New Guinea, landed in Leyte, and battled on to a devastated Manila. Lieutenant Ishizuka and General Yamashita's Fourteenth Army were waiting.

23

TOO LITTLE TOO LATE

The year following the Battle of Midway in June 1942 marked a decisive reversal of Japanese fortunes. Defeats in the Solomons and New Guinea and the symbolically charged shooting down of Admiral Yamamoto, the planner of Pearl Harbor, following his location by American code breakers in April 1943, led Emperor Hirohito to proclaim with no risk of hyperbole that his country's situation was now "truly grave." Mounting casualties meant that able-bodied men were needed for combat duty, no matter how many or difficult their previous tours of duty. A soldier of Sergeant Ishizuka's experience and fitness was not likely to be overlooked. Late in 1943 he was recalled to active duty and was promoted to candidate for commission, assigned to the field artillery school near Chiba City, east of Tokyo.

Ordinarily a one-year period of instruction, the course—and the probationary period following its completion—was shortened under pressure of manpower shortages. Compressed though it might have been, neither rigor nor rigidity of course training was sacrificed to time. If anything, the training of a young officer was more draconian that that of an enlisted man. Beyond physical, drill, and swordsmanship training, a candidate rehearsed infantry tactics and practical field problems and received specialized instruction in his selected technical field. Officer candidate Ishizuka's training emphasized operation of 75mm and 105mm field howitzers and 81mm mortars. Candidates also received ample amounts of indoctrination training on the Imperial Army's expectations of officer conduct, emphasizing first and foremost that an officer's proper position on the battlefield was in one place only: in front of his troops.

Sometime in the second half of 1944, now-Lieutenant Ishizuka deployed for his new assignment in the Philippines. The atmosphere surrounding Ishizuka's departure for the front in 1944 was in marked contrast to his send-off to China in 1940. In place of boisterous, jingoistic, celebratory reveling, troop departures were now (as they had been since Pearl Harbor) conducted in secrecy.[107] Rigid controls on the media's dissemination of "defeatist" coverage could not prevent pullulating funeral processions and attritional food shortages from imparting an oppressive air of fatalism on the country. Lieutenant Ishizuka's sunny assurance, says his family, concealed from no one the approaching endgame. Watching the receding Honshu coastline from the deck of a troopship, his sense of déjà vu must have been laden with the looming consequences of a grand strategy gone bad. If he was galled by the country's bloody-minded leadership building a charnel house out of his generation's fealty, he—like most of Japan—interred the resentment deep within.

Ishizuka reported for duty with the veteran Fifty-eighth Independent Mixed Brigade, an amalgam fighting unit comprising motorized infantry, artillery, engineering, and support elements. It formed part of the Fourteenth Area Army Shobu Group, commanded by General Tomoyuki Yamashita, the Tiger of Malaya under whom Ishizuka had served during the conquest of Singapore. Yamashita, shortly after the brilliant success of the Malayan campaign, had fallen victim to the jealousy and longstanding enmity of Prime Minister Hideki Tojo. He was exiled to a backwater command in Manchuria where he languished until Tojo's fall from power after the loss of Saipan in mid-1944, when he was placed in command of the defense of the Philippines. Yamashita arrived in Manila barely a week before MacArthur launched the Leyte invasion. He inherited an order of battle not of his own making and from which he could at best hope to salvage the honor of delaying the inevitable.

Samar Island lies in the eastern Vizayas region of the central Philippines. Joined hip-to-shoulder with Leyte Island like a better-nourished Siamese twin, it hovers protectively over Leyte Gulf at its feet to the south. San Bernardino Strait to the north and Surigao Strait, swinging around southern Leyte to merge with the gulf, form aquatic pincers around Leyte and Samar and are the only two egresses from the central Philippines to the Pacific Ocean. In October 1944 they provided the maritime avenues by which two advancing Japanese naval fleets, in coordination with a third passing northeast of Luzon, attempted to converge on Leyte Gulf and snuff MacArthur's incipient liberation of the Philippines.

The success of MacArthur's culminating stroke to retake the Philippines, a strategic denouement to his island-hopping campaign, relied on the 738 ships and amphibious forces of Admiral Kinkaid's Seventh Fleet and the screening force of Admiral Halsey's Third Fleet to support the Sixth Army as it landed at Leyte. The Japanese, in a defining act of inspired desperation, committed to thwart the Leyte landings with a three-prong defense: a Northern "decoy" Force under Admiral Ozawa, a Southern Force to slip undetected through the Surigao Strait under Admirals Nishimura and Shima, and the Center Force, the main strike force targeting the Seventh Fleet through the San Bernardino Strait, under Admiral Kurita.

In a series of epic naval actions remarkable for their martial intrepidity and culture-driven, End-of-Days ferocity, American tactical competence was in no small part abetted by a healthy dose of Caesar's luck and uncharacteristic Japanese vacillation. The Japanese and American fleets lunged, parried, and feinted for tactical advantage in a high-stakes game of blindman's bluff. In a near-fatal ploy, the Japanese decoy fleet, relying on Admiral Halsey's well-known combative impetuosity, lured the Third Fleet north and away from the Leyte Gulf landing area, leaving the San Bernardino Strait completely unguarded. Although a surge by the Southern Force through the Surigao Strait was beaten back by a superbly executed American defense from Seventh Fleet forces, the Center Force sailing through the San Bernardino Strait completely surprised the Seventh Fleet's escort carriers assigned to protect the landing beachhead and invasion shipping, threatening a decapitation of the still-vulnerable body of landing infantry.

Reminiscent of the Spartans at Thermopylae, a small group of six escort carriers and seven escorts under the command of an American Leonidas, Admiral Clifton Sprague, unflinchingly intercepted Kurita's powerful Center Force of four battleships, seven heavy cruisers, and a multitude of escort ships, sacrificing themselves to protect the Seventh Fleet's escort carriers and MacArthur's invasion force. In a frenetic two-hour battle that saw the launching of the war's first organized kamikaze attacks, with the Japanese on the verge of annihilating Sprague's forces, Kurita suddenly and inexplicably ordered his ships to break off action. The valorous defense had succeeded; the invasion force was secure; and the Imperial Japanese Navy had effectively ceased to exist, leaving the U.S. Navy in undisputed dominance of the seas.

The Battle for Leyte Gulf was Japan's Armageddon. The debacle of Corregidor was redeemed, MacArthur's honor salvaged, and his strategic judgment exonerated. Beyond the inevitable loss of the Philippines, the battle had wider significance for Japan. In the words of Admiral Yonai, the Japanese Navy Minister, while the defeat at Leyte "was tantamount to the loss of the Philippines," in a broader context "I felt that it was the end."[108]

From the outset of his command, Yamashita was adamantly opposed to the defense of Leyte, considering it a squandering of scarce resources of manpower and materiel. Knowing that Imperial General Headquarters would sooner or later have no choice but to write off the Philippines as a strategic loss, he wanted to marshal his forces for a protracted defense of Luzon, utilizing a static defense to pin down as many U.S. divisions as possible in the hope of slowing the Allied advance toward Japan. He anticipated that MacArthur would, following the securing of a Leyte foothold, launch his invasion of Luzon at Lingayen Gulf, located on the west coast of Luzon where the fertile Central Plains of Luzon open onto the Luzon Sea. By yielding Leyte and evacuating Manila, Yamashita intended to meet MacArthur head-on, stopping him on Lingayen's beaches. Instead, he was overruled by his high command, Leyte was lost, and with it irreplaceable aircraft, cargo ships and transports, and troops drained from China and Luzon. No less ominously, his orders to evacuate Manila were largely ignored by the Navy contingents under his nominal command.

The Japanese recognized that the battle for Luzon, including Manila, would prove decisive to the outcome of the Pacific War. An elaborate defense of Luzon had been planned well ahead of the Leyte invasion, and Japanese air forces were reinforced with fighters and bombers from Burma, China, Formosa, Manchuria, Japan, and the Kuriles—some 884 aircraft of all sorts operating from over one hundred airfields. Only a few months before Ishizuka's arrival in the Philippines, American carrier-based fighter aircraft and antiaircraft fire destroyed over four hundred Japanese aircraft, three aircraft carriers, and Japanese naval air power, at the cost of some thirty planes, in the apocalyptic Great Marianas Turkey Shoot. This time around it took no more than a matter of weeks for the war's greatest concentration of Japanese air power to suffer wholesale destruction at the hands of U.S. naval and army air forces. The Americans then proceeded with "a systematic reduction of enemy communications and ground installations in a display of air-ground coordination unparalleled in the southwest Pacific," wrote the official journal of the U.S. Army Air Forces.[109]

The imbalance in losses appeared emblematic of a terminal attrition in the capacities of the Japanese war machine. The Japanese will to fight, though, was undiminished. As an official U.S. military history recounts, "[The enemy] continued to fight with the same fanatic zeal and tenacity of purpose that characterized his fighting in the early days of the war."[110] Japanese resistance in Saipan, Guam, the Philippines, Okinawa, and Iwo Jima, stiffening inversely to the prospects of ultimate victory, savaged any nascent hope of early surrender.

Ishizuka moved directly from Manila to the Fifty-Eighth Independent Mixed Brigade, located in the hills above Lingayan Gulf to the west of Baguio. With the mountains at their backs, some 152,000 Japanese troops, including Ishizuka's brigade, prepared to meet the accelerating Allied advance north through the Philippines. It is hard to believe that Lieutenant Ishizuka did not find both comfort and irony in déjà vu. He had returned to service under the command of Japan's ablest general, the architect of Japan's greatest triumphs of the war, victories in which Ishizuka was proud to have played his small part. But he would also have realized that Yamashita's return to center stage, like his own, was an instance of too little, too late. Both men would play with honor their assigned roles through to the final curtain call, but neither would have entertained hope of an encore performance.

24

THE MINDERBINDER EQUILIBRIUM

23 December 1944
East New Guinea

Dear Family,

Another fellow and I are working to make a refrigeration unit. I furnish the plans, he furnishes the work. Ideal n'est-ce pas? We are using ordinary piping from the many crashed planes here about. For a compressor we swiped an electric driven hydraulic (gear) pump. I'm not sure that it will have the necessary capacity, but we can find that out by experimentation. We use a small pipe for pressure chamber, a larger size pipe for the expansion or cooling chamber. I'll have to experiment with the expansion nozzle, fitting it to the capacity and pressure differential of the system. I think I can get some from a short ways up the coast. If not, I know I can get the necessary chemicals to manufacture some ammonia. Our object is...to cool any beverage down to a comfortable drinking temperature. As it is now, we...put a can of beer near a drainage crack on my plane, let high-octane gas drip on it for a couple of hours...making it very cool and tasty...

...You've heard about the black market racket in Europe—well, Nadzab [New Guinea] has the worst set-up you can imagine. Little

organization, no one knows where all the supplies go. A lot of the sergeants sell the supplies, pocket the money. Since it is the only way transients get much, they get away with it. Our outfit broke up one such beer racket...

If America's greatness is an engine fueled by ingenuity, initiative, enterprise, and incentive, then Milo Minderbinder, the charismatic rogue in Joseph Heller's *Catch-22*, is its runaway hijacker, careening full throttle switches thrown. As the author describes him, "Milo['s]...was the face of a man of hardened integrity who could no more consciously violate the moral principles on which his virtue rested than he could transform himself into a despicable toad. One of these moral principles was that it was never a sin to charge as much as the traffic would bear."[111]

Milo himself, justifying his "syndicate's" bombing of his own squadron, articulated his *Weltanschauung* in terms that would have done proud the "invisible hand": "In a democracy, the government is the people... We're people aren't we? So we might just as well keep the money and eliminate the middleman. Frankly, I'd like to see the government get out of war altogether and leave the whole field to private industry. If we pay the government everything we owe it, we'll only be encouraging government control and discouraging other individuals from bombing their own men and planes. We'll be taking away their incentive."[112]

The fecundity of the World War II black market is ample testament to the all-too-often happy cohabitation of ingenuity, improvisation, and illegality. With the mass movement of men and materiel to overseas battlefronts, scarcity on the home front and surfeit in the field created serendipitous job openings alike for the connected, the conscientious, and the conscienceless. On both fronts, authorities—military and civilian—struggled mightily to impose system and order on markets dynamically inclined to find and impose their own equilibrium: the Minderbinder equilibrium. Whatever the commodity—meat, whiskey, gasoline, cigarettes—illicit market-makers scratched every itch...and charged what the traffic would bear.

The black market on the home front sprouted spontaneously from the fertile ground of price controls and rationing. The Wall Street financier Bernard Baruch, drawing on his personal experience of national shortages in World War I when chairing the War Industries Board, published a 1941 article in the *Harvard Business Review* entitled "Priorities: The Synchronizing Force," proposing a rationing classification system based on priority of expenditure (running from Class AA to Class D). Acknowledging that any rationing system by its very nature "short [circuited] the laws of supply and demand" and was therefore inherently inflationary, he went on to advocate a comprehensive system of national price controls to be administered by a central authority.[113] This authority ultimately emerged as the Office of Price Administration (OPA).

Rationing products as diverse as gasoline, meat, tires, typewriters, sugar, nylon, silk, eggs, shoes, butter, and coffee to ensure military needs were met, the OPA-imposed and enforced regime encountered opposition at all levels. Organized crime counterfeited rationing coupons; corner gas station operators sold extra gas on the sly to Americans skeptical of alleged shortages (the typical ration allocation was three gallons per week); butchers and housewives colluded over beef steaks and pork chops; restaurant owners reaped windfalls from satiating scarcity-driven cravings. Not surprisingly, public support of the war effort at an abstract level assumed distinct limits when it came literally to food on the table.

On overseas fronts, the astonishing acceleration of wartime production, generating mountains of supplies and materiel, often outpaced the administrative controls required to ensure their efficient distribution and accounting. Those with "gateway" access to supplies parleyed their positions as market-makers for both civilian and military consumers. War-ravaged and war-deprived occupied territories provided the most lucrative outlets for contraband sales. An intelligence report of the U.S. Strategic Services Unit immediately after the war quoted an American Army officer in Berlin who furnished a menu of items that he provided to Soviet soldiers in exchange for dollars:[114]

- Carton of American cigarettes: $200;
- Army wrist watch: $1,000;
- Five-cent chocolate bar: $5;
- Bottle of whiskey: $150;
- Low-grade French cognac: $80;
- Pair of army boots: $200.

Another officer wrote that "nobody who sold a few cartons was considered a criminal. It was the big wheeler-dealers who dealt in cars, diamonds, and tens of thousands of dollars that the CID [Criminal Investigations Division] was after. This army organization might call on you if you ordered one hundred cartons of cigarettes a week from the United States (at one dollar a carton) and enquire politely whether you were really such a heavy smoker. But they were too busy to investigate something like twenty cartons a month. For four packages of cigarettes you could hire a German orchestra for an entire evening."[115]

Within the government, attitudes to black market operations, and their prosecution, were ambivalent. The U.S. Senate in early 1941 established the Special Committee to Investigate the National Defense Program with a mandate to investigate "excessive profits, fraud, corruption, waste, extravagance, mismanagement, incompetence, and inefficiency in expenditures connected with the prosecution of the national defense program…"[116] Initially chaired by Senator Harry Truman, the "Truman Committee" held hundreds of meetings and conducted extensive field investigations into all aspects of wartime profiteering and abuse. Its work has been characterized as "the most successful investigative effort in the history of the United States and from an initial budget of $15,000 is estimated to have saved the country in excess of $15 billion.[117]

At the other extreme, according to a former OPA Enforcement Department Director, the Justice Department, charged with investigating and prosecuting black marketers referred by the OPA, routinely refused to cooperate with the OPA on enforcement issues, considering the criminal sanctions against black marketeering as overly harsh. He comments that "Attorney General Francis Biddle decided not to prosecute black marketers in food because he felt 'OPA regulations were unfair and invalid.'"[118] President Roosevelt refused to back the OPA in its bureaucratic struggle with Justice, perhaps sensing the limits of popular self-abnegation.

Given the remarkably contracted timeframe in which the United States mobilized and fought a two-front global war, it is not surprising that a "chasm between plan and operation" not infrequently resulted in "administrative chaos," "administrative anarchy," and "trial and error fumbling," as the authors of an authoritative study on the

wartime planned economy have described it. They conclude not un-
fairly that "the successes of the wartime planned economy were 'less a
testimony to the effectiveness with which we mobilized our resources
than they are to the tremendous economic wealth which this nation
possessed.'"[119]

25

"GEM OF THE SEA OF THE ORIENT"

17 May 1945

Dear Folks,

Flew down to Manila, a few days ago…I've seen pictures of [war damage in] England and Europe, but I've never seen anything that compares with Manila. The old walled city, formerly very beautiful as well as historic, is completely ruined. Fighting did some of it, naturally, but most of it was burned and blown up by the Japs. In the entire walled city, there isn't a single building in good enough shape to be repaired. Every single one is a complete wreck. The rest of Manila was about normal. All the big buildings were blown up or ruined by the fighting, but small homes weren't too badly off. Don't let anyone kid you, though. There was some of the toughest possible fighting took place in Manila. It was a beautiful city, but it will take a long time to rebuild it…I've driven over a pretty large part of [Luzon] and every town has the same story—at minimum, all large buildings destroyed. Often most of the town is ruined…

Incidentally, saw MacArthur with his wife. Naturally I just waved and said "Hi, Mac." Well, anyway, I did say it under my breath.

Like its larger Indonesian neighbor to the south, the Philippines is an archipelagic state. And like Indonesia, governance in the Philippines is hostage to the ineluctable geopolitical reality of land broken by water—7,000 fragments of land strewn randomly over eleven seas washing the Asian landmass. Matters taken for granted in territorially unified states pose Sphinxlike policy conundrums to political leaders already hobbled by sectarian differences of culture, language, and religion. A cost-effective, unified transport system is a physical impossibility. The infrastructure of power, water, and communications is a luxury sought, not a right presumed. Distinctions polarize; national cohesion eludes.

Manila is both emblem and capital of the Philippines. A particularly hapless victim of Japanese atavism and American carpet bombing, its emergence from the rubble of 1945 has been less controlled evolution than spontaneous combustion. From a mere 900,000 inhabitants in 1945, a city of 13 million teeters today on the cusp of dysfunction, enduring air of Augean filth, gridlock of both political and arterial varieties, and cascading waves of unemployable provincial migrants. To catalyze job creation in the provinces and stem the flow of the hopeless, I was mobilizing private sector capital for a nationwide rural electrification and development program I had devised and was implementing throughout Southeast Asia.

As I crisscrossed the country canvassing sites and organizing grassroots support, I could not escape a hovering sense of parallel universes. I was inadvertently retreading my father's progress through the Philippines in 1945: in Samar, a fighter base cut out of the jungle, in Ilocos Norte another base at Laoag, in Batanes the site of a fateful strafing mission over Batan Island, in Leyte the site of his wartime recuperation from combat wounds, and, of course, in Manila and its walled city of Intramuros. And each crossed path, like each new province with its seemingly immutable problems, reinforced how thoroughly the ghosts of the past inhabit our present.

159

17 May 1945

Dear Folks,

> *I have quite a bit of stuff to send you. One of the things is an article, given to me by the father of a Filipino Lt. who fought and was taken prisoner in Bataan. It is very interesting; this father is an old Army man, fought against the Americans in '98, for the Americans in '01, and with us in the world war in '17. He is an interesting old duck...[The other] is a Philippine flag...with yellow stars representing Luzon, Mindanao and the Visayas group of islands (Leyte, Cebu, etc.). The sun is yellow and has eight groups of radiating rays, each representing one of the original provinces which fought the Spaniards in '98.*

P.D. James has written "At the heart of the universe there is cruelty. We are predators and are preyed upon, every living thing."[120] One could be excused for thinking she was writing of a half-millennium of Philippines' history. Whether at the hands of rapacious Spanish colonialists, nascent American imperialists, homicidal Japanese occupiers, or acquisitive homegrown ruling elites, fratricidal division has made the Filipino people serial hostages. In Stockholm syndrome writ large, the populace, benumbed by an interminable stream of scandal and political theater, has been exploited so long their sense of self has become dependent on their exploiters. The Catholic Church ignores the Malthusian inevitability of unchecked, impoverishing population growth with its inflexible opposition to family planning and devil-may-care "go forth and multiply" advocacy.

The historical antecedents were not promising. Magellan, with his landing in Cebu in 1521, set the tone for the next four centuries of colonial development. He promptly converted the first natives he encountered to Catholicism and formed an alliance to subjugate a nearby chieftain for purposes of exacting tribute. When the ill-planned and executed venture cost the great explorer and a significant number of his command their lives, the surviving crew proceeded to alienate their hosts with graceless attention to the local women. Many were dispatched, presumably by piqued cuckolds. The balance departed posthaste—a temporary retreat.

In 1565, Spain-in-the-islands redux, rearmed and renamed (after Philip, King of Spain, leader of the Counter-Reformation, sponsor of The Armada, and colonizer of Florida), suffered none of Magellan's extemporization. With sacred complicity underwriting secular coercion, the Spanish systematically orchestrated the near universal conversion of the population to Roman Catholicism (excepting a large Muslim chunk of Mindanao) and the creation of a landed elite. The oligarchy of landholders and the "friarocracy" of priests were the twin pillars of colonial society. Spanish transplants and co-opted local leaders formed the core of a ruling elite persisting to the present day, as much a source of social tension now as four hundred years ago. The proselytizing, opiating efforts of Augustinians, Dominicans, Franciscans, Recollects, and Jesuits provided the moral underpinnings for a truly catholic land grab.

The traditional system of governance and land ownership in the Philippines pivoted on the barangay dato, or village chief, overseeing a traditional kinship structure with communal use of land. The Spanish introduced feudal notions of land tenure, the *encomienda* system, essentially a division of the entire country into parcels, each overseen by landed nobility responsible for the spiritual and economic welfare of landless tenants or vassals. To ensure effective centralized control without creating unsustainable costs in men and material, village chiefs were in essence "elevated" to the position of landed nobility. The socially unifying bond between chief and community was broken; henceforth the chiefs looked to Manila for legitimacy.

01 May 1945

Dear Family,

I've wandered around a little. The Japs are several miles back, so we can visit quite a few towns. The Spaniards did a lot around here. Every town still has its large and once-beautiful Spanish cathedral and bell tower. In spite of their condition, you can't help but be impressed by the size and massiveness of the structures. They built pretty well. A lot of the old Spanish roads, culverts, roadside shrines, bridges are still in use, too. I think their principle contribution was Catholicism. Americans brought education, but every thing else seems to be dropping apart, whether as a result of or in spite of Americanism, I don't know.

I've met quite a few nice families here. I don't remember whether I mentioned it before, but a while back I went to the home of a very wealthy landowning doctor here. Their home would be almost a palace, even back in the States. We had dinner, played cards for a while, then we all sat down and were entertained by the girls. Over here, in the poor homes, the men do the entertaining. In the better homes, though, the women do it all. In this family's case, each of the daughters was an accomplished pianist, sometimes accompanying themselves by singing songs. It was very interesting.

The Filipinos were divided and ruled but not inert. During the two centuries following the cementing of Spanish rule, at least six major uprisings disturbed the felicity of the Spanish overlords. Three grievances in particular prompted revolt. All Filipinos were required to pay a tribute to Spain—one family, one tribute. All Filipinos were subjected to forced labor (*polo*); a prospective *polista*, or laborer, could avoid conscription only by paying an exemption fee. All Filipinos were subject to the *vandala*, under which native farmers were forced to sell their produce to the government, which abused the monopoly system when setting prices. The uprisings failed because the Spanish effectively exploited internal regional, tribal, or clan divisions. Northern Tagolog speakers were enlisted to quell southern Visayan speakers, and the favor was returned as need arose. No national identity existed.

National consciousness in the Philippines, as in restive European colonies in the twentieth century, first formed and spoke with the voice of a Western-educated, liberal local elite. The Propaganda Movement, led by the charismatic Dr. José Rizal in the last decade of the nineteenth century, was far from revolutionary. Its aims were more akin to those of a loyal opposition: representation of the Philippines in the Spanish Cortes; legal equality of Spaniards and Filipinos; creation of a public school system independent of the friars; abolition of the polo and the vandala; guarantees of freedom of speech and association; secularization of the clergy; and equal access for Filipinos to government service.[121] A remarkable intellect and humanist, Rizal embraced the new study of anthropology to refute with scientific arguments the friars' stereotypes of Filipinos as racially inferior.[122] His two great *cris de coeur, Noli Me Tangere*[123] ('Touch Me Not) and *El Filibusterismo*[124] (The Reign of Greed), damning Spanish rule in the islands, earned him a national following and the lasting enmity of Spanish church and state.

The Spanish were intractable; genuine reform was blocked at every turn. With Rizal's arrest for sedition and rebellion, the national, nonviolent movement for reform and peaceful evolution was eclipsed by a plebeian constituency espousing revolution and national independence. The *Katipunan*, or revolutionary society, patterned on Freemasonry and initially led by Andres Bonifacio, launched the Philippine Revolution, the first against Western colonial rule in Asia, in 1896, with the famous "Cry of Balintawak," the tearing up of identification certificates symbolizing vassalage to Spain.[125] The Spanish responded with a reign of terror, executing many, including Rizal, imprisoning thousands, and shipping others to Spanish colonies in Guam and Africa.

The revolutionary Katipunan, with the fratricidal self-destructiveness later to typify Filipino self-governance, broke into two factions, one led by Bonafacio, a grassroots leader, and the other by the brilliantly ruthless Emilio Aguinaldo, like Rizal a member of the educated *illustrados* class. Outmaneuvering Bonafacio, Aguinaldo ultimately gained control of the revolutionary government, in the process having Bonifacio and his brother, Procopio, executed for sedition and treason. Despite initial battlefield successes against the Spanish, the Filipinos under Aguinaldo were unable to achieve a *coup de grace*. In a move that came to symbolize the primacy of class over national interests, Aguinaldo, in exchange for the receipt of 400,000 pesos, agreed to a truce with the Spanish and to voluntary exile in Hong Kong.[126] Later in his life, as expedience dictated, Aguinaldo would similarly submit to the Americans and to the occupying Japanese. The morally neutral instinct for self-preservation of the *illustrados* and wealthy *hacienderos* classes in the Philippines has successfully co-opted or rebuffed every encroachment on their ruling prerogatives.

The truce was short-lived. With reciprocal duplicity, the rebels refused to disarm and the Spanish to implement promised reforms, both biding time to husband resources and resume the conflict. Aguinaldo's exile was short-lived. The timely intervention of a *deus ex machina* seemed to promise delivery. In 1898, the United States declared war on Spain, moving against Cuba, Puerto Rico, and the Philippines. Sailing from Hong Kong with Aguinaldo, Commodore George Dewey's squadron arrived in the Philippines and on May 1 destroyed the Spanish fleet in Manila Bay. Lacking the men and firepower to carry the battle ashore and take Manila, Dewey awaited the arrival of the U.S. Army at the end of June. Aguinaldo, in the meantime, was put ashore to organize Filipino forces, the *insurrectos*, preparatory to an assault on Manila and to set up an independent government.[127]

Newcomers though they might be to the take-no-prisoners world of *realpolitik*, the Americans were quick learners. Aguinaldo had succeeded in surrounding the city but with Dewey withholding support from his naval guns was unable to force a Spanish surrender. The Americans, at war and unprepared to contemplate a handover of the Philippines to anyone, least of all a group of revolutionaries, feared the Spanish would surrender to the insurrectos before the Army arrived. They cooperated with Aguinaldo but avoided any written commitment to Philippines' independence. On June 12, the newly organized Filipino national government formally proclaimed Philippines' independence.[128]

The three-way stand-off was broken with the arrival of U.S. troops south of Manila in late June. Aguinaldo reluctantly admitted U.S. troops to the trenches fronting the walled city. Dewey was meanwhile negotiating with the Spanish what has come to be known as the "Mock Battle of Manila." The Spanish governor-general, fearing a loss of reputation and reprisals by the insurrectos, agreed to surrender conditional upon an exclusively American occupation of Manila following a face-saving exchange of fire. Most of the American commanders were unaware that the battle was to be a sham. In the event, Dewey's vessels bombarded abandoned Spanish forts and American troops charged Spanish positions, only to find that the defenders had withdrawn. Only General Arthur MacArthur, father of Douglas, took casualties, unaware that the Spanish had surrendered to Dewey at least an hour before his assault. None were aware that Spain had signed an armistice one day before the "battle" for Manila.[129]

With the Spanish removed, the Americans quickly occupied and assumed control of the city. After excluding Aguinaldo's government from the battle planning, the Americans refused him permission to occupy parts of Manila.[130] Adding insult to injury, they then excluded the Filipinos from negotiations leading to the Treaty of Paris in 1898 and the transfer of the Philippines, with Guam and Puerto Rico, by Spain to the United States for twenty million dollars. As the leading insurrecto military commander, General Antonio Luna acerbically asked, "People are not to be bought and sold like horses and houses…[T]he traffic in Negroes [was abolished] because it meant the sale of persons; why is there still maintained the sale of countries with inhabitants?"[131]

Furious, Aguinaldo defied the Americans and seized control of several strategically important districts of Manila. Inevitable hostilities erupted in early 1899. In a self-defeating calculus, Aguinaldo, once again opting for personal over national interest, had Luna, by far his most competent field commander, murdered.[132] Knowing he had no chance of defeating the Americans head-on, Aguinaldo dissolved the regular army and established decentralized guerilla commands, furnishing perhaps the first U.S. lesson in the asymmetric warfare encountered a century later in Iraq. By the time the conflict ended two years later with Aguinaldo's capture, the rebellion had engaged 126,000 American troops and claimed the lives of 4,000 American and 16,000 Filipino soldiers, not to mention perhaps 200,000 civilians who died of famine, disease, and crossfire—all in a country of (at the time) only 7 million people. Aguinaldo, nothing if not astute at reading shifting winds, quickly swore allegiance to the United States and issued a proclamation calling on his compatriots to lay down their arms.[133]

The Americans were, by the standards of their Spanish predecessors, a relatively benign colonial overlord. President McKinley, in 1898, had proclaimed U.S. policy to be one of "benevolent assimilation in which the mild sway of justice and right" would replace "arbitrary rule."[134] A Filipino journalist wrote in the *Philippine Daily Inquirer* in 2004, "For all their faults, these new [American] imperialists—compared to their Castilian predecessors—taught our masses to read and write…and soon enough we were writing our own history."[135] In Muslim Mindanao, the Americans outlawed slavery and, in presentiment of future grievance, replaced sharia law with a new legal system, introduced schools teaching a non-Muslim curriculum, and organized local governments to challenge the authority of traditional community leaders. The Catholic Church was disestablished as state religion and the holdings of the friars were sold off—albeit in large part to the landed haciendero class. Under Governor William Howard Taft, a future U.S. president, representative institutions developed at breakneck speed, the guiding development philosophy being Taft's "Philippines for the Filipinos." Universal suffrage was introduced in 1933 and the Filipinos elected their own commonwealth government in 1935. Full independence was promised in 1945, a timetable only slightly delayed by the intervention of war.

———————

6 March 1945
Luzon

Dear Art,

I've been talking to three Spanish fellows who have been in Manila for the last three years. They really went through hell, especially when we took the city. At one time, there were 50 civilians in one small area. The Japs massacred them (they were under machine gun fire for 1 ½ hours once), both sides shelled them. They were trapped there for almost two weeks under constant shell fire. When the Americans finally arrived, nine out of the 50 were alive, four of those badly wounded. The Japs used to stop the men in Manila, search them, and then stupidly ask "Are you a spy?" They just generally beat up people. They caught one guerilla, subjecting him to the tortures you see in movies—this actually often happened—burning off fingernails, breaking arms and legs in several places, burning them, and as a climax they made this one fellow swallow hot oil. They aren't very pleasant, to say the least. I don't know whether I'd let myself be captured alive or not...

Yamashita inherited and was later hung for—by most accounts un-justly—the sins of a nearly three-year-long occupation regime, climaxing in the frenzy of atrocities preceding the Allied retaking of Manila. As they had in Singapore, the Japanese in the Philippines ceded through gratuitous abuse whatever "liberationist" moral high ground they might have claimed over the displaced Western colonialists. Occupation policy, in the Philip-pines as elsewhere in the newly minted Co-Prosperity Sphere, was steered with episodic bipolarity: velveteen ingratiation cohabiting with iron-fisted martial brutality. Local survivors identified three main phases of the oc-cupation: military cruelty, both intentional and inadvertent, in the initial exuberance following the surrender of Corregidor; attempts to win the friendly cooperation of the civilian populace interspersed with spasmodic anger at guerilla resistance; and latterly the generalized hysteria, inducing more systematic atrocities, triggered by the American landings at Leyte.[136]

Japanese mismanagement of the occupation alienated putative sup-porters even in the Philippines, where the local elite was predisposed to dance with the devil if it preserved their ruling prerogatives. As Paul Line-barger, a U.S. intelligence officer, wrote after the war, "[The Japanese] bankrupted all non-Japanese business so that Japanese carpetbaggers could buy their way in cheap; businesses owned by white foreigners were expropriated out of hand...The Japanese did not have enough sense to be satisfied with 100% return on their money, but wrecked the conquered economic systems with inflation, poor management and excess exploita-tion. Even the quislings became restless under the poor occupation poli-cies of the Japanese, and before the war was over a considerable number of the Japanese quislings re-quislinged back to the [Allied] side."[137] Noth-ing is as predictable, or as unprincipled, as a quisling's nesting instinct.

24 January 1945
Philippines

Dear Family,

[The Filipino] women are still pretty darn clean morally...They
all hate the Japs thoroughly and...refer to them as "little monkeys."
When the Japs were here, most of the women went into the hills, for

they were raped too often if they stayed. The women are exceptionally pretty, but not too bashful when it comes to walking around camp areas—guess the Japs fixed that. They walk around, fellows in every stage of dress and undress. A couple girls came into my tent the other day to get laundry, all I had was a pair of shorts handy so I laid them across my lap, went on with the hanging. Somehow, I don't seem to be as modest as I used to be.

Air raid alert. Lights out.

Supported by an "independent" puppet government, the Japanese orchestrated a comprehensive "hearts and minds" campaign combining active propaganda, public relations of the army and navy, complete control and censorship of the media—newspapers, magazines, film, radio, music, and cultural events—and a thorough revamp of the school curriculum. Throughout the country the Japanese formed neighborhood associations with designated leaders responsible for organizing and conducting nightly patrols to notify the Japanese of the presence of guerillas. In the morning the same leaders assembled their members for morning exercises known as the "Bushido system" and exhortatory ministrations on the duties of the flock. Curfew, blackouts, and other orders of the occupation authorities were carried out by the association leaders and infractions were dealt with summarily.

In the realm of education, the Japanese military occupation authorities issued the Basic Principles of Philippines Education[138]:

1. To establish the Philippines as a part of the Greater East Asia Co-Prosperity Sphere;
2. To eradicate Western thought, particularly that of the United States and Great Britain, and to promote a culture based on Filipinos' identity as Asians;
3. To cultivate morality and to eradicate the evils of materialism;
4. To spread the use of Japanese and eliminate the use of English;
5. To promote elementary and vocational education; and
6. To encourage people to be industrious.

Because of the shortages of Japanese-language teachers, front-line soldiers who had teaching experience back in Japan were often relied upon. Had Ishizuka arrived in the Philippines at an earlier stage of the war, he might have found himself back in the classroom. And as in Japan, he would have relied on textbooks espousing the same nationalist ideology:

> …Our national language is spiritual blood flowing through our nationals…The goal of Japanese language teaching [is]…to strengthen the unity of various people in the Great Japan Empire…Kokugo [national language, i.e., Japanese] has great power…Japanese culture is just like a river wide and long. It flows out from the deep heart of the mountains, and joins together with many rivers and flows down…Japan has become a father of a new [Co-Prosperity Sphere]. Asia will become a large house, and all of its members will have nice meals in the house, talking in Japanese…The power of [Japanese] will make a new Asia.[139]

---

4 July 1945

Dear Family,

Every Sunday night there is quite a formal dance. The Filipino girls are usually beautiful (I think there is a little Spanish blood mixed up) when nicely dressed in Spanish-type formal gowns. We have a pretty good time, though we usually leave the girls there. It is too much work when you have to take chaperones along, too…No profit in it…Even with chaperones, the better girls won't go for rides, etc. It is really a tough war. [Thought you might be interested to see an invitation I recently received…]
"Invitation: LIEUTENANT ROBERT E. LACROIX
U.S. Army Air Corps
4th Squadron, 3rd Air Commandos

The Municipal Council, The Collegiate, Secondary, and Ele-mentary School Teachers of Laoag request the honor of your presence at a July Fourth Dance at the Provincial Auditorium on Wednes-day, July 4, 1945 at eight o'clock in the evening. (Note: In event of rain, the dance will be held at the Provincial Capital)

Special Features

1. *Colorful Costume Depicting—*
   a. *Evolution of the Filipina Dress*
   b. *Regional Costumes in Revue*
2. *Pageant of the United Nations*
3. *"V" Grand March led by Miss America and consort*
4. *Vocal Solo*
5. *Dance, Dance, Dance"*

With independence on July 4, 1946, the old grudges of colonial class resentment merged with the new resentment of wartime collaboration, ensuring decades of future grievance. Manuel Roxas, the first elected president of the Philippines, was an acknowledged collaborator, having served in the wartime Japanese-sanctioned puppet government.[140] The wellspring of popular anger with Roxas was the elite's lamentable record of wartime enrichment as the populace suffered starvation and brutal-ity. In exchange for collaboration, the Japanese had preserved the rural land tenancy status quo, securing the property rights of the elite. While his fellow collaborators were held in jail in the run-up to the presi-dential election, Roxas rode to victory on the support of his old friend and Filipino icon, Douglas MacArthur. As president-elect, he promptly pardoned the lot. Roxas and his successors governed in accordance with the guiding maxim of that model of unprincipled, cynical resilience, Talleyrand: "Since the masses are always eager to believe something, for their benefit nothing is so easy to arrange as facts."

It need not have been so. In his *Last Farewell* before execution by a Spanish firing squad in 1896, the courageous patriot Rizal evoked a future whose potential he mortgaged with his life.

My dreams, when scarcely a lad adolescent,
My dreams when already a youth, full of vigor to
attain,
Were to see you, gem of the sea of the Orient,
Your dark eyes dry, smooth brow held to a high
plane…

…Hail! How sweet 'tis to fall that fullness you may
acquire,
To die to give you life, 'neath your skies to ex-
pire…[141]

Five decades and three wars later, Douglas MacArthur, sharing
Rizal's affection for the Filipinos, envisioned the same bright future on
"…soil consecrated in the blood of our two peoples."[142] Within fifteen
years of MacArthur's pledge, the Philippines would become one of the
most prosperous countries in Asia; within fifty years it has become one
of the poorest. That soil watered with the sacrifice of so much promise
should yield a crop so unpromising speaks to "an extreme of wicked-
ness or folly," in Lincoln's phrase.

As with many nations formed in the crucible of independence
struggles, early national identity is often clearer for what it opposes than
for what it supports. Filipinos themselves characterize their national leveling trait—the tall poppy syndrome by which ambitious individuals
(and policy innovation) are kept in check—as a "crab in the basket"
mentality. Their unwillingness to coalesce around an articulated vision
of national development threatens to relegate the Philippines to permanent barrio status in an increasingly up-market Asian neighborhood.
The consummating act by which the Filipino people were to be liber-
ated, so long yearned for, threatens to consume them at the moment of
fulfillment, leaving only a dreamt abstraction of a pure ideal.

26

THE SKY RAINED HEROES

2 January 1945
Hollandia – New Guinea.
One night stand.

Dear Family,

Well, our outfit is finally going to have a chance to prove itself. We have more training—both individual and collective—then any outfit to-date in modern warfare—straight commandos probably the only exception. It should show up in combat results.

You know, I've been doing quite a bit of traveling. Frisco, Hawaii, Guadalcanal, Biak, East New Guinea, Biak, Moratai, Leyte, Peleliu, Biak, here, and back to our base. [Leyte]…is really rough on the ground troops, but [they]…love the air corps…for we save their necks in numerous ways. As the newspapers told you, the Japs had temporary air superiority in Leyte at the very beginning. Once the air corps moved in, the ground troops were able to move ahead without the extremely costly harassing, strafing raids that the Japs are so adept at.

Prior to the American invasion of Leyte, Japanese naval pilots fed wildly exaggerated reports to Imperial headquarters in Tokyo claiming the destruction of 1,200 American aircraft and eleven aircraft carriers. The delusion was amplified, immediately following the Battle of Leyte Gulf, by Tokyo's erroneous perception that a decisive Japanese victory had seriously crippled the American carrier force. These misapprehensions led the Imperial command (notably excepting General Yamashita) to conclude that a decisive concentration of forces in Leyte could drive the Americans back into the sea. Despite their victory in the Battle of Leyte Gulf, the Americans by late 1944 had yet to achieve complete air or naval supremacy and the October monsoon rains prevented the construction of new airfields critical to effective Air Corps support. The Japanese were able to reinforce Leyte with two divisions and, in tacit acknowledgement of their waning air power, launched the first kamikaze attacks of the war. Japanese tenacity, always formidable, was bolstered by the deadly—if ultimately fatal—combination of sensed opportunity informing forlorn hope. MacArthur's battle for Leyte, in the understated words of an official military history, "lasted longer than expected."[143]

4 January 1945
Leyte-Philippines

Dear Family,

Finally got here [from New Guinea]... These killing, five-hour hops, most of it over water and enemy territory. The nervous strain is plenty, and the physical strain's just as tough. If you don't believe it, simulate our conditions—take a straight-backed wooden chair—the back can have a little padding. The rest must be hard as wood. Strap yourself in—one belt around your waist, or a little lower. Bring two straps down over your shoulders and tighten up so you have about two inches play in the straps. Now sit like that for five hours, always looking around in every direction. Don't forget to lag about 40 pounds of equipment from your shoulders, legs, and the parts of your body. Before long your tail begins to numb and soon feels as though you're sitting on needles.

Things aren't as tough as they might be... The Japs pulled a raid on New Year's Eve which lasted quite a spell...all the ack ack in the place cut loose at midnight. Since they didn't seem to get too close, we stayed in bed. That is, for a while. A couple of the Jap bombers dropped a few bombs near us, one bomber being shot down just a little further. It was all rather interesting, but not as awesome as you might expect. The mosquitoes bothered me a lot more, for I woke up in the morning with my hands and forearms swollen. It may have been a scorpion, though, since mosquitoes never did this to me. It isn't especially painful, just annoying.

Incidentally, we set a record on the way here. Only lost one ship in 28 which is exceptional. And the pilot wasn't even scratched. The pilot, Lawrence, was back at Bartow with me. He is known as "Safety"—a mockery, for he has wrecked his last three planes in as many months, through no fault of his own. When he left Frisco, he shaved off all his hair, leaving a black fuzz. He looked so tough they named him "Safe Cracker," which was abbreviated to "Safety."

Goodnight, now. I'm in pretty good spirits right now, for we have come to a definite combat commitment (can't tell you where or when, though) and we have something to look forward to.

The physical discomfiture of long-haul fighter patrols was compounded by the emotional stress of weather, navigational, and terrain conditions allowing little or no margin for error. World War II fighters lacked on-board radar and, unlike bombers, an on-board navigator. Navigation was limited to visual reference points, often based on inaccurate charts, radio communication, and celestial navigation with rudimentary charts. Storms in the Pacific theater, accompanied by massive vertical cloud formations and unpredictable weather fronts, would develop with startling speed and intensity. Fighters on long missions and low on fuel could easily become disoriented and lost. Beneath lay vast expanses of shark-infested water or, worse, impenetrable, malevolent jungle. Pilots parachuting into the latter normally simply disappeared. Bergerud estimates that more than half the aircraft lost in the Pacific theater fell afoul of accident or simply disappeared. He comments that we are still discovering wrecked aircraft in the New Guinea jungle.[144] My trek through the Borneo jungles with Majid and his fellow Dayaks in the late 1980s yielded just such a discovery. The pilot is most likely still listed as "Missing in Action."

> *8 January 1945*
> *4ᵗʰ F.S. Commando*
> *3ʳᵈ Air Commando Gp*
> *Leyte, Philippines*

> *Dear Family,*

> *Since [arriving in Leyte], we've been working at a furious rate on our new planes. I've got a pretty good one. When I lost the last one, I swore I would do a minimum of work on this one until I was sure I'd be able to keep it. However, as soon as I got it, I began puttering around, now have it all painted and running with a purr. We are getting mighty anxious to get...to the combat zone. To you in the States, I imagine New Guinea sounds like a combat zone, with all the raids on Wewak, Rabaul, and other places. However, except for the few involved [in combat], New Guinea was a zone of peace and rest and extreme quiet. To the permanent personnel, it is a haven where they can become heroes to the folks at home, the easy way. To the rest of us, it is a stepping off place to the combat we've been preparing for for so d_____ long.*

[We have one "problem child" in the squadron—obnoxious, arrogant], I don't expect the fool to live long…Up in Peleliu in the Palaus…we were out on part of the untouched battlefield. The child picked up a Jap hand grenade—it might have been booby-trapped—then he calmly proceeds to bang it on a rock, jiggle it near his ear. Then to top it off, he pulled the pin. Luckily he had enough sense to throw it into a dugout, so the explosion didn't hurt anyone. Right now he has made himself the most disliked person in the outfit. He is right talented in that direction.

Flew my plane up to Finchaven [New Guinea] the other day to paint it up. While there we went into the officers club, had a fine dinner on plates and tablecloths, with real ice water. Later, just before flying back, we went back into the bar. Before we had a chance to say a thing, the sergeant in charge sidles up, says "sorry sir, but we can't sell you any of our officers' liquor since it is rationed." Then he gets the bartender to one side, slips us a couple of real tall, cool, Tom Collins—they even had a double shot of gin in them. After that, we got talking with the bartender, told him that we were just back from Leyte. That opened him up—he was kind of sick of the paddle feet (non-combat officers, non-flying). He got right sociable and generous. The main thing we craved, since we had to fly back, was ice water, so he cracked up some ice, and we had five glasses of ice-water apiece.

Sent a plane down to Australia the other day. It came back laden with steaks and fresh eggs. We had a real feast. I had four beautiful tender steaks, just as tender as any in the States. To round it off, I had four eggs fried, several pieces of bread and butter, onions, coffee. Finished a perfect evening by waddling back to our tent, polishing off a quart of Aussie beer. Wonderful life. Cooked five eggs last night, and finished my last few tonight…I'm in pretty darn good shape—haven't even had dysentery in two weeks.

19 January 1945
Leyte, Philippines.

Dear Family,

It has been raining all night and all day, so we had no missions. We were up at 4 as usual, though. Spent the morning on alert; am spending the rest of the day catching up on my correspondences. The tent area looks like a lake with tents sticking up out of the water. We have two war tents. We managed to appropriate a tarpaulin, use it as a floor. Serves pretty well, for what water comes in runs down and out the other side. We have cots. With all our luggage, mosquito nets, cots, blankets, bed rolls, etc., our tent is a little crowded and of course most of our clothes are wet at this point…Anything other than clothes rots down here anyway. Liquor is the most important item, even if you don't drink. You can trade a quart of whisky for almost anything. A bottle of Scotch here is worth almost $50.

Saw my first cock-fight last night. Rather interesting. You heel them with a razor spur. Get them mad by holding them back, letting them peck at each other. Then when they are good and mad, you throw them into the pit and let them fight until one is killed. I suppose it is rather brutal, but it is really interesting. Cock fighting results in some real bets, even more so than poker or black jack.

My only complaint is that we have missions averaging several hours—your seat gets so sore you can't sit down the rest of the day. I've rebuilt all the rest of my equipment and plane so I am pretty comfortable. Even put a special cold air duct in my plane.

Food's good, but irregular. We usually eat at 0415, 1130, and 1700. When we have diarrhea, we are so busy flying we forget about it. Usually, though, we have constipation, so a long hop isn't the least uncomfortable.

I sound like a walking encyclopedia of trouble. We are really enjoying life…The going isn't too tough right now, so we are get-

ting broken in in a lot easier fashion than we expected. The food is 100% better than before. We have all our equipment and clothes again—that helps. We get laundry done by the Filipino women, and their women are very attractive to look at. Our men are with us, so the load is a lot less. All in all, we are quite happy.

Guess I'd better stop, now, Goodnight.

24 January 1945
Leyte, Philippines

Dear Family,

I am writing you, surrounded by luggage, tent, and mosquitoes on the other six sides. The big luscious kind that need runways to fly off of.

Have been reasonably busy. Got myself some high ranking Japs the other day—direct hits dive bombing. We really did a job on the b___. Only bad part about it all is that we have to make long missions to get to our targets…I think that will be remedied in the very, very near future. This life is enjoyable other than the fact we can't sit down for two hours after a mission. The food is good—a lot of dehydrated vegetables, potatoes, rice, eggs…We have had no spam, usually beef, since we left New Guinea. Life is muddy and dusty. You know, our air mattresses make all the difference in the world. The mattress, combined with our food, really makes things enjoyable… At any rate we are now on combat rations, eating pretty well.

We are weighed down with more equipment—jungle pack, rubber dinghy, parachute, Mae West, gun, knife, emergency kit, oxygen mask, gloves, silk scarf (not for looks, but for wiping face, stop bleeding, clean canopy, and numerous other uses), ammu-

nition pouch, helmet, goggles, and a few other assorted things. There is a new kit out that, in two small flasks, combines medical equipment and food supplies and other odds and ends that cover every possible contingency. You could live a week on the food alone in it. The medical supplies would last several months for any condition, whether wounds, constipation, dehydration, malaria, a score of other possibilities. This scientific warfare is wonderful, within certain limitations consistent with any type of combat.

Air raid alert. Lights out.

29 January 1945
Note the change—APO 70
Luzon, Philippines

Dear Family,

As you can see, I've moved again. We are up where there is a little going on.

We have a pretty nice set-up here. A new air strip, the surrounding country hasn't been too marred up, except for a few craters, etc. We have set up our quarters in dried rice fields. These fields are about 150 ft. by 200 ft., are separated from each other by small dirt ridges about 12" high. They are dry, flat, are pretty nice. Few mosquitoes or flies, quite the antithesis of Leyte.

The Filipinos here are, as yet, unspoiled. The Japs have left here so recently that they still have almost nothing. The Japs took almost all their clothes so they have only rags. We get them to work for clothes, candy, cigarettes, etc. We have hired a lot of them, at 1 ¼ pe-

sos (about $0.62) a day, to build us thatched, bamboo huts. We put our pyramidal tents on top as roofs, using bamboo and palm leaves for framework, floor, thatching. Makes a pretty nice set-up. They do a darn good job. You know, the more I see of the Filipino, the more I like and respect them. They are, in many ways, just like Americans. It is amazing how well-educated some are. Also, every Filipino of about seven years up to 25 speaks both English and their own language. Imagine an American child of seven being able to speak two languages fluently. It is also amazing how they hate the Japs. They all carry machetes and bolo knives, which they use to good advantage when they find a Jap. Before anyone can interfere (who would want to), the natives have sliced him into more pieces than you can imagine. Typical of their attitude is a little episode that happened in Leyte. A Jap was executed, a grave day for him. The grave turned out to be a foot too short. One of the helpful Filipinos, attempting to save the work of enlarging it, simply cut off the legs, threw them in on top. Enough horror stories, though. You may like to sleep nights.

It gets cool here at night, pretty comfortable. The guns roaring in the distance have, by now, become so habitual as to be virtually unnoticed… We are finally near a town… The towns here are rather beat up, but [better than] those in Leyte [which] were so beat up, muddied, and dirty as to be quite unpleasant.

Met a Filipino boy yesterday who was a Pfc in the Am-Phil. Army, fought at Bataan. When it fell, he escaped to the hills, has been doing guerilla work since. Now that Allied troops are here, he is reporting for duty again.

Flew nine hours yesterday, was about worn out. Normally, we only fly about 5 hours a day. We either fly early, get off late afternoon, or sleep late and fly late.

Enclosed is a Jap five peso note…I got it for 8 American cigarettes. We get five cigarettes, matches, gum, candy, and other assorted luxuries, free. I use most of it to trade for work, luxuries of various kinds. Don't ever doubt the Red Cross. They do more over here to make life enjoyable than any other three agencies. They supply coffee, sandwiches to transit personnel. They have candy to take on missions, which is a real life saver. On a four-hour mission, you get mighty hungry and tired, and a little water and chocolate bar peps you up and relieves tension. The Red Cross helps get word through to expectant parents, even when there is no way for the soldier to do it. We had two boys here whose wives were having babies. After two months of worry without mail, Red Cross got word through for the men...As you can see, the Red Cross is really popular.

In an era when war posters attained the status of iconographic art, "The Greatest Mother in the World" must rank among the most affecting and effective images ever produced. Evoking the reverence and sublime peace of Michelangelo's *Pieta* in St. Peter's Basilica, the Red Cross WWI War Fund Campaign poster features a seated nurse clad in cascading white robes. As she gazes with transcendent quietude into the distance, she clasps in her arms a reduced-in-scale stretcher, cradling a recumbent soldier, blanketed, with heavily bandaged head and hands. Behind her right shoulder is juxtaposed a large red cross. At her feet is a plaque on which is inscribed "The Greatest Mother in the World." Like the marble Virgin gazing at the unresurrected Christ, the image is profoundly moving.

As many a veteran will attest, it is difficult to overstate the contribution and achievements of the Red Cross in World War II. It exemplifies "voluntarism" at its most selfless, as inspired national movement. At the time of the dedication of the National World War II Memorial in Washington, D.C., in May 2004, a special exhibit paid tribute to the wartime role of the Red Cross. The Red Cross was active on both civilian and military fronts. More than 7.5 million Americans volunteered for the organization, and it is estimated that by war's end "nearly every family in America had connected with the Red Cross—either as a supporter or beneficiary of Red Cross Services."[145]

The Red Cross was a vital link between the home and battle fronts. They transmitted more than 42 million messages between U.S. military personnel overseas and their families and friends in the States. The American Red Cross prepared and shipped over 27 million parcels to the International Committee of the Red Cross for delivery to U.S. and Allied prisoners of war. The first nationwide blood donor service was organized by the Red Cross, collecting some 13.4 million pints of blood from 6.6 million donors during the war.[146] These blood drives led to the development of the first mobile blood collection unit and a method for producing dried rather than liquid plasma, improving shelf life and transportability.[147] Millions of volunteers knit socks and clothing, prepared bandages, visited wounded soldiers, and counseled their families at home. It was motherhood's proudest day.

3 February 1945
Luzon, Philippines

Dear Family,

I asked for action, and I'm really getting it. We had our toughest mission to-date, yesterday. It was a bombing-strafing job on destroyers, and they really threw up the fireworks. It gives you a funny feeling to see all the ack-ack coming and still have to keep on going in. It is a feeling of acute anticipation and mild curiosity—the latter as regards whether it is your turn to get hit.

There's a movie on, I'll finish this later...I've seen the movie. Besides, this combat movie stuff isn't too hot, although once they get set up they usually get a fair show.

To continue the previous train of thought, I like combat pretty well. I guess it is a natural desire to like destruction. If you've ever seen six streams of tracers hosing into a target, I think you'd know what I mean. I've flown an awful lot lately (9 hours a day), and hope I can keep it up. However, some replacements came in today, so they will probably ease up a little on the rest of us. I'd rather keep up the steady flying, though.

Had a freak accident the other day. A tribute, incidentally, to American planes. A light bomber caught a frag bomb in the fuselage, almost severing the tail. The pilot flew it back. Just as he landed, the shock of landing broke the tail section completely off. In spite of it, he kept it rolling straight and no one was killed. It was a real miracle. War brings out all sorts of queer accidents. I'll tell you some others, sometime.

Yes, Bong returned to the States. McGuire—the second leading ace—pushed his luck too far, was killed a few weeks ago. You know, a pilot is good for one tour of duty. Most of those that come back for a second or third tour almost always get killed. Wish we could see some Jap planes in the air. We've shot them up on the ground, but they seem to fly only in the night (ruining our sleep, incidentally). You ought to see us during an air raid. Normally, we don't get up, just lie awake and ready to jump if necessary. One night, though, we were strafed. Most of us hit the foxholes totally naked, our only articles being our 45's and helmets. It struck me so funny. Even the slowest jumped that night. However, the flak was really pretty.

It is late. I've got to get some sleep. I'll write again when I have time.

P.S. Guess you've been praying for me quite a bit. At any rate, someone has. Keep it up. There really are no atheists here.

The World War II fighter ace is a near mythic figure, aerial incarnation in lineal descent of medieval chivalry's combat *a l'outrance*. In his underrated classic, *The World Set Free*, H. G. Wells foretold the future as the world tottered on the edge of abyss in 1914:

So it was that the war in the air began. Men rode upon the whirlwind that night and slew and fell like archangels. The sky rained heroes upon the astonished earth. Surely the last fights of mankind were the best. What was the heavy pounding of your Homeric swordsmen, what was the creaking charge of chariots, besides this swift rush, this crash, this giddy triumph, this headlong sweep to death?[148]

While all services—and all sides—had their bona fide heroes, few lodged themselves in the public imagination as vividly as fighter pilots. Fighter pilots competed, usually with external modesty, for the mantle of top ace. Major Thomas McGuire, America's number two ace with thirty-eight combat "kills," died chasing with unquenchable, and uncharacteristically open, lust for fame the record of top ace Major Richard Bong, who stayed just ahead with forty kills. McGuire was awarded the Congressional Medal of Honor posthumously; Bong received his Medal of Honor while alive, but died shortly thereafter, test piloting a jet prototype on the day the Hiroshima A-bomb was dropped. Both men flew the twin engine P-38 Lightning in the Pacific theater.

The top Japanese ace, Chief Warrant Officer Hiroyoshi Nishizawa, had 103 combat kills while his fellow Mitsubishi Zero pilot Lieutenant Saburo Sakai had 64 kills. Sakai, of Samurai descent, possessed the combination of warrior skill and luck that most fighter pilots would equate with longevity. During an attack on a squadron of American Douglas Dauntless bombers, a .50 caliber round deflected off Sakai's flight goggles, crushed his skull bone and left him covered in blood, blind in one eye, and barely conscious. Flying for four and a half hours without a canopy, Sakai returned to base, landed, and underwent surgery without anesthetic. Reconciled with his former foes after the war, Sakai was asked why the records of Japanese aces so outstripped those of his American antagonists. He explained that "There were only a few Japanese [aces]. The American aces were sent home as instructors, but the top Japanese pilots, because of our shortage of manpower, were left in combat to die."[149] Of the 150 pilots who began in Sakai's unit, only three survived the war.

Nothing comes close to the staggering combat records of German air aces on the Russian Front. The top German ace, Major Erich Hartmann, had 352 kills, crash landed 14 times, and lived by the motto "When he fills the entire windscreen, you can't miss." Germany (including Austria) had 15 aces each with over 200 kills and 105 aces with over 100 kills each. Certainly the most colorful was Colonel Hans Ulrich Rudel, a dive bomber ace and Germany's most highly decorated war hero. Over the space of four years, Rudel flew 2,530 combat sorties, destroying 519 Russian tanks, 150 artillery guns, 1,000 vehicles, a battleship, a cruiser, a destroyer, seventy landing craft, and eleven planes. He was shot down thirty times, lost a leg (which interfered not at all with his combat flying), and was the only recipient of Germany's highest decoration, the Knight's Cross with Golden Oak Leaves Swords and Diamonds.[150] He lived to a ripe old age. German combat kills were in no small part abetted by two factors: Stalin's obsession with numbers—throwing ever-increasing quantities of brave but poorly trained pilots in mediocre planes against superior enemy pilots and equipment—and Soviet air warfare stressing low-flying tank killers (Il-2 Sturmoviks), lethal against German tanks but no match for German Messerschmidt and Fokker-Wulf fighters dropping from above.

The matinee-idol derring-do of the propeller plane fighter pilot was a historical adrenalin rush, produced in the early days of manned-flight-as-warfare. It was short-lived and ultimately tamed, as in any rapidly evolving discipline, by the steady flow of ever-increasing technical sophistication and operational complexity. The "scientification" of aerial warfare, an increased public sensitivity to combat casualties, and the advent of technology obviating the need for humans in the air all number the days of the fighter pilot. Until that day, the words of General "Billy" Mitchell, crusading visionary of aviation in war, will remain as true as when he spoke them in 1924: "It is probable that future war will be conducted by a special class, the air force, as it was by the armored Knights of the Middle Ages."[151] The "Right Stuff" still rules.

5 February 1945
Luzon, Philippines

Dear Family,

Just received your letter of 7 January, Dad…a total of 72" of snow during November and December. You know, it has been three years since I've seen snow.

We are having more or less a holiday here. The field has been too wet for flying, so we have had a welcomed rest. Sleep. Also, I've gone to town—this afternoon, as a matter of fact. The town is only a hollow mockery of what it must once have been. Very few entire buildings, and those in pretty bad shape. You know, I don't mind killing Japs…Don't mind destruction. Don't mind taking chances. Don't mind poor food, heat, work, etc.…but I hate to see Filipinos waiting to get the remains of our mess (chow to you). Most of them fish and eat other common varieties of food. A few, however, seem to prefer begging than trying to fend for themselves. Don't know why. Maybe they have to. At first it bothered me a lot, but now I'm getting used to it. When we first got here, we were so close behind the Japs that there was some excuse. Now, however, they have had almost a month to get re-adjusted, with every possible aid in the line of food and clothing. Most of them are much better off than they were when the Japs took over. The others evidently prefer to beg. So, I am losing pity for them. It still remains the hardest part of war, I guess.

What a doc we have. After missions we get a "medical" shot of whiskey. The other day, after a mission where we really needed it, was he to be found? Hell No. He is one of the laziest men I know. I drink a little—one shot a day—but not very much. A little steadies your nerves and relaxes you so you can sleep well. Too much, however, ruins your judgment. Since a lot of our flying is at tree-top level (to avoid flak), we need the best possible judgment. I've had nightmares once since I've been here. [After one nine hour day] I had a roaring noise in my ears that night. After I went to sleep, every once in a while the roaring would suddenly stop and I'd bolt upright, ready to bail out. That happened three times that night. I'll never fly nine hours again in one day. It is too much.

You see, running out of gas always scares you. On long trips we always run each tank dry. We know within a couple of minutes when it will quit. I've actually sat in my seat watching the fuel pressure gage drop before changing tanks, yet when it actually stops, the sudden silence scares the hell out of you. Another thing that gets you, particularly out over water: On long trips you more or less relax. Then when you unconsciously turn your head or otherwise move it changes the set of the helmet on your head, causing a slight change in the engine sound. You sit upright, check all the switches, and suddenly realize what the trouble was. These all sound and are trivial things, but they are coldly realistic at the time. What they actually are is an outgrowth of the continual (though sometimes subconscious) alertness of a pilot to any changes in his plane. I've always said aviation is a fertile field for psychologists.

Remember our problem child? We got here on Luzon and no one will live with him. He is now living alone. Not very pleasant for him, but he asked for it.

I'm pretty happy as long as they let me fly all I want to. To me, a little skip or dive bombing combined with strafing is one hell of a lot of fun. I got a Jap staff car the other day on a highway. More fun. You see, this is the culmination of two years' practice. We are finally using it and we are really getting up a good group record. Hope we get a group citation. We should, if we keep up the good work.

Time to quit now. Hope to have some good missions tomorrow.

27

THE CATERPILLAR CLUB

Letter received by my grandparents shortly after receipt of a Western Union telegram advising that my father was "Missing in Action":

6 July 1945

Mr. Arthur E. LaCroix
970 Center Street
Newton Center, Mass.

Dear Mr. Lacroix,

I have just learned of the very sad news you received concerning [the death of] your son. There is not much which I might say that would be of comfort to you at this time, but I do want to express my sincere sympathy for you. Should you find that I can be of assistance in any way I hope you will not hesitate to call on me.

Most sincerely yours,
/s/
Christian A. Herter
10th District Massachusetts
Congress of the United States
House of Representatives
Washington, D.C.

The Batanes Islands[152], midway in the Luzon Straits between the Philippines and modern-day Taiwan, are flotsam churning in the wake of two receding landmasses. Seen from the air, alternating cascades of white-crested aquamarine waves, push-pulled by dueling currents, buffet the cast-off islands known as "The Home of the Winds." As the allies moved north through the Philippines in an accelerating arc toward the Japanese home islands, my father's fighter squadron ranged north into and across the Luzon Straits: to Batan Island and Formosa.

Backlit by the rising sun on February 12, 1945, an eiderdown of spent storm clouds over Batan was abruptly rent by two saber-gray P-51H Mustang fighters. The roar of the low-passing planes swept with tsunami violence over the sleeping Japanese airfield. Sharp staccato bursts from the Mustangs' six .50 caliber wing guns hacked swaths across the red clay runway. Moist globs of spit earth registered an angry, impotent response. Two Mitsubishi Zero fighter planes and a big twin-engine "Dinah" attack bomber burst into flames.

The four pilots of D-Wing, Fourth Fighter Squadron Commando, following a rushed breakfast of spam and coffee, took off for Formosa just before dawn bearing wing tanks but no bombs on a long search-and-destroy mission. They flew low to evade radar detection, low enough to see the prop-wash on the water under the adjacent plane. As they approached the coastline of Formosa, they climbed to two thousand feet, scanning for a pilot missing since the day before. Following a fruitless search, the wing split: two pilots flew on to Formosa; my father and his wing man headed for Batan and the airfield at Basco, the capital city. Midway to Batan, the American fighters overtook a lumbering Japanese Dinah bomber. Dropping from above, LaCroix fell on the rear gunner, and in aerial high noon fashion the two men blazed away. The gunner's compartment burst into red. Another pass and the bomber's starboard engine exploded in flame. The American followed the bomber down until it splashed and splayed on the sparkling Pacific waters.

The airfield at Basco, set against the cloud-enveloped Mt. Iraya volcano, lay in a small valley surrounded by hills crested with anti-aircraft nests. Diving out of the sun, the hornet-nosed planes made three roaring passes through the gauntlet and over the runway. They broke off, surveyed the havoc, and decided on a fourth run. The pheromoned hive of Japanese .31 caliber anti-aircraft guns lashed out in defensive fury. Lethal black mushrooms blossomed around the attacking planes.

As LaCroix pulled back on the plane's stick three hundred feet above the runway, searing lead rivet-punched the vulnerable underbelly of his P-51. Blood splattered and his foot jerked off the rudder pedal as a .31 caliber round drove up through his ankle, lodging in his calf. Hot coolant and the liquid metallic odor of oil, redolent with burn-alive terror, surged through the cockpit. Oil-sprayed goggles, pain, and the spin of the wounded plane disoriented him. The 1,790 hp Packard/Merlin engine in the distinctive shark-shaped fuselage sputtered, choked, and vomited oil and smoke. The plane's ruptured fuel line ignited, and the exhaust vents spewed fire.

Fighting back to 1,000 feet, the pilot struggled to blow the canopy, freeing the jammed mechanism in a frenetic barrage of curses and blows. He loosed the center-clasped seatbelt and shoulder harness with a single mid-chest whack, rolled the plane over, and launched from the cockpit. Instead of free fall with parachute billowing, he slammed repeatedly against the side of the burning, plummeting plane. The plane was falling with him, locking him on the armor-plate, half in and half out of the cockpit. Reaching up with his foot, LaCroix kicked the stick, tore loose, and fell. Sudden silence. He pulled the ripcord—nothing—and figured, as he wrote, a telegram was going to his family.

The jolt of the opening parachute brought short-lived comfort: he was upside down, his shoulder gun harness caught in the parachute shroud. He tore it lose, swung upright, glimpsed the whining dive and cartwheeled splintering of his plane on the water and plunged into convulsing, fifteen-foot seas. Groping instinctively he popped his Mae West, cut loose the chute, and, battling a water-laden flight suit, heaved himself into the raft. His .45 was gone, as were his emergency water and one of the two paddles, a result of sloppy workmanship back in the States. As he stuffed the bullet hole in his ankle with medical powder, he registered the sharp crack and splash of automatic weapons fire ripping the surrounding sea. His watch had stopped at exactly 11:00 a.m.

Four hours by boat off the coast of Batan lies Itbayat Island, largest island in the Batanes group and first landfall of the 1941 Japanese invasion of the Philippines. Wholly outside the angst-ridden discourse of nations and commerce, the peaceful and isolated Batan and Itbayat Islands are priority development targets of the Philippines Department of Energy. Ostensibly to canvas native Ivatan support for a community electrification program, my trip to the islands was in reality a personal rite of passage, returning me to the waters from which my father had so narrowly escaped death.

With no scheduled air or boat service from Batan, getting to Itbayat was the first challenge. Already lowering thunderheads and building seas presaged worsening conditions, but the exhilaration of the looming crossing trumped sounder judgment. We trolled the shoreline near Basco for a fisherman intrepid or greedy enough to risk the impending tempest. The round-sided, flat-sterned *falowa* fishing craft of the Ivatan are technicolor splashes on the white canvas of the Basco beach. Unlike the ubiquitous double-outriggered, canoe-shaped *bancas* that dominate inter-island transport in the rest of the Philippines, the falowas are unique to the Batanes islands, hollowed seaworthy tubs from pre-Hispanic days designed for the treacherous seas that limit fishing to three months a year. Manually constructed from diminishing stocks of local *palomeria* wood and powered by small two or three cylinder engines, the falowas are generally open-decked with a small hold and a center-stepped mast for a stabilizing sail. The tough, wiry, kelp-brown Ivatan pilots display remarkable adroitness in maneuvering and maintaining the falowas in squally seas with primitive tools and navigational aids limited to instinct and memory.

Soon enough relieved of the price reserved for the compulsive and the foolhardy, my two Filipino compatriots and I secured a twenty-five-foot, blue-and-white-striped fishing falowa whose singular merit was that it floated. Following the crew's storage below deck of our already soggy baggage, we carefully removed our shoes and socks, rolled our pants to the knee, and waded gingerly to the slippery plank leading to the falowa's deck. We situated ourselves comfortably on the open, chairless deck, unwrapped our waterproofed supplies of fruits and *empanadas*, tasty local pastries, and were instantaneously smashed by a five-foot wave arching over the bow of the still-tethered vessel.

For the next four and a half hours, in cocktail-shaker violence of pitch, plunge, yaw, and roll, we clung like forlorn mollusks to the slightly rotted horizontal spar just above our heads. As winding walls of water engulfed us, the absence of guardrails, harnesses, life preservers, or anti-slip decking was less diverting than the absence of a head. It was a liberating sensation to answer the call of nature where we stood, comforted by the knowledge that we would be scrubbed and scoured within two minutes.

Our voyage started with the vivid hues, beloved of landscape artists, created by a brooding storm's artful play of sun, sea, and sky: waters of crisp sea green, teal, turquoise, and beryl; cumulus masses etched in foreboding black with luminous penumbrae; a mobile carnival of fishing boats splayed over a fixed jungle green and umber backdrop. But mid-crossing, the elements conspired in hostile assault. Sky and sea in alternating fits drove searing microbursts of shard-like rain in black vertical columns. Wavecrests atomized in scything horizontal sheets. The forward hatch cover slipped its plastic twine bonds and nearly reduced me to jetsam. Prostrate on the deck, a fisherman and I struggled to cover and secure the gulping hatch.

Throughout the crossing, our phlegmatic crew of three appeared happily oblivious to the imminent prospect of seaborne interment. The captain was wrapped mummy-like in a shredding pancho whose sole purpose appeared to be to obscure his view. Aft of the captain was the apparent second-in-command. A doughty and indefatigable brick of a fellow, his charge was the manual bilge pump at which he furiously and unceasingly extracted quarts of water from the below-deck luggage compartment while gallons rushed in through the forward hatch and assorted rents in the devil seam. Perched in the forepeak, like a placid tern riding out a seaborne tempest, a heavily mustachioed fisherman bearing a disconcerting resemblance to Pancho Villa periodically and without warning lunged aft along the gunwales to avert looming catastrophe. Returning to his perch, he would roll, light, and smoke a native cigarette, a feat no less remarkable to my mind than our continuing buoyancy.

When the rain-clouded mass of Itbayat Island hove into view, I could only wonder at my father's thirty-odd hours' immersion in conditions much more perilous and less asked-for than my own. Sailing over the same waters where he had fought, pursuing development in the same islands whose liberation he had sought, my sense of affinity, of familial continuity and purpose distinct from the vague connectedness imparted by old photographs and the family Bible, outlasted the adrenalin rush of the journey.

Vainly searching for a dock or landing ramp, the skipper, with evident relish, advised us in Tagalog that to avoid a risky beach landing on the rocky coast we would anchor some fifty yards offshore, just inside the reef line, whence we would wade ashore. As he let go the sand-filled kerosene can anchor, throngs of Ivatan villagers emerged from the coconut palm grove littoral, chattering and gesturing volubly. Overcome with historical déjà vu, I puffed my chest portentously and stepped off the four-foot freeboard of the fishing boat, expecting to stride ashore with MacArthur like gravitas. Instead, miscalculating the depth, I disappeared to my eyebrows and bobbed to shore like a malfunctioning periscope. Overlooking the mortification of my lèse-majesté, the local native children, apparently intuiting their role in this historical recreation, rushed exuberantly to the beach line: "Hey, Joe! Hi, Joe! What's new, Joe!" I too had returned.

The bright yellow survival raft, only a few hundred yards windward of Batan, drew steady fire as the defenders dispatched a patrol boat to recover the American. The flowing tide and onshore winds threatened to draw the raft onto the razor-sharp coral. Rising with each inhalation of the ocean, LaCroix watched as the Americans strafed the shoreline. An erupting orange-red-yellow fireball aborted the incipient capture mission. Over the next twenty-six hours, daylight and refueling permitting, American fighters flew cover for the downed aviator, heaving seas preventing a seaplane rescue.

Late in the afternoon he was jolted from his torpor by the sound of a plane passing overhead. An American C-47 circled low and lazy, apparently assessing landing conditions on Batan. Above, the American fighters cut sharp loops like predatory falcons appraising a plump grouse. Buoying to the crest of a swelling wave, LaCroix was stunned to see the C-47 lower its landing gear and swing into position to land on the island. Abruptly an American fighter plane dropped from formation in a sharp dive on the rescue plane, guns ablaze. The C-47, in a gradual descent toward the Japanese-held island, billowed smoke, veered to the leeward side of the island, and disappeared. The exhausted fighter pilot reflected sardonically on the eternal verities of SNAFU[153].

As night fell and the "friendlies" returned to base, the seas mounted and a gale blew up, threatening to capsize the semi-submerged raft as it surged from wave crest to trough and back again. LaCroix's legs and stomach bunched in excruciating knots. He played out a sea-anchor and secured himself to the dinghy. A one-man dinghy, as my father later wrote, "supports you but is like a bathtub as far as keeping you dry— you are under water all the time." During the night he drifted among reefs and small islands, miraculously avoiding the razor-sharp coral. He sunk deeper into semi-consciousness.

Where the Atlantic menaces with paternal sternness, the Pacific lulls with maternal warmth. Stirred to wrath, the Atlantic inspires predictable dread while the savagery of the Pacific terrifies as aberration. In the aftermath of emotional outburst, the Pacific, recovering its wonted composure, reverted to sheltering form. A shift in tide and wind drove the pilot's life raft out of range of the island's defenders. Salving saltwater cleansed a wound that in the jungle would have festered, turned septic, and killed. Convulsive heaves gave way to quieted breathing.

In the early hours of the second day, LaCroix, bleached and desiccated as sun-scorched papyrus, thirsty and hungry, half-sensed, half-heard the rising drone of an approaching aircraft. He yanked the raft's blue cover over himself to avoid detection. As the swell thrust him temporarily free of the imprisoning churn, he glimpsed the welcome profile of a P-51. He flashed his survival mirror and put out die-marker, but he had drifted further than he realized. The pilot passed by unawares.

By noon of the second day, the ocean calmed to ten-foot swells, inviting a seaborne rescue. A sudden adrenaline rush of fear surged through the pilot. From the direction of Batan two mast-tips appeared on the horizon. Japanese? He had no weapon. Paddling furiously he attempted over the next hour to distance himself from the approaching masts. With his strength ebbing, the closing vessel fired a warning shot. He assessed his choices: over the side to the sharks or surrender to the Japanese. Fearing capture but having no means of evading it, he slumped with resigned exhaustion into the water-filled raft. It was a lucky decision. The masts belonged to two five-man dinghies tied together—the pilot and crew of the C-47 downed the previous day by LaCroix's squadron leader.

The C-47 had set out from Leyte the previous morning, bound for an airfield on Luzon. With no field in sight and running low on fuel, the pilot opted in desperation to land at the first airfield he spotted—Batan. The American fighter pilot assumed, as he put it, that "the damned Japs had patched up one of our buggies and didn't even have the grace to take the markings off." When the Japanese guns on the island opened up on the P-51 but not the C-47, the pilot's fears were confirmed. He took out one engine after another on the big transport plane and watched it settle on the water. It was only when he returned to strafe the survivors as they clambered aboard life rafts that he saw their American uniforms. He dropped a message telling them of LaCroix's location on the opposite side of the island. They sailed around the island during the night. The squadron leader was later awarded the Distinguished Flying Cross for downing the American plane. Ironically the C-47 contained a nurse with whom the squadron leader was to have had a date the night before.

The Americans by now made up a small flotilla: a fighter pilot, two transport pilots, a crew chief, three crew members, and two Army nurses, overseen by circling fighters. A PB-Y finally located the flotilla and landed in the still-heavy seas. With all aboard, the PB-Y misjudged its take-off, crashed into a swell, and only by jamming full power avoided sinking under the weight of in-rushing water. The PB-Y flew its varied cargo to Lingayen where, it was reported, the nurses were given much care and attention. Lieutenant LaCroix was flown on to a front-line hospital in Leyte, treated for a broken tibia and burns, given a plaster cast after removal of the Japanese bullet, and awarded an Air Medal and a Purple Heart. Having saved his life with a parachute, he was also officially inducted into the exclusive Caterpillar Club. Every year thereafter my father celebrated two birthdays: the one of his birth, the second of his rebirth.

28

A Peculiar Humor

16 February 1945
Field Hospital—Luzon

Dear Family,

Dad—I got that Jap plane for you. I was the third in our squadron to get a Jap plane. It was a big twin engine job. I looked over, saw the big red sun on it, almost got buck fever. She made the prettiest dive and splash you've seen. I felt good. On the way back we got some more, but they were on the ground. That was what sent me here. I have a minor wound—got a Jap machine gun bullet through my ankle. It's pretty inconsequential, but I have to wear a cast—mainly for the burns I got on that leg at the same time. All in all, it was a profitable day. I will get the air medal for the plane, the Purple Heart for the wound. I can't fly for six weeks, which should make you happy. Two weeks here and then two or three weeks in Sidney for rest-leave, after which I'll spend a little more time resting. It is a pretty good deal. To top off my accomplishments, I'm also a member of the Caterpillar Club…As soon as I can, I'll take a picture of myself next to my plane with the Jap flag painted on it. Real impressive.

We had a sad thing happen today. Two boys, addle-brained incompetents, fooling around in their tent—with unloaded guns, naturally. One of the guns went off, shot the other boy through the stomach. I believe if they could make every fool who is careless with a gun watch the death agonies, there would never be any more accidental shootings. The boy died this noon. Getting shot by Japs is one thing, but when your own men don't have enough decency and common sense to be careful—that makes me boil like all hell. A man like that ought to be court-martialed.

Goodnight, now.

18 February 1945
Field Hospital—Luzon

Dear George,

You probably would be interested in this place. Since I'm in the surgical ward, I see a lot of interesting cases. Had one here the other day. A boy got shot from left to right through the stomach. Pierced the intestines twice. Got infection in there, his intestines bloated up, gradually restricting his breathing until he died. About 18 hours, I think, altogether. Interesting, but not very pleasant to lie here and listen to. Several fellows with minor bullet wounds of the type I have. There is a brain fracture close that is pretty well healed up. Several splint cases.

In a more humorous vein...the boy near me takes penicillin treatments—they inject it in your rear-end with a needle about three inches long. The corpsman stands back, throws it like a javelin. The poor receiver just lies there and grunts...It is really interesting to watch the medical procedures. Incidentally, guess I'd make a good doctor, in one respect. I can look at any mess and not get a weak stomach.

Seems strange to realize a lot of the fellows are sent from here back to the States. I like it pretty well over here, except that I don't like all the over-water flying. I can tell you first-hand that it is no fun, sitting in the water, wondering when and if you'll be found, and whether the Japs might get to you first. I'll be a lot happier when we get more over-land flying.

When a soldier in the First World War was hit in the head, lungs, bowels, or large bones of the leg, the wound was normally fatal. Learning from this experience, the Army during the Second World War decided to move major surgery as close to the front as possible, operating without delay.[154] The less seriously wounded were moved to evacuation hospitals in the rear. Thus was borne the mobile field hospital, the precursor of the Mobile Army Surgical Hospital (MASH) units of the Korean War. Field hospitals, each comprising three platoons of sixty enlisted men, six nurses, and an equal number of surgeon officers, were assigned as divisional support units, one platoon to a division. Doctors and nurses performed triage at the field hospital's receiving tent. A field hospital could perform perhaps eighty operations a day and records indicate that over 85 percent of soldiers operated on in field hospitals survived. Field hospitals in Leyte saw the highest ratio of killed to wounded (1:3) in the war, including casualties from kamikaze attacks on Liberty ships attempting to enter Leyte harbor.[155]

The U.S. Army Medical Department oversaw the provision of medical and surgical care for the massive force spanned across the globe. The Medical Division of the Air Corps was constituted as a separate, but affiliated, entity in recognition of the distinctive physical qualifications required of fliers and the diseases and injuries peculiar to, or more common among, fliers. In one more example of experimentation and innovation driven by exigency, the Medical Department devised the "chain of evacuation." Defined as "the entire group of successive installations engaged in the collection, transportation, and hospitalization of the sick and wounded," the chain comprised in succession: (1) company aid men, (2) litter bearers, (3) battalion aid stations, (4) division collecting and clearing stations, (5) field hospitals, (6) evacuation hospitals, (7) hospital trains, planes, and ships, (8) general hospitals, (9) convalescent hospitals, and (10) general hospitals in the United States.[156] As one historian wrote of medical treatment in World War II: "There [was] nothing rigid about the field medical service. Improvisation and adaptation were the rule…"[157]

The diseases most common among soldiers during World War II were gangrene, malaria, staphylococcus, and streptococcus infections. In the Pacific theater, where monsoon rains and tropical conditions proved fertile incubators, scrub typhus, dengue fever, and tropical dysentery alone caused four times as many casualties as did battle wounds. Medical personnel also encountered diseases with which they had little prior experience: yaws, leprosy, bubonic plague, and cutaneous diphtheria.[158] Gas gangrene was particularly feared. Flourishing in damaged flesh in the absence of oxygen, it was usually fatal and remained largely undetectable until a wound was opened. But the putrefaction was instantly recognizable, and at the shout of "Gas," a hospital tent galvanized to isolate the wounded soldier, fearing contagion with other wounded men, disinfect the tent, and re-sterilize surgical instruments.[159]

18 February 1945
Field Hospital—Luzon

Dear Family,

My main achievements, since I got here, are writing, reading, and sleeping. I've written so many letters I'm thinking of adopting a pen name. I've read every book in the place. So now I'm trying to learn the Philippine language. In the Philippines, each province (much like states) has its own dialect. However, the government here adopted a universal language for the Filipinos. This is the Tagolog dialect, which I'm trying to learn. Only trouble is that at one minute a native is teaching me Tagolog, and a few minutes later I've mixed up words of the Pangasinan dialect. I am learning slowly. Ex. Bring me some water, food. Kumuha ka ng tubig, pag-

kain. Etc. The Filipino ward boys here are teaching me, but much prefer to teach swear words and love phrases.

I'm in pretty good shape again. Naturally, I can't walk yet, but most of the steady pain is gone. I get just about everything I want in the line of drinks (both alcoholic and otherwise), candy, and usually, reading material. The fellow in the next bed is a Marine pilot. We get along right well except when we discuss planes. Then it gets a little bit hot going.

Looks as though I'm going to get my [rest] leave to Sidney. Hope so, for it probably will be my only chance to get to Australia. I imagine that before long, rest leaves will be taken in Manila. Providing the Japs left anything worth-while. Before the war, of course, it was quite a play-town. Manila was the peacetime playtown and Baguio was the wealthy summer resort. You can pick Baguio out on the maps; it's in the mountains north of Lingayen and Rosario. There is supposed to be food, swimming, fishing, resting there. It is high enough in the mountains so that there are no mosquitoes or flies there. Don't know, or rather I can't tell, just how much of it is left.

About time to stop. It's sundown. A cock is crowing, some chickens cackling. The Filipino boys are rattling off their lingo while they adjust our mosquito nets. So, guess I'd better stop.

3 March 1945
Luzon

Hello, Proud Parents,

Twenty-five years ago today your prize possession came into the world—me. Allow me to sincerely congratulate you and commend you on your superb taste. Well, it sounds good, anyways.

I'm out of the hospital. However, I don't believe I'll stay here. The docs think it would be better for me to be evacuated to Leyte so I can get more complete medical care, nurses, and good food. I could stay here, but…at Leyte…my leg would heal faster and I'd be able to get back to action sooner.

After I wrote and told you about my little escapade [being shot down], I was sorry. However, I'm glad now, for I've been told you were sent a "wounded in action" telegram. I believe you were also sent a "missing in action" telegram, but I think that it was probably stopped before it got to you, for I wasn't missing too long (although at the time, it seemed like years)… Well, now you know the whole story. I wasn't going to tell you it all, but since the newspapers did, I thought you might like a first hand report.

I'll be pretty well-healed by the time I come home. Already I have four ribbons. Pacific theatre ribbon with four stars. (major campaigns participated in.) Philippine ribbon. The purple heart and air medal—I'll get them within a few days or weeks. Now if group would get magnificent and give me a promotion, I'd be quite satisfied. Fat chance of that, though. At least, not until I can get back into action and that may be almost two months.

We had a darn good bombing raid a couple of nights ago. The best the Japs have given us here on Luzon. The darn thing kept us awake most of the night. Can't say I particularly enjoyed stumping my way to a fox hole with my cast, but the fireworks were really beautiful. If those darn Japs aren't careful, though, they are liable to hurt somebody. They are exceptionally discourteous in that way. However, we taught a couple of them manners that night. The raids don't bother me when I fly every day, but when you are just an observer with a peg-leg, they get annoying.

4 March 1945
Luzon

Dear Dad,

Well, at long last Manila is just about all taken. It amazed me, though, to see the newspaper reports that Manila was in our hands. At the time the original report came out, we were having the toughest fight of this war just hanging on to the outermost suburbs. MacArthur is doing a wonderful job, but the casualties are a lot heavier than your newspapers indicate. We have air superiority, of course, but it has been an exceptionally tough fight on the ground, where and when the Japs have chosen to fight. Strangely, or maybe not so, MacArthur is very unpopular with the troops, mainly for obvious reasons. Also, when Manila was taken, he wouldn't allow anything larger than small arms in [the city]. Since the Japs had fortified many parts of the city, it proved rather expensive and the original order was, I believe, eventually countermanded. However, the bad taste is still in the troops' mouths. I guess the original idea was to save the city, but the troops didn't give a damn about the city, for which I don't blame them.

I guess I'm a little cynical, but I'll shoot anyone (except Americans) and destroy any and all property before I'll give up my own life. Naturally, a direct order to the contrary would change any given situation, but when it is up to me, that is my attitude. Also, I learned my lesson the hard way. The reason I was shot down was that I went back too many times, strafing. You see, there were more planes and troops out in plain sight than I've had the pleasure of meeting before and the two of us couldn't resist going back. Actually, even if I hadn't been saved the damage we did on that mission far outweighed the cost of our one plane and pilot. However, from now on they will call me "one-pass LaCroix." There are plenty of other fools who will go back extra times, so there is no use of my doing it…Although it is a dubious pleasure, I have the first Purple Heart that has not been awarded posthumously. It is the one decoration that I don't want any clusters on…

You know, it is interesting watching people over here. I've watched fellows in air-raids. Some that are big, strong, healthy are the ones, many times, that go weak and panicky with fear, crying in the bottom of a fox-hole from the time the warning shot sounds until the all-clear. Although not entirely true, a fellow's actions seem to reflect a great deal on his upbringing. Boys that never had to think for themselves, never had to use any self-control or self-discipline, are the men who break at the times of strain. Pilot training is quite a help, incidentally, for although I've seen many pilots really almost scared to death, I haven't seen one break yet…

Goodnight, now.

6 March 1945
Luzon

Dear Art,

Life here is pretty good…It is a lot of fun, when you can forget the possibilities of capture. There are no particular worries over being killed—you either are or aren't, but the idea of being captured has caused a lot of sleeplessness and not only by myself. Combat itself is fun. We have a lot of new replacements and so we older ones have a lot of time off. We get a lot of reading, sleeping done…For a week or so after I went down, I didn't give a good damn whether I ever saw the ocean again…I had a mild sort of nightmare the first night when I woke up suddenly, listening to the surf. I enjoy the ocean now as well as I ever did.

They are supposed to evacuate me today. At least there will be nurses in Leyte. Hope I can make it to Australia where the food is good and the women aren't.

Few issues are calculated to provoke explosive territoriality as predictably as the perception that "foreigners are taking our women." The deluge of American troops in the U.K. and Australia during the Second World War was the origin of the overused popular epithet "Overpaid, oversexed, and over here." In Brisbane, Australia, a town of 300,000 inhabitants became almost overnight host to more than 300,000 American troops, both white and black. Tensions between Australians and Americans had their genesis in three uncomfortable realities: race, women, and differential economic status.

Black American troops, excluded from combat units and assigned mainly to transport and service units, were segregated on the south side of the Brisbane River and not permitted to cross the Victoria Bridge to the city's civic center on the river's north side. The troops resented their discriminatory treatment and the maintenance of order resulted in periodically heavy-handed treatment by baton-wielding American military police (MPs). While the Australians treated the local Aborigines at least as discriminatorily as the Americans did their minorities, the Australians' instinctive libertarianism resented the visible exertion of authority by the MPs and inclined them to a "typical Digger [Australian infantryman] concern for the underdog," as one Australian veteran put it.[160]

The inevitable competition for few women by many men was exacerbated by the outward manifestations of American affluence and exclusiveness. The "Yanks" had well-tailored uniforms, were well-paid, and in consequence drew favorable attention from local women short on food, fuel, and the amenities of everyday life. While Australian units had "wet" canteens within their unit lines, U.S. forces had well-appointed PX clubs offering food, drinks, cigarettes, and merchandise at discount prices. Australians were excluded from these clubs. Despite the generally well-mannered behavior of American troops, the Aussies resented "running second on their own turf."[161]

Tensions erupted in frequent brawls between American and Australian troops, one local authority estimating as many as twenty fights a night in late 1942. The "Battle of Brisbane" erupted in November 1942 when two Australian infantrymen came across an American MP applying his baton to a drunken U.S. soldier. As the Aussie veteran explained, the American MPs used batons for riot control; their use in the Australian Army would have provoked a riot.[162] The Australians went to the aid of their belabored comrade-in-arms, doubly happy at the prospect of evening scores with the military police, a group generally resented among the local populace for their arrogance and perceived over-readiness to resort to force. A crowd of Australians gathered to support the two "good Samaritans," as a witness put it, and the MP retreated into a nearby American PX. MP reinforcements arrived, followed shortly by the fire brigade with its riot-quelling hoses, all to no effect. The battle raged for three hours until the MPs opened fire, killing one Australian and wounding several others. Alliances may form globally but they fray locally.

09 March 1945
Back on Leyte—Another hospital.

Dear Family,

What a racket this life is. Have been sent to the convalescent hospital. I'm in my tent on the shores of the beautiful Pacific, listening to the plentiful supply of liquid sunshine coming down. It is right on the beach, looks like a "Join the Navy" advertisement. The tents are set about fifty feet back from high tide. They are in the middle of a nice coconut grove. The beach itself is a gray sand—a little oily from the scores of ships in the harbor. The water is the clear blue I've raved about before, always with waves just choppy enough to make good swimming. I'd give anything for a sailboat to float around in in the harbor. There is always a good stiff wind blowing that makes sailing conditions ideal. Clean sheets on a real bed with real springs with real white nurses. A life of leisure and comfort.

This hospital has all the surgical cases from the front. There are a lot of badly wounded infantrymen. It is really amazing how they keep some of them alive and well. Cases with bullets in arms, legs, lungs, stomach, etc., all in good shape. By use of drugs they have little pain, are able to enjoy this life, somewhat, after a few days.

I am the only air corps pilot here, so I am having an interesting time. Some of these boys have darn interesting stories to tell. You know, it is funny how much more unbelievable some true stories are than the pulp adventure magazines of the States.

It amuses me how the newspapers say "mopping up operations are in effect," many times before the troops have gotten to their objective. Some of the infantry boys here, although not bitter, are pretty cynical about it all.

12 March 1945
Leyte Hospital

Dear Family,

Raining again. On Luzon it never seemed to rain. Here it always does.

Took off the cast yesterday. Can't walk on it yet, though, for they haven't taken an x-ray. The burns are healing pretty well, new skin covering about ¾ the area, the rest healing as rapidly as might be expected. As for the break, I don't know whether I'll have to have another cast put on or not, but the x-ray will tell. I'm feeling pretty well and pretty spry. The nurses keep life interesting and I fit a little chess and reading in.

Saw Irving Berlin a couple of days ago. He and his troops put on a ½ hour show in each hospital ward. They were pretty good. I noticed one thing, though, although the boys here want to laugh, it is hard for an outsider to make them laugh. Wounded men have their own brand of humor. We have a lot of fun and laughs but it is a different brand. Berlin's show got the men loosened up, but it took some time and even then, it wasn't completely relaxed amusement. Boys in here laugh at things that would seem awfully callous to an outsider. For example, one fellow came back from an operation half under the weather. He kept slapping himself, moaning "wake up, wake up" etc. It is quite a laugh when somebody moans with pain. I guess it is a sort of defense to keep yourself from getting moody about it, for everyone having gone through the same pains, they can fully appreciate the discomfort and by laughing at it keep their minds off the actual agony. It is a little complicated, but you probably can follow the trend and thought.

Time to stop now.

"The great intangible of America's wars beyond logistics, beyond strategy, beyond wonder weapons and generals, is the spiritual force of its fighting men and women—that is the force that the USO so magnificently serves." So the United Services Organization describes its strategic mission. The USO, with its wistful slogan "Until every one comes home," was yet another, albeit the most colorful, face of the vast civilian edifice buttressing America's two-theater war effort. President Roosevelt, ever-attentive to the "great intangible" of the men and women he governed, proposed that private, rather than governmental, organizations assume responsibility for the entertainment of the Armed Services on-leave. The USO was formed in response in 1941 and by 1944 operated over 3,000 clubs in which the famous and not-so-famous, volunteers all, provided service personnel a welcome respite from war.

But the USO's most memorable innovation was the traveling camp show, the moving carnival of Hollywood celebrities recruited as front-line troop morale boosters and war machine propagandists. Between 1941 and 1947, the USO put on more than 428,000 camp shows for Allied military personnel. *The Stars Go to War* captured the public imagination, the enthusiastic gratitude of the troops, and the vitriol of Tokyo Rose and Axis Sally, who were no less concerned with the morale of American troops. Bing Crosby crooned, Jack Benny chiseled and fiddled, Larry Adler harmonicaed, John Wayne swaggered, Bogart Marlowed, and Cagney Cohaned, Marlene Dietrich sultried, Ruby Keeler Ziegfelded, Fred Astaire pirouetted, George Burns deadpanned, The Andrews Sisters harmonized, Kate Smith accordianed, Benny Goodman puffed and Glen Miller huffed, Mary Martin warbled, and Irving Berlin, while "Puttin' on the Ritz," opined how he "Hate to Get Up in the Morning." But none could touch the dedication and sheer force of personality of the doyen of USO stars, Bob Hope. During the summer of 1944 alone, Hope traveled over 30,000 miles, giving more than 150 performances as he hopped hazardously from Pacific island to island. Several million miles and all of America's wars later, during the umpteenth honorarium from a grateful country, a retired commandant of the U.S. Marine Corps referred to Hope as "this magnificent soldier in grease paint who had a way of bringing a little bit of home to troops in faraway places." An intangible gift of very tangible value.

28 March 1945
Leyte

Dear Dad,

Last night I was lying on the beach, alone, listening to the surf and thinking. It was one of those perfect nights; a full moon glistening on the breakers, small scud clouds drifting by, etc. (maybe I should be a poet) At any rate, I got to thinking what I would like to do when I get home again.

As you know, I will probably get a thirty-day leave. I will want to spend the first part of that leave just lying around the house, just reaching the ultimate in laziness with you, mom, and grandma. After that I would like to take a trip of about two weeks with you alone. We could head up towards [New Hampshire], maybe wander over to Pittsburgh. Anywhere we feel like; nothing definite. We might spend the entire time at one place, or we might go to five places. Just fishing, swimming, eating, drinking as the whim strikes us.

I can't remember any time when we have been together, alone, for more than a couple of hours. I would like a chance like this to get together; to talk things over completely. Heretofore we have often started conversations but have never been able really to finish them.

As for equipment, all we would need would be old clothes, fishing tackle, and a couple of cases of scotch and other assorted beverages. I would undoubtedly be a long ways from sober for the first few days, but it wouldn't matter, for we would have no wifely, brotherly, or sisterly distractions and admonition to cause undue inhibitions. I figure that by the time I get back to the States, I will have earned a good bender. The kind of bender where you get a warm glow on and maintain it for several days. Never overdoing it, but never sober.

Each day we would load up the boat with tackle, bait, scotch, and crackers and sardines. Come time to eat, we would leave the boat and cook some of our fish—providing we weren't too lazy, that is...

Goodnight, dad.

All my love,
Bob

29

A HAPPY PRINCE OF SERENDIP

The big debate of the second half of the war in the Pacific was Luzon versus Formosa: would the principal objective of the drive that had brought the Allies into the western Pacific, preliminary to an assault on Japan itself, be the northern Philippines or the future Taiwan? American military planners anticipated that an invasion of the Japanese home islands would be necessary to end the war. This, in turn, would require coordinating intensive aerial bombardment of Japan with air and sea operations to cut Japan's resource lifeline with the Dutch East Indies (Indonesia). The best place from which to launch such attacks would be airfields in eastern China and a seaport on the south China coast, the latter substituting for the logistically difficult supply routes from India and Burma. This strategy presumed control of the South China Sea, which depended upon securing air, naval, and logistical bases in the strategic triangle formed by Luzon, Formosa, and the south China coast.

Earlier debate over possibly circumventing the Philippines entirely on the march to Japan was resolved in favor of MacArthur's invasion of the central Philippines at Leyte in late 1944. Seizure of either Luzon or Formosa would depend upon staging areas in the central and southern Philippines. Just prior to the launching of the Leyte invasion, Washington was notified by General Joseph Stilwell, Allied chief of staff to Generalissimo Chiang Kai-shek and commander of U.S. Army forces in China, Burma, and India, that Japanese offensives in southeastern China had deprived U.S. Army Air Forces of the bases that were to have been expanded in preparation for the assault on Japan. With the disappearance of the bases went the urgency of securing a southern Chinese seaport and Formosa as a stepping-stone to the Chinese coast. Ultimately a shortage of manpower resources and MacArthur's argument that bypassing Luzon would be disastrous to American prestige in Asia and the world decided Washington in favor of seizing Luzon, bypassing Formosa, and targeting Okinawa.

The battle for Okinawa, commencing on April 1, 1945, marked the first use of massed formations of hundreds of kamikaze aircraft called *kikusui*, or "floating chrysanthemum" for the symbol of imperial Japan. These flights originated from airfields in Kyushu and Formosa. The Army Air Corps rejected a request for a heavy bombing campaign against the airfields, arguing that it was an unwarranted diversion from the strategic bombing campaign. In the event, kamikaze attacks were primarily responsible for sinking 34 Allied ships and crafts and damaging another 368, the largest losses in a single engagement in U.S. naval history.[163] Fighter aircraft flew continuous interdiction and suppression sorties over Formosa and the South China Sea strategic triangle until the end of the war. My father's squadron was part of this effort.

28 April 1945

Dear Family,

At this point I am rather tired, so I don't know how this letter will turn out. I'm flying again, usually flying two days and off the third. It makes it pretty nice that way, although I did fly today—my day off... Went down south today to pick up a new plane for myself. It is a sweet ship—has the smoothest engine I've heard in a long time. Has a lot of new, fancy gadgets on it that are rather helpful.

Main thing bothering me right now is that I don't have my own chute, have to borrow one each time I fly. I had just gotten a new one, shipped it up here on a plane. The damn thing crashed, burned, so I lost quite a bit of equipment. No, I was not on it.

Late on the morning of June 20, 1945, my father's P-51 flight, following an "on-the-water" flight from Laoag in the Philippines, was scouting for targets of opportunity just above ground level over the west coast of Formosa. Formosa was ceded by China to Japan in perpetuity following the Sino-Japanese War of 1895. The Japanese heavily fortified the island in the intervening half-century. The Americans encountered little anti-aircraft fire until the four Mustangs, in formidable line-abreast strafing formation, pounced on a large railway yard marshalling Japanese troops. My father picked "an innocent looking village tower" near the tracks. Gun flashes erupted from the upper windows of the concealed flak tower. As he returned fire, the cockpit canopy suddenly shattered. His goggles protected his eyes but fragments of the canopy sliced into his exposed face.

Passing out of range of the tower's guns, LaCroix climbed to two thousand feet and had another pilot check him over for leaking coolant. He tested his machine guns with the idea of revisiting the target. Six .50 caliber machine guns only a few feet away on each wing, without the noise attenuating Plexiglas of the canopy, were deafening. He headed for home as soon as his hearing returned.

He made a good landing but on touch down there was an explosion and smoke in the cockpit, both seeming to originate behind the armor plate. It might have been the result of undetected damage or a delayed explosive. An inspection revealed the radio set, designed to detonate in a crash to prevent enemy retrieval, had exploded. The canopy had taken a burst of machine gun fire from the front, missing the pilot by inches. His borrowed parachute was packed differently than his own, so he was flying without the extra cushion he normally used. Sitting five inches lower than usual, the ersatz parachute saved his life. It was the second time he avoided a posthumous Purple Heart.

At the time of the incident a photograph was taken of my father still in his plane on the flight line. Several years after the war a fellow pilot enlarged the photo and placed it in a frame made from remnants of the shattered cockpit. The blow-up revealed a bullet hole near the left-rear part of the canopy. As he was passing over the flak tower, the tower gunner pivoted and fired over the plane's retreating left wing. The trajectory of the bullet passed within an inch of his head. Sitting on his own parachute, the bullet would have caught him square in the head. I keep the Plexiglas-framed picture on my desk. "All chance, direction which thou canst not see."

30

THE HUMAN REMAINS HIGHWAY

Midway between Mandalay and Lashio lies a small village like all small villages in rural Burma: an agglomeration of atap and wood bungalows squatting on thick bamboo poles above pillowy red dust seasonally inundated by torrential monsoon rains. Majestically disdainful hogs, cackling fowl, omnivorous goats, and mangy dogs rule insolently. They yield sullenly to the kinetic disruptions of elfin girls and mischievous boys. In a symphony of dissonance, squawks, bleats, barks, and clucks merge in unlikely harmony with droning Theravada Pali chants. The tinkling bells of lumbering water oxen mingle with the untainted laughter of the young. The ebb and flow of Burmese conquest—Mons, Shan, Mongols and Arakanese, Siamese, Chinese, British, and Japanese—have cyclically inundated this village to as little enduring effect as the biannual rains. The villagers absorb what is useful and, like proverbial reeds in the stream, bend gracefully until the waters recede, knowing full well they will return with the inevitability of the planting season.

In 1985 I was making my way through north central Burma, visiting Buddhist monasteries to study the peacefully xenophobic monks whose role as glue in a fraying social fabric impressed me. My Burmese guide, Than, and I were attending a rite of passage for Burmese boys, the *Shinpyu* or ceremony of initiation as Buddhist novices. We followed the novices, heads newly shorn, clad in novitiates' yellow robes, and carrying alms bowls, into the blinding glare of a mid-September afternoon. A throng of proud families swept us along to the celebratory slaughtering of a large pig and a meal of sparrows—beaks, wings, feet, and all—chick peas, rice, and tea. My self-consciousness was artfully disarmed by the simply given trust of people who asked nothing in return.

With parting congratulations, we headed for our World War II-vintage U.S. army jeep parked on the outskirts of the village. Stopping to thank the village headman for his hospitality, we emerged from his hut to a funereal silence. Even the animals were subdued, as if in homage. On the fringe of the village, adjacent an ancient shattered wall, in a location as remote in Burma as a foreigner could legally travel, a group of uniformly elderly Japanese men were surrounded by villagers both young and old. Despite the palpable excitement on the faces of the villagers, the gathering possessed a sobriety at odds with the happy abandon of the village festivity. At the core of the concentric circles formed by the Japanese and the villagers were large open canvas suitcases brimming with radios, videocassette recorders, small appliances, ornaments, and cash. Sensing a somber religiosity about the gathering, Than and I paused at a distance and watched.

In 1944, this Burmese backwater lay directly in the path of the Japanese Imperial Army retreating eastward into Siam and Cambodia before an avenging British, American, and Chinese juggernaut. Shortly after Rangoon fell to the Japanese in March 1942, the Eighteenth Division, which had fought alongside Ishizuka's Fifth Division in the conquest of Singapore, was redeployed to Burma. Ishizuka was mustered out around this time, returning to civilian life in Tokyo until recalled for service in the Philippines. The Eighteenth was assigned the task of holding a line from northeast of Mandalay to Lashio against the advancing British XIV Army, commanded by the brilliant but modest and therefore, unjustifiably, forgotten General William Slim.

By late 1944, the aura of invincibility around Japan's military machine had long since faded. On top of relentless and well-provisioned Allied pressure, the Japanese were fighting in what Slim has described as "some of the world's worst country, breeding the world's worst diseases, and having for half the year at least the world's worst climate."[164] The local Burmese exiled their serious offenders to parts of this region, knowing the environment would surely kill them. Because of Allied control of the sea lanes to and the skies over Rangoon and southern Burma, the Japanese were desperately short of supplies. As the Allied advance gained momentum, the Japanese retreat assumed the nightmarish features of Napoleon's retreat from Moscow. Called by Japanese soldiers the "Human Remains Highway," one soldier described it as a "vision of hell."[165] Soldiers in their twenties were stooped like old men. Tens of thousands were left to die and decay, the rest too weak to assist them. Many took their lives, frequently in "double suicides," embracing one another with a grenade between them. Allied soldiers, rather than contribute unnecessarily to the appalling carnage, detoured around the retreating forces. Out of 305,000 Japanese soldiers who fought in Burma, only 118,000 returned to Japan.[166]

The attitude of the local Burmese during the war, typified by the Burmese nationalist Aung San, father of the democratic activist Aung San Suu Kyi, was practical in the extreme: when the Japanese were winning, they favored the Japanese; when the Allies, more specifically the former colonial power Britain, nosed ahead, they switched horses. In the early stages of the war, the Japanese effectively played the race and Burmese nationalist cards, promising liberation from the "white" colonial power under a new Burmese Government. Prior to the war, Aung San was a political activist at Rangoon University, becoming in 1939 secretary of the extreme Nationalist Minority Group, for which he served seventeen days in prison. When his organization was proscribed by the British, he fled to Japan where he received military training in a Japanese officers' school. Aung San and his colleagues accompanied the Japanese in the invasion of Burma, forming the nucleus of an irregular Burmese force that evolved into the puppet Burmese National Army. The Japanese made Aung San a major general and commander in chief of the BNA.

Early in 1945, Aung San and his men agreed to defect to the Allies. Despite early hopes and promises, the Burmese quickly discovered that Japanese and Burmese concepts of self-governance shared little more than nomenclature. As one Burmese leader put it to General Slim, "If the British sucked our blood, the Japanese ground our bones!"[167] When Aung San discovered that Japanese policy was more noose than rope, he turned to the British. His patriotic pragmatism was reflected in an exchange with Slim, quoted in the latter's memoirs, *Defeat Into Victory*. When Slim remarked that Aung San and his men came to the British only because the latter were winning, Aung San replied, "It wouldn't be much good coming to you if you weren't, would it?"[168] Slim had to agree. Aung San proved good to his word, supporting the Allies in their advance against the Japanese, disrupting Japanese communications, ambushing small parties, and killing Japanese stragglers. Slim, later field marshal, viscount, and chief of the British Imperial General Staff, always believed that had Aung San received continued British support following the war, he "would have proved a Burmese Smuts."[169] Aung San's vision and integrity might have catalyzed Burmese development. Instead, in a great historical "what if," Aung San was assassinated in 1947. His daughter and her people reap the harvest.

Aung San's concern was political survival after the war; his people had more pedestrian preoccupations. Slim explains it well in his memoirs, "[T]o the main mass of the peasant population the invasion was an inexplicable and sudden calamity; their only interest was, if possible, not to become involved in it and to avoid the soldiers of both sides." Burmese hill tribes were intensely loyal to the British; Burmese on the plains, where most fighting occurred, were generally apathetic.[170] Apathy was hardly an effective shield. As the Japanese retreat turned to rout, shelter was sought where it could be found. The shattered wall in the village was the scene of a vicious firefight between advancing British and retreating Japanese infantry. Most of the village had been leveled. Over a broadly advancing front, it was a terrifying reality that combatants and non-combatants were indistinguishable, or at least indistinguished.

Anticipating a death in which it might prove impossible to recover their bones for cremation, Japanese soldiers would often place fingernails or hair in a small wooden box, sealed with bamboo nails, to be returned to their families in Japan. If comrades fell and time and battle permitted, the survivors might cut off a finger or hand of the slain soldier, carrying it in their mess kit or pack until it could be ceremonially cremated and the ashes returned to Japan. In Burma, the scale and speed of the Japanese collapse precluded even these vestiges of religious observance. As men fell, their comrades would rip a piece of cloth from an already rotting uniform and make a crude notation locating the fallen body. Through mud, leach-infested swamps, blinding monsoon rains, starvation, and harried retreat, over decades of haunting recollection, the survivors preserved the tattered cloth and the memory of men left behind. And they returned.

Forty years after they straggled out of Burma, a cluster of veterans of the Eighteenth Division returned to a place they had never really left. They came in search of reconciliation: with their unburied comrades, with their ghosts, with the innocents whose lives had been shredded indifferently. Their contrition took the only form they knew to transcend the barrier of language and resentment. They offered reparation. Carrying suitcases the weight of the packs they bore as young soldiers, they gave to the villagers a life's worth of possessions. It seemed to me at the time too neat, too cold and indifferent. I see it differently now. Leaving the village elders to distribute the gifts, a few of the oldest villagers accompanied the veterans to the smashed wall on the edge of the village. They gently raked, shoveled, sifted earth, muffled exclamations marking a recovered remain, piece of equipment, shell casing. Gently placing the bone fragments in ceremonial urns for the return to Japan, the veterans bowed their way out of the village for the final trip home.

31

"Namu-Amida-Butsu"

14 April 1945
Luzon

Dear Family,

Our life of leisure at the convalescent hospital finally was termi-
nated. We celebrated it with a two day drinking party…It was our
final celebration before returning to combat and we did it proud.
Even had a date—my only one since I left the States. Of course, two
of us had the only women, along with eight other men. All we did
was sit there on the beach, drinking and singing.

At any rate, as all good things do, the vacation ended…I then went
up to the front lines [at Baguio] with [a friend from the 32nd Divi-
sion—infantry]…It was very interesting, both because of Baguio's fame
and because of the fact it was one of our old dive bombing targets. It was
the first time I've been able to see the actual targets I've bombed…made
me happy I was on the giving and not the receiving end. There isn't
much left of Baguio. The one remaining building, it so happened, was
the Catholic Church. A beautiful structure with hand carved wooden
furnishing. The people in Baguio didn't have too bad a time. It was one
of the few places where the Japs had not mistreated the people too badly.

Spent three days…in the front lines. Had a pretty rough time, for the fighting is pretty severe. [We were] under shell fire, mortar fire, and…sniped at. The main reason I went up there was to observe our group in action…dive bombing, skip bombing and strafing…[and to provide control for close air support of the infantry]. It was very interesting and valuable inasmuch as I found some of the defects in our technique and also got the infantry's view point on our close support…I learned a lot…Frankly, though, I prefer to stay in the air. Smells a lot better and the sleeping is better. Can't say I appreciate sleeping all night in a foxhole. When the artillery isn't firing, the Japs are infiltrating…I wish you could see the country they are fighting through. It is so rough and mountainous that the average person in the States would consider it too rough for normal mountain climbing.

The Air Commandos pioneered techniques of close air support for frontline advancing infantry in conditions requiring utmost precision. Frequently positioned no more than fifty yards from the enemy in terrain of serrated ridges, caves, jungle, and ill-defined battle lines, American troops in an air strike found themselves in a precarious position. A tactical withdrawal to widen the margin for error risked open exposure to enemy fire; remaining in position risked friendly fire casualties. The Air Commandos initiated the practice of embedding flight leaders in infantry command posts and front line positions to consult with ground commanders, radio back pilot briefings, and supervise actual strikes. The results of this unorthodox approach were summarized in a commendation from the commanding general of the Thirty-second Infantry: "On several occasions we were forced to ask that…air strikes be made within fifty to one hundred yards ahead of the infantry…these strikes were, to my mind, perfection itself…It is my belief that this is the first time that pilots of the supporting arm have visited the forward ground units in the combat zone to view terrain and study the tactical situation in which they were to be employed."[171]

Taking off in two-by-two or four-by-four formation, full power at 3,000 rpm, a close air support flight skimmed at treetop level toward the target area. As the planes approached the objective, the forward controller, usually identified by a large yellow umbrella near the target area, directed the attack by radio, pinpointing the targets directionally or with smoke bombs. The flight remained under the controller's direction until released or until ammunition was expended. In a strafing mission, adrenalin rushing, full power applied, the Commandos would come in on the deck and open up with six .50 caliber guns each, the violence of the attack intensified with napalm, rockets, and five-hundred-pound bombs. Pilots claim that strafing missions were the most exciting—but at a cost. Coming in low out of the sun the planes might catch an enemy unawares, but as they passed over the target, tremendous ground fire exacted the highest proportion of fighter losses, even with evasive action. Strafing runs were often preceded by dive-bombing, the P-51s peeling off in echelons from eight to ten thousand feet, releasing five-hundred-pound bombs, and pulling out at two thousand feet. The violence of the assault was such that, as one commander around Baguio put it, the infantrymen "moved forward immediately after the strike and took the position practically standing up."[172]

General Walter Krueger, MacArthur's Sixth Army commander, sent a commendation to the Air Commandos following the Baguio action:

> Close air support by...air forces of operations of this division past two days has been magnificent. Strikes against [named targets] have been particularly effective, enthusiastic cooperation of air force personnel to include visits by pilots to front line troops has materially improved coordination between ground and air forces. Request this commendation be forwarded to personnel concerned.[173]

———————

The island of Luzon sits atop the Philippines like a severed thumb straggling the ligaments of a once-intact limb. At its base lies Manila, gateway to the central plains, a verdant swath whose northern egress is Lingayen Gulf. On the northeast-facing pad of the thumb is the Cagayan Valley. It is a long, narrow swale between two ranges of mountains, and the Cagayan River winds and twists up the center until it falls at last into Luzon Strait. Perched between these two agricultural Edens, the top food-producing areas of the Philippines, on a southwestern spur of the rugged Cordillera Central Mountains, the summit eyrie of Baguio looks down with Olympian detachment on the defining mortal rituals of sow and reap. It was to Baguio, pre-war summer retreat of the Philippines' elite, that General Yamashita withdrew his headquarters in late 1944.

Known variously as the City of Pines, City of Flowers, and City of Lovers, Baguio was established during the Spanish colonial era as a minor link in a chain of *rancherias* forged to pacify and exploit the rich commercial potential of northern Luzon. Early in the twentieth century, the Americans, sensing its recreational potential and seeking respite from summer's sweltering lowland heat, greatly expanded the town and linked it by road with Manila. In the purest traditions of Asia's famed colonial hill stations—Dalat in Vietnam, Bogor in Indonesia, Fraser's Hill in Malaysia, Maymyo in Burma, Simla, Darjeeling, and Ootacamund in India—cool, beautiful Baguio, 5,000 feet above sea level, indulged the colonialist fantasy of Asia-become-home. Architecture, weather, and social custom converged to feed a comforting security of connectedness to all that was familiar. The whimsical artifice of the hill station was exemplified by "...the heights of God," an anonymous poem published in a 1917 edition of the *Darjeeling Advertiser:*[174]

> Ah! Yes, 'tis good to be up here
> In this thrice blessed clime,
> Where Jacks and Gills [sic] may climb the hills
> And have a jolly time.
> 'Tis good to watch the babes we love
> who to our heart chords cling,
> To see them grow in beauty's glow,
> Like flowers in the spring.
> 'Tis good to see the virgin snows
> No man has ever trod
> The saints alone around His throne
> May walk the heights of God.

In the last year of World War II, the Imperial Japanese Army sought respite of a different sort in Baguio. With Leyte lost, and most of his air and sea support with it, Yamashita rushed to implement the plan he had advocated from the outset of his Philippines' command. He would abandon Manila and retreat behind the natural shield furnished by northern Luzon's geography. He established his defense of Luzon in three sectors centered around Baguio: his own Shobu Group defending northern Luzon in the mountains west of the Cagayan Valley, Kembu Group overlooking Clark Field and the mountains west of the Central Plains, and Shimbu Group covering southern Luzon from the mountains east and northeast of Manila. Shobu Group's principal objectives were to prevent an Allied landing on the west coast of Luzon north of Lingayen Gulf, threaten the American advance through the Central Plains, deny the Americans access to the Cagayan Valley, and conduct a protracted defense of the mountainous terrain it held.[175] It was a measure of his plan's effective use of the formidable Luzon terrain that Yamashita and more than 50,000 of his men surrendered only after the close of the war on August 15, 1945, thus evading the annihilation visited on the remainder of his army.

---

16 June 1945
Luzon

Dear Family

If you know anyone in Chicago, ask them if they saw an article in one of the Sunday papers (probably Chicago Daily News) back around mid-April about how the brave and courageous P-51 pilots took an airfield behind Japanese lines, occupied it with the aid of guerrillas, and have been using it since. I understand they really made a wonderful story about it. Incidentally, for your peace of mind, the lines finally caught up with us so now we even get supplies by land, occasionally. I'm trying to get a copy of it, or at least send you the exact date of the paper and its name. Although

I haven't seen the article, I understand they did us full and lavish justice. Don't believe it all, though.

Headline, *Chicago Daily News*, 23 April 1945:

Fliers Steal Jap Airfield

An advance fighter base in Luzon...American airmen, working on their own, have snatched a valuable base from under the noses of the Japs. Usually the fliers wait for the infantry to take an airstrip. This time...the special [Air Commandos] which have landed with assault forces on many beaches...[went in ahead and seized the field]...Japs are on three sides... supply is handled entirely by air...[Filipino] guerrillas are guards...

The tactical brilliance of MacArthur's retreat from Manila through Bataan to the fortress of Corregidor at war's dawn found its Japanese counterpart in Yamashita's retreat from Manila to the mountain resort of Baguio at war's twilight. Yamashita had anticipated the American landing at Lingayen Gulf, twenty-five miles southwest of Baguio, but he expected to have at least another two weeks to position and provision his troops. Though he never intended to defend Manila, his trifurcated defense of Luzon depended on his ability to move seventy thousand metric tons of supplies stockpiled in the capital to defensive positions further north before the Americans arrived. By January 9, 1945, when the Americans landed at Lingayen, he had moved only four thousand tons of supplies.[176] His logistical difficulties were exacerbated by command problems. Not until mid-January did Tokyo headquarters give Yamashita fully consolidated command of the defense of Luzon, a thankless gesture by then and one that certainly contributed to Yamashita's post-war trial and execution.

Considering Manila indefensible, Yamashita had ordered his Shimbu Group commander not to attempt a defense of the capital but to cover the evacuation of supplies, destroy all bridges and vital installations, and evacuate the city as soon as the Americans appeared. By withdrawing to the mountains east of the city, the Shimbu Group would also retain control of the dams and reservoirs that supplied Manila's water.

Unfortunately the Japanese naval commander for the Manila area, Rear Admiral Sanji Iwabachi, at that point still independent of Yamashita's command, countermanded the general's order and vowed to defend the city to the last man. Shimbu Group, in contravention of Yamashita's orders, contributed three battalions to support Iwabachi's rash decision. Had Yamashita's orders been followed, much of the city's destruction and many of its worst atrocities would have been averted.

The men under Yamashita's command were some of the best Japan fielded, battle-hardened veterans like Lieutenant Ishizuka. But by early 1945 these forces were understrength, underfed, and under-equipped. And the leadership, organization, and coordination of ground combat forces reflected the eleventh-hour attempt to salvage a losing position with Yamashita's command appointment. As Yamashita put it in testimony after the war, "The source of command and coordination within a command lies in trusting your subordinate commanders. Under the circumstances, I was forced [to defend Luzon] with subordinates whom I did not know and with whose character and ability I was unfamiliar."[177]

The already formidable logistical complexities of Yamashita's retreat to Baguio became virtually insurmountable under pressure of unremitting American air attacks and unforgiving terrain. Luzon's highways and railroads were before the war the finest transportation network in the Far East outside Japan. By early January 1945, American land and carrier-based air attacks, supported by guerrilla sabotage operations, had so severely damaged the system that Yamashita could move only a trickle of essential supplies overland. Bridges were destroyed, highways cratered, railroad beds and marshalling yards damaged, railroad rolling stock and engines knocked out, and trucks destroyed. Japanese troops suffered under growing shortages of munitions, construction equipment, medical supplies, communications equipment, and food. Even before the American invasion, the Japanese had imported rice from Thailand and French Indochina to make up domestic shortages. After the invasion, shortages became acute.[178]

The terrain that abetted Japanese defense also impeded the movement of forces on both sides. Fog, torrential tropical downpours, serrated mountain ridges, mudslides, and washed out roads made the simplest movement time-consuming and therefore hazardous. Air power in these circumstances served as the great leveler. As if to drive the point home, the Fourth Fighter Squadron Commando on January 23 attacked General

Yamashita's headquarters at Baguio, strafing and dropping 32,000 pounds of bombs. A message center, administration buildings, quartermaster buildings, and the general's personal quarters were demolished. Shortly thereafter the squadron was astonished to hear Tokyo Rose announce that the entire Third Air Commando Group had been wiped out by Japanese paratroopers. The general and his men were not to be so fortunate.

Excerpts from daily life during the Battle for Baguio:

...One of our best ground officers died yesterday—polio or spinal meningitis. He was one of those loud, happy, hardworking, life of the party fellows who impressed you as having enough energy for five people. Three days ago he complained of a sore throat, yesterday he died. We sure will miss him.

...I seem to have hit a new low. One of my best friends was killed today, I got [a "Dear John"] letter from [my fiancé], and I'm fed up with being a 1ˢᵗ Lt. when I could be a Captain...Oh well. Such is life.

...The "Dear John" Letter
6 March 1945
Washington, D.C.

Dear Bob,

Hope your leg is well-healed by now and that soon you will be on your way to Australia and two or three weeks of civilization before returning to the life you seem to enjoy so much. Wish you all sorts of luck—but I guess you have plenty of it. This is the last letter you will ever have from me and I'd prefer that you don't write to me any more. Think it will be best for all concerned…You have changed so much that I don't think I ever want to see you again…I will send your fraternity pin to your mother to keep until you get home…Best of luck to you always.

Tillie

…All the little things are going wrong. I got shot up yesterday [over Baguio]…The rainy reason is setting in, so our flying for the next few months will be pretty erratic.

K___ C___ [close friend] is transferring out of the outfit. He is very unpopular with some of the fellows. The whole thing was brought to the climax when he led a flight through a heavy flak area we were told to stay away from. One of the boys (…a boy from Bartow, also) was pretty badly shot up, just barely made it home before he collapsed. He is, incidentally, in the hospital now, doing very well, and will go home as a result of it. At any rate, K___ is leaving because of this (the second time he has done it). I'm darn sorry to see him leave, though.

[Another friend] is going home before long. The damn fool put the plane into a vertical dive with full throttle and rpm. Result—by the time he got it under control again he had received a minor brain concussion which will ground him for several months. He is OK except he has severe headaches a lot.

…I'm still thinking of coming back for a second tour of duty…but I have one serious handicap—my right eye is definitely getting hard astigmatism, may prove a handicap in my next phys-

ical exam. I've managed to talk my way out of them for the last 15 months, but eventually I'll have to have an exam—at least when I go back to the States…Incidentally, my flight leader and I (excuse the bragging) have never wasted a bomb yet. We have more direct hits than almost anyone else around here.

Guess it is about time to stop. The boys are getting together over in the mess hall for some…fruit cake and coffee. I do very little drinking of anything but beer. I get sick. I guess it must be partly the climate, but mainly my physical condition. None of the boys are able to drink much.

…I'm very much interested in two articles that have come out, although they haven't been verified officially. One is that Russia has given Japan a 21-day ultimatum. The second is that some of the higher-ups in Japan conclude the war is now lost. If the two are true…there is a very good chance that the Japs may quit before any of us expect it…If Russia throws in actively with us against the Japs, the results may be a fast and furious break up… The Japs are fanatic but they are also clever and may not be willing to lose everything just for the sake of fighting.

I wish we were able to get more news. Our radio was lost in a crash a while back, so our outside contacts are only through official sources.

By mid-March frontline Japanese troops like Lieutenant Ishizuka were getting less than a quarter of a pound of rice a day, a far cry from the minimum daily requirement of nearly two and a half pounds. The rains made it impossible to cook what little rice they had. If they managed a fire, men collected edible wild grass from the field, boiled it with salt and felt gratitude for temporary relief from clawing hunger pains, paying later with continuous diarrhea. Shelter during air attacks and shelling was sought in "octopus traps," holes dug in the ground to the height of a soldier, but men were soon submerged in chest-high rainwater and had to climb out, exposing themselves to a concussive lacerating death from exploding shrapnel. Drinking water, even with the rain, became scarce as well-sated hoards of maggots spilled from unburied corpses into puddles, streams, and rainwater collection cans.[179]

...Raining again. Every day it starts raining in mid-afternoon, rains until about midnight. One consolation—it keeps things a lot cooler than usual.

By end-March, starvation and diet-associated diseases filled hospitals and sapped the strength of combat units. Baguio area hospitals, their malaria prophylaxis exhausted, stood by helplessly as malaria prevented replenishment of the strength drained by dysentery. Allied air strikes on supply roads to Baguio, combined with impossible terrain and Allied ground attacks, made it virtually impossible for the Japanese to bring any food into the Baguio area. A soldier described the steady debilitation of starvation, bombardment, strafing, and close-quarters fighting:

Our losses were dreadful...the heavily injured...would regret overtaxing their mates...[and die] apologizing and weeping...[180] I could not imagine that [one comrade I saw] had fought successfully in Hong Kong and Singapore. He looked to be deep in thought; in fact...he had reached the limit of mental exhaustion and was merely gazing intently at the water trickling down to his feet...He passed away [shortly thereafter]...[250]In increasing numbers our soldiers fell, physically emaciated and crippled, yet mentally alert.[251]

———————

In the fourth week of April, Lieutenant Ishizuka and the Fifty-eighth were ranged with other elements of General Yamashita's Shobu Group in a defensive arc around Baguio. The tightening vise claws of the U.S. Thirty-seventh and Thirty-third Divisions, ascending from the south, and a northerly descending force of Filipino guerillas led by an American officer who refused to surrender in 1942, promised a long-anticipated coup de grace. Yamashita, intending to prolong his resistance indefinitely, had evacuated Japanese civilians and the Filipino puppet government from Baguio in March and on April 19 departed with his command. His subordinate left in command then ordered all troops along the main line of resistance to fight to the last man.

By this stage of the battle, the combatants were separated in places by fewer than three hundred yards. Against imbedded defenses in naturally defensible terrain, the distance might as well have been a yawning chasm. The decisive impact of American air power in these conditions was described by Yamashita in testimony after the war: "If we had had your artillery and your air support, we would have won."[252] He described the close coordination of air power and artillery to protect the flanks of the attacking divisions, coordination that had effectively neutralized his own plan to infiltrate and harass: "We weren't ready for that type of fighting and you beat us with it."[253]

Weather permitting, the air commandos were flying nearly continuous missions in support of the infantry's brutal advance through the mountains surrounding Baguio. Following his visit to the front lines in mid-April, my father rejoined his squadron and on April 25 joined the final assault on the hill station. Captain John Rhode, a support aircraft controller for the Fifth Air Force, recounts a Fourth Squadron's attack on the Baguio defenders:[254]

> We are situated on a rise of a hill…overlooking the Jap front line. Our radio-equipped jeep is at the foot of the hill and beside us is a field telephone. From our foxholes…we can see the Japs at their guns, covered with weeds…A distance of 600 yards separates us from the Japs, but there is a valley in between and the situation is stalemated. If we advance now, we will get machine gun fire full in the face. If we try to steal up the steep sides of the opposite hill, Jap snipers…
>
> H-hour [ground attack time] this morning is 0900…it is time for the show to begin, and also time to call in our planes for close air coordination with the ground troops. We pick up the field telephone and call "Red Leader," code word for the commander of our already airborne fighters. We identify our aircraft controller station as "Rhinestone." Nothing but a crackling sound responds. We repeat, "Rhinestone calling Red Leader. Come in, please. Over." Still nothing.

As we wait for a reply, we wonder if the P-51s will be on time. This split-second timing is a ticklish business, the worry of keeping our fighters from strafing our own troops.

Still no contact with Red Leader. One last look around, a final check. We can see our front line and the big white panels indicating our forward positions. There is one off to the left, two on our right, and two more in front of us and a little below. Just behind and a little above us is a big white arrow pointing to the opposite hill, today's objective.

We make a check with the artillery. "Artillery from aircraft controller. Are you ready? Over." The answer comes promptly. "Ready for your instructions. Over."

This means the artillery will have smoke shells set to put the finger on our Jap neighbors as a guide to the fighter planes.

Five minutes to go. Where the hell are those P-51s? Another call. "Rhinestone to Red Leader. Come in. Come in. Over." This time we make contact. "Red Leader to Rhinestone; Roger. What are your instructions?" The curtain is ready to go up... "Rhinestone to Red Leader. Orbit off to the west, and I'll silence artillery to clear the target for you."

Artillery is told that the planes are heading in. The guns are to fire only white phosphorus to mark the target. Another peek over the edge of our foxhole at the Jap lines. All quiet. "Red Leader from Rhinestone. Do you know your target? Have you the correct photos? Do you want any further instructions?"

"Rhinestone from Red Leader. We know the target; we have the correct photos, and will follow your instructions. We are orbiting west of target area and have it spotted."

"Rhinestone to Red Leader; good boy. Artillery will mark the target with smoke in two minutes. Target is at three o'clock from your present position. Will you make a dummy run over the bald spot on the hill, directly opposite the white arrow marker? Trajectile path is south to north at your present altitude and position. You are clear on this path?"

"Roger from Red Leader; we understand."

"Artillery from aircraft controller; planes are ready for you to mark the target."

"Back to aircraft controller from artillery. Smoke is on the way. Will be on the target in 60 seconds."

"Rhinestone to Red Leader, your target will be smoked in 50 seconds. Do you have it? Forty seconds, thirty…twenty…ten…there it is Red Leader. Do you see it, Red Leader?"

"Roger. We see it."

"Back to Red Leader. There are heavy machine guns, caves and dugouts in that area. The wooded spot 100 yards west has a battalion of Nips. Behind the hill are artillery and mortar positions. You are to attack and destroy them. The target is all yours. Go get 'em."

We listen in as Red Leader instructs his planes:

"Red Leader to Red One, first flight will attack after me. I'll make a dummy run to be sure of the target and have Rhinestone give me an OK on the spot."

The Japs know what is going on, and their tracers start coming up from their positions. This fire further defines the target for us. Red Leader dives in at 400 miles an hour and the P-51s buzz the target right in the face of their fire.

"Go get him. Get him. Get him. Don't let that guy get away. There he goes, dammit! Go in and get him."

"I got him now. Take it easy. If I don't hit him I'll sure scare him to death."

We have more instructions for Red Leader. "Rhinestone to Red Leader. Our troops just got some fire from the hill, two o'clock from the bald spot."

Red Leader passes the dope along to his boys. "OK, let's get our friend over there, gang.—Dammit, [pilot's name]. That was too close to our troops. I told you not to fire if you don't know where our troops are."

"Hell. I saw them. I saw them."

It goes on and on, for about 15 minutes and then…"OK, Rhinestone, we're through. Hope we did some good."

"Roger, Red Leader. You did a swell job. The troops are up three quarters now, and moving right along. Red Leader, can you make a few dummy passes to keep the Nips in their holes until the infantry gets the rest of them."

"Roger, can do."

Already 200 Japs have been killed in this air attack, and one ammo dump, three supply dumps and seven to ten machine guns and gunpits knocked out. The infantry is taking the objective without loss of a single life. The majority of the remaining Japs are [sic] just sitting in their foxholes, bewildered and dazed—not even knowing the air attack is over until the ground troops go right into them with bayonets.

Baguio fell on April 26.

Lieutenant Yasyuki Ishizuka fell on April 25. Men died en masse, the shock and violence of the air attacks expunging, erasing. Some murmured "Namu-Amida-Butsu"—homage to the Buddha of Infinite Light and Life—and died; most just died. The lieutenant, as the rents in the flag that was subsequently taken from his body show, died from blast shrapnel. Or he might have been killed by concussion and the shrapnel was an afterthought, the scorn of the victor. It has been observed that severe battles are frequently followed by heavy storm showers. The rain is called "the tears of joy for the victor, and the tears of sorrow for the defeated, the tears of mourning for the dead."[255] It washes away all impurities of the battlefield. On that April day in 1945, on the cusp of the dry season in the Philippines, the skies had nothing left to give.

---

17 May 1945

Dear Folks,

I'm temporarily grounded, and I'm traveling around a lot. It seems that when you are hospitalized, you can't fly until cleared by the air force. I didn't know that. So, after flying combat for a month [following release from the hospital], they caught up with me and I have to wait until the papers come through, which is mere formality…Since I'm grounded, another fellow and I are taking a few days off, going back to Baguio…to see actual damage I've done myself.

On his return visit to the Baguio front, my father, during a reunion with a company of the infantry troops his squadron had supported, was presented with Lieutenant Ishizuka's flag. It was a memento of gratitude from men who had risked their lives together in combat. He treasured the flag's associations, subtly transfiguring over the decades, until he passed it to me.

---

27 June 1945

Mr. Arthur E. LaCroix
970 Center Street,
Newton Center, Massachusetts

Dear Mr. LaCroix:

Recently your son, Lieutenant Robert E. LaCroix, was decorated with the Air Medal. It was an award made in recognition of courageous service to his combat organization, his fellow American airmen, his country, his home and to you.

He was cited for meritorious achievement while participating in aerial flights in the southwest Pacific area from January 16, 1945 to May 11, 1945.

Your son took part in sustained operational flight missions during which hostile contact was probable and expected. These flights included interception missions against enemy fighters and bombing planes, and aided considerably in the recent successes in this theatre.

Almost every day your son, and the sons of other American fathers, are doing just such things as that here in the Southwest Pacific. Theirs is a very real and very tangible contribution to victory and to peace.

I would like to tell you how genuinely proud I am to have men such as your son in my command, and how gratified I am to know that young Americans with such courage and resourcefulness are fighting our country's battle against the Japanese aggressors.

You, Mr. LaCroix, have every reason to share that pride and gratification.

Sincerely,

/s/

George C. Kenney,

General, United States Army,

Commander.

Lieutenant Ishizuka, along with thousands of his comrades, was bulldozed into an unmarked mass grave to avert the spread of disease. Without ceremony or afterthought, the jungle reclaimed the burial site, the Americans left, the world moved on, and the echoes of a life ceased to ripple. The lieutenant's family received a wooden chit to mark his passing. It contained nothing but his name.

PART IV

THE PRISM OF MEMORY

The will cannot will backwards; that he cannot break time and time's covetousness, that is the will's loneliest melancholy.

—Friedrich Nietzsche, *Thus Spoke Zarathustra*

32

INVETERATE SCARS

On a late afternoon in 1943, a Japanese schoolboy and his fifth grade classmates surged past their beckoning teacher and, shielding their eyes against the glare of the setting sun, scanned the western horizon. A trembling of sound was quickly swallowed by a roar as a gunmetal gray Zero fighter emblazoned with blood-red discs on its wings plunged toward and over their heads, sweeping upward. The children, open-mouthed in rapture, followed the pilot's face as he careened from dizzying heights, pulling up and over the power lines once, twice, three times. One little boy, effulgent with pride, traced entranced the rising falling arcs of his elder brother's fighter plane. At long last and too soon, with seeming reluctance, the plane rose slowly into the sky, circled overhead several times, dipped its wings to either side, and disappeared over Osaka Bay on its way to the front.

In later years the little boy, ageing as his brother did not, "wondered what the pilot thought as he looked down upon the familiar mountains and rivers and what heartrending sorrow his parents must have felt as they bade farewell to their son."[256] On that afternoon in 1943 he vowed to become a fighter pilot and like his brother take flight to defeat the hated Americans and British. The dream evaporated with Japan's war machine. He was left a lifetime, one month at a time at his brother's graveside, to muse on the ephemeral hold of an ever-less-recalled animus and the undiminishing throb of loss that was its residue: "Army Air Corps Captain Masaaki Kawano, Killed-in-Action on 28 October 1944, while on a mission from Tacloban, Leyte, Philippines; age 23."

April 10, 1944
Foster Field, Texas

Dear Family,

I've finally found one thing I'd just as soon have as combat, almost. If I can ever work it to get assigned to a jet-propelled squadron, I'll grab it… You may remember how, while at Wright Field, I raved about the possibilities of jet propulsion—not as auxiliary units but as the propelling force. Since then I've grabbed every chance to learn more about them [sic] and am more and more convinced as to the future of such work. At present, naturally, the practical applications are in fighter work, but as it develops, it will swing toward heavy stuff. You probably realize the implications. A propeller is efficient only at comparatively low speeds and ceilings. Jet propulsion approaches highest efficiency at great speeds and high altitudes, thus giving unlimited possibilities. These possibilities—either military or commercial—are limited principally at present by fuels, a high specific gravity fuel being required. Anyway, by staying in the army, I'll be able to do both the flight and engineering work which is what I'd give my neck to achieve.

True to his dream, my father returned to Wright Patterson after the war to design and test pilot jet aircraft of the future. His enthusiasm for a job combining flying and engineering was unabated, and as the Korean conflict approached, he contemplated a return to combat flying, this time in jet-propelled aircraft. For reasons he had explained in a letter to his father a decade earlier, his marriage to my mother in 1952 put paid to these plans. With a family on the way he concluded that aerial bliss and domestic bliss were incompatible. He joined Westinghouse Electric and in ventures with Rolls Royce Engines, based in Pittsburgh and in Derby, England, engineered jet turbines. When Westinghouse exited the jet engine field, he switched to the company's then-promising nuclear power field. It was during this period, when Westinghouse and Mitsubishi Electric formed a joint venture to develop power systems, that he met and became close friends with Captain Hiro Matsuda, formerly a fighter pilot of the Imperial Japanese Navy and now an executive with Mitsubishi.

Captain Matsuda (not his real name) was a scion of a venerable samurai family, a bona fide hero and survivor. His visits to our home, along with those of another friend and fellow Westinghouse executive, a former U-Boat captain in the German Kriegsmarine, were eagerly anticipated by my brother and me, both young boys. Dinners were frequently raucous. The U-Boat commander thrilled us with ferocious-sounding Teutonic commands during mock naval drills with my father's 400-year-old Portuguese harquebus. My mother shuddered and gasped discreetly as the fifteen-pound blunderbuss soared, swooped, and circled over her Baccarat crystal and Spode porcelain. My brother and I filled out the drill team with a Civil War musket, bayonet attached, and a Kentucky long rifle, replete with loading plunger. My father counted the cadence and furnished useful tips on the handling of antique arms.

Dinners with Captain Matsuda (the Axis representatives were never united, my parents perhaps fearing the emergence of some Entente Uncordiale) were, at least through the main course, more sedate. He exuded a personal aura redolent with authority. Seductive modulations of voice and gesture conveyed a deep power, mesmerizing his listeners. But by dessert unseen impulsion was displaced by very visible martini and claret-driven kinetics. My father knew the captain loved to sing and was fond of pointing out that the P-51 fighter pilots of the Air Commandos were known affectionately (at least to one another) as "The Singing 51s of the Fighter Sections." This assertion he would promptly put to the lie with an atonal rendition of a wartime me-hearty musical limerick. The captain rose unfailingly to the bait, unleashing in ersatz combat an orotund assault of Nipponese barracks ballads typically in the airy style of this excerpt from the Imperial Navy's anthem:

Across the sea, water-drenched corpses;
Across the mountains, grass-covered corpses.

We shall die by the side of our lord,
We shall not look back.

My mother tried not to look appalled. My brother and I cheered for more.

Neither the captains nor my father ever discussed the war in the presence of my mother and the children. But my brother and I would evade kitchen duty to position ourselves over a backroom heating duct venting into my father's study where the men, over cigars and brandy, would quietly recount their lives in combat. The adults would have been furious with our trespass but this risk was insignificant next to the thrill of vicarious participation in what seemed to us superhuman exploits.

Flying assorted versions of the famous Mitsubishi Zero fighter plane from both aircraft carriers and, when Japan lost most of these, land, Captain Matsuda battled in the air from the Coral Sea to Leyte (places and events I only made sense of later in life). The Zero, flown by most Japanese aces, was legendary. In the early years of the war, no Allied fighter could match it. The Zero was designed by Mitsubishi for the Japanese Navy to satisfy requirements for high speed, long range, rapid climb, and, first and foremost, superior maneuverability. It was the first long-range escort fighter in the world. It has been said that if the Germans had the long-range Zero instead of their short-range ME 109, the outcome of the Battle of Britain might have been different. Superior fighting agility, though, was purchased at the expense of safety: the Zero was designed with less pilot armor, no self-sealing fuel tanks, and low wing loadings. My father commented that while a Zero was impressively maneuverable, as soon as it was hit it would simply disintegrate. Despite early warnings from General Chennault (of Flying Tigers fame) in China before Pearl Harbor, the U.S. Army Air Corps was slow to recognize the Zero's remarkable fighting attributes. Only in the second half of the war did U.S. fighter aircraft design catch and then surpass the Japanese with planes like the P-38 Lightning, the P-51 Mustang, the Grumman Hellcat, and the Vought Corsair.

The captain's conversations with my father were remarkable, particularly to children of our age, for their collegial warmth. Two former enemies from the same theater of combat, once bitter as my father's letters attest, confided with no trace of rancor their memories and sensations of combat. The Japanese are reticent by nature, my father by upbringing. Yet only twenty years after the war the two men discussed fear, anger, resentment, loathing, euphoria, black sorrow—emotions that my father would never have revealed to, much less discussed with, his children. The captain was wounded several times, the last—during an aerial dogfight over Leyte at the time of the invasion—so severely that he barely made it back to his Tacloban airfield. He was evacuated to Japan, in all probability saving his life. He was convalescing outside of Tokyo when the first bomb was dropped on Hiroshima. In the rippling circles of coincidence, I much later discovered that Captains Matsuda and Kawano had served in the same unit during the Leyte invasion. But that coincidence paled against the one that cost my father his friendship with the captain.

The Japanese flag my father received following the battle of Baguio had remained in his possession, packed away in an army foot locker with the other memorabilia of a former life. His conversations with Captain Matsuda rekindled an interest to discover more of the flag's owner. It did not occur to him to return the flag to Japan; the war's associations had not yet abated to comfortable abstractions. But he assumed that his deepening friendship with the captain, one whose mutual candor and trust had evolved out of mirror-imaged experience, would "objectify" a discussion of the flag's origins as it had their discussions of friends taken in the fever of mutually sought destruction. The captain assented.

My father removed the carefully wrapped and preserved flag and spread it on the desk before them. The captain rose and, leaning over the desk, carefully scanned the kanji circumjacent the sun's representational disc. His body flexed and tensed, he straightened and with deliberate effort pivoted toward my father. Mournfulness and anger vied on his now wan face, only moments earlier ruddled under the brandy's influence. With preemptive formality of which the Japanese and the British are masters, he bowed stiffly to my father and announced, "Robert-san" (in lieu of the casual diminutives the men normally employed), "I must leave at once." My father was, rightly or wrongly, thunderstruck. It was clear the Japanese was mortally offended, but the American was mystified and requested an explanation. The captain volunteered only that he had known the soldier personally, both men hailing from the town whose identity was disclosed on the flag. Having settled after the war in Tokyo and his parents long-dead, he had not known of the soldier's fate, just one among so many of the lost. He departed without more, my father never learning either the soldier's name or his hometown. The captain and my father never spoke again. "Only through time time is conquered," wrote Eliot. "The trilling wire in the blood / Sings below inveterate scars / Appeasing long forgotten wars."[257] Some scars are more than inveterate, they are invisible.

33

SAIPAN—THE SERVITUDE OF MEMORY

Public remembrance is reserved for the victors. The losers are left to honor their heroes surreptitiously, in whispering shadows, or in public ceremonies shrouded in remorseful apologia. On the islands of Saipan, Tinian, Guam, and Peleliu in the western Pacific, I watched groups of aging Japanese veterans and family members quietly assemble in Shinto ceremonies, popularly termed "bone collecting" trips. A Shinto's spirit remains at the site of death and will rest only on completion of a full and unvarying burial ritual. In the latter phases of the Pacific War, Japanese soldiers sacrificed in massed banzai attacks on entrenched U.S. positions or brutal last-ditch stands—honoring their oath of fealty to the emperor and the inflexible dictates of samurai Bushido—were bulldozed into unmarked communal graves. Hundreds of thousands of Japanese soldiers unquietly awaited spiritual closure. Through a combination of incomplete military records, local native recollection, and serendipitous discoveries during civil construction, remains lost for decades were recovered and ceremonially interred.

In the Shinto belief system, a proper burial consists of at least twenty phases. The body is cremated on the funeral day, removing death's impurities and transforming the corpse into purified ancestral spirit. The *kich-fuda* is the succeeding period of serious mourning when family and friends wear black and carry stringed prayer beads. In the *koden* phase, the mourners offer monetary gifts to the immediate family to defray funeral expenses and receive a small gift in return. The bones of the deceased are placed in an urn and kept on the family altar for thirty-five days. During this period, incense sticks are burned and visitors pay their respects. In a final stage, the *bunkotsu*, family members are given the deceased's ashes for placement in a family shrine. Daily rituals are performed at the shrines to bring the spirits of the dead back to earth, including offerings of drink and food and the burning of incense. The house and family are sprayed with purifying salt. Deified and enshrined, the dead are remembered.

On Saipan and Tinian in the Northern Marianas Islands, 200 miles north of Guam, nearly 30,000 of the islands' 33,000 Japanese defenders died at a cost of 3,100 American dead. On the northern end of Saipan, the slaughter reached its apogee in "mass ecstatic outbursts, communal frenzies...thinkers, poets, peasants...fallen, shrieking...in an anonymous exalted mass," to borrow an apt description from Mailer's *The Naked and The Dead.*[258] Site of the last redoubt of the doomed Japanese command, it is also the location of the Banzai and Suicide Cliffs.

Saipan, a volcanic and limestone island of virile beauty, was taken from its colonial overlord, Germany, following the Treaty of Versailles ending World War I and mandated to Japan by the League of Nations in 1920. Between the two world wars, the Japanese built a vibrant local economy based on sugar cane and copra. A burgeoning population of Japanese merchants and laborers coexisted in uneasy harmony with indigenous Chamorros and Caroligninans. With the outbreak of war in 1941 and the seizure of nearby Guam, administration of Saipan was assumed by the Fourth Fleet of the Imperial Japanese Navy. Concerned less with the hearts and minds of its subjects than with their unwavering, laboring obedience, the Greater East Asian Co-Prosperity Sphere quickly transformed native resentment into seething hatred, further isolating the civilian Japanese population. By the time the American invasion fleet appeared off the Saipan coast in mid-1944, military propaganda depicting the Americans as barbarian, child-eating cannibals had ratcheted up the natural trepidation of local Japanese to full-blown terror. By the time the first wave of U.S. Marines hit the beaches, the local populace was in a state of unreasoning frenzy.

From lowlands in the south, Saipan rises abruptly 1,600 feet to Mount Tapotchau in the center of the island and proceeds north along a spinal column of forbidding, cave-riddled ochre bluffs, pockmarked from American artillery blasting snipers and gun emplacements embedded tick-like in the rock face. The running ridge terminates abruptly in the titanic, sheer, three-hundred-foot Suicide Cliff, glowering over a coastline of thirty-foot wave-incised bluffs fronting hypnotic sapphirine waters. As the U.S. Fourth Marine and the Twenty-seventh Infantry Divisions advanced north on either side of the island, driving their prey before them, the civilian Japanese population fled, with the army, their imagined fate. When they reached the end of terra firma, they leaped into oblivion.

One of the most tragically memorable filmed images of the Second World War is that of a young Japanese mother, infant child clutched to her chest, rushing to the precipice of the Suicide Cliff and without hesitation casting their lives to the winds. Like demon-driven lemmings, ignoring the bull-horned pleas of nearby American troops, some eight thousand civilians plunged from both the Suicide Cliff and the lower, seaside Banzai Cliff. Many survived the watery fall from the lower cliffs but surf, sharks, and shock vitiated rescue efforts by American ships. Benumbed veterans of neolithically elemental combat wept at the site of dead women, children, and old men roiling in the surf or crushed on an anvil of volcanic rock.

We Americans perceive ourselves as liberators. We are troubled by much of the world's refusal to see us as we are convinced we are—rational, altruistic, and egalitarian. Yet standing on the ledge from which the young Japanese mother unflinchingly launched herself and her most precious possession, one senses the guiding, commanding power of collective memory, its prism refracting, altering perception. The child's mother, in death as in life, submitted with ancestral fidelity to an ethos she neither questioned nor understood. Mailer understood: "For a thousand years or more the Japanese had tilled the land, expended their lives upon it, and left nothing for themselves…With nothing in their lives but toil and abnegation…they had renounced even the desire to think about joys they would never have…They were abstract people…knowing nothing about the vehicle that moved them…who lived in the most intense fear of their superiors that any people had ever had."[259]

Collective memory had become collective servitude, the past imprisoning, not animating the present. The silent eloquence of infant victims at the Suicide Cliff censures inaction, exhorts the unceasing, thankless engagement of democratic ideals. Cultural relativism, a docile endorsement of the status quo masquerading as tolerance, is a malicious fiction, refusing the battle for ideals from which hope arises. Kanji-inscribed bronze, ceramic, and cement memorial plaques embedded along the cliff line divide the world of what might have been from the world of what can be. In an era of infinitely shading grays, they remind us that moral truth still persists with achromatic clarity.

The expressions of the Japanese veterans clustered near the Suicide Cliff are impassive, each immersed in the melancholia of remembrance. For two weeks a team of specialists has shifted through bone fragments at the base of the cliffs. The bones, sorted and identified, as far as practicable, have been cremated. A Shinto priest carrying a flat, tapered wooden mace of office, the *shaku*, and clad in ceremonial *saifuku*, white silk kimono, ankle-length divided skirt, and outer robe, with *kammuri*, a rounded black paper hat with vertical protuberance rising at the back of the head, *tabi* and *asagutsu*, stiff white socks inside black lacquered clogs of paulownia wood, intones ritualistic prayers. Smoke rising from the crematory and incense sticks mingles, morphs in the distant eyes of the veterans with the acrid acetone of spent cartridges, detonated jungle clay, and fetid rot, the soul-shuddering violence of unremitting bombardment, screams of dismembered, blasted comrades, the glimpsed terror of a relentlessly vengeful foe. Shimmers of emotion flit across faces otherwise insensible. The priest concludes his prayers, and with visibly anguished effort the men emerge from a deep, inaccessible dark. Not all will share the peace they have brought their fallen comrades.

34

Yasukuni—The Dissonance of Memory

The solace of one people's remembrance is the pain of another's recollection. Looming out of the early morning mist, bespeckled with dew drops glistening like ocean spray on a dreadnought, the massive steel-plated *torii* of the Yasukuni Shrine, the largest Shinto gate in Japan at one hundred tons and eight stories high, conveys the steadfastness of age-old authority. Beneath its outstretched arms, a small group of nine elderly men, formed in military parade order with two buglers and a drummer in the vanguard, prepares to enter the grounds of the shrine. They are dressed in the winter uniforms of the World War II Japanese Manchurian-occupation Kwantung Army and carry period Model 99 rifles. Despite the involuntary bow of age, the men are alert, intense. To the slightly dissonant notes of the bugled march, they move in rhythmic step past two giant lanterns and the guardian lion-dogs, under the torii and down a long avenue lined on either side with smaller octagonal stone lanterns.

Midway to the shrine complex, the men in unappreciated irony detour around the imposing bronze statue of the Confucian vice-minister of war in the Meiji period. A samurai who was himself assassinated by discontented samurai, he oversaw the defeat of the shogunate's troops, the Westernization and modernization of the Japanese military, and the design of the first Western warship in the Japanese navy. Moving in succession under two smaller *torii* and through monumental wooden shrine doors bearing giant gold chrysanthemum bosses, the honor guard passes through the *somei yoshino* cherry trees lining either side of the avenue in the inner grounds. Each spring as the "cherry blossom front" advances across Japan, the blossoming of Yasukuni's cherries, tracked expectantly on public television, marks the official entry of the front into Tokyo. The fleeting flowering and early fall of the *sakura* blossoms is an apt symbol of the fallen souls venerated by the Shrine. The *ooka* WWII attack bomber, used on suicide missions and displayed at the Shrine, was named for a cherry blossom. "And their lives were scattered over the water's surface as so many cherry blossoms," wrote one veteran.[260]

Past the purification trough outside the Shrine doors, used ritually to cleanse hands and mouth, the troop halts before the offering hall fronting the main hall holding the Shrine's sacred remains. While the troop stands at silent attention, supplicants of every age and gender approach the offertory trough, toss coins as votive offerings, bow twice, clap their hands twice, bow once more, and retire. At length the soldiers bow, volte-face and march out, their martial air met in counterpoint by the incongruous strains of a Mozart symphony emanating from a shrine outbuilding. The *basso continuo* for this cross-cultural fugue is furnished by a Shrine drummer energetically assaulting an enormous *miya-daiko* shrine drum, made from the hollowed trunk of a keyaki tree with a cowhide skin, nearly two meters in diameter, and used for offerings to the deities.

The Yasukuni Shrine rises north of the Imperial Palace grounds in Tokyo, across a moat from the Nippon Budokan—the massive martial arts hall built on the site of a samurai dwelling depicted in a Hokusai landscape and better known in the West for Bob Dylan's "Live at the Budokan." The shrine is the vortex of competing, unstanched passions, outgrowths of Japan's wartime adventurism. Erected in 1869, at the time of the Meiji Restoration, the shrine was originally dedicated to those who fell in battle securing the modernizing Meiji regime against the decaying 265-year rule of the Tokugawa shogunate, civil conflict romanticized in the film *The Last Samurai*. It later enshrined the souls of soldiers and civilians, including women and children, who died in Japan's international conflicts: the 1895 Sino-Japanese War, the Russo-Japanese War of 1904–05, the First World War, the Manchurian conflict, the Sino-Japanese War of 1937–45, and World War II, known in Japan as the Pacific War. In the form of Kanji-inscribed mortuary tablets, some 2.5 million ancestors are worshiped at Yasukuni—including fourteen Class

A war criminals convicted by the International Military Tribunal for the Far East, the Japanese equivalent of the Nuremberg Trials.

Yasukuni is to Japanese as Arlington is to Americans—the heart of a nation's remembrance. But where Arlington unites, Yasukuni divides: Japanese and foreigners alike. Unlike the little-known Chidorigafuchi, Japan's tomb to the Unknown Soldier, an austere concrete structure next to the Imperial Palace holding ashes symbolizing nearly 350,000 unknown Japanese soldiers who lost their lives in the Pacific War, Yasukuni has become a byword for unrepentant Japanese nationalism. The Shrine's truculent defense of Japan's war role, and its apparent endorsement by senior Japanese leaders, is the source of unremitting international furor. Shrine publications refer to the "'Martyrs of Showa' (Emperor Hirohito's reign) who were cruelly and unjustly tried as war criminals by a sham-like tribunal of the Allied forces" or to "Some 1,068 people, wrongly accused as war criminals by the Allied court, enshrined here." Yasukuni's ritual defense of the war sounds oddly discordant in the pacifist Japan of today: "War is a tragic thing to happen, but it was necessary in order for us to protect the independence of Japan and to prosper together with Asian neighbors."

Before the Second World War, the shrine was run by the Army Ministry and played an important role in unifying popular sentiment around war and the military. Spirits of the war dead were viewed as heroic and apotheosized. During a visit by Emperor Hirohito to the shrine in 1938, the English-language *Japan Times* described the political-cultural significance of the shrine:

> Enshrined as *Kami* (demi-gods), [the soldiers] become deities to guard the Empire. They are no longer human. They have become pillars of the Empire. As they are enshrined at Yasukuni, they retain no rank or other distinction. Generals and privates alike, they are no longer counted as military men, but as so many "pillars." It is because they are the pillars of the nation that they are worshipped by the Emperor and the entire populace.[261]

Although Yasukuni's connection with the state ended after the war and the abolition of Shinto as a state religion, the shrine continued to treat the war dead as fallen heroes. This would likely have remained unexceptionable but in 1978, Yasukuni secretly enshrined 1,068 convicted war criminals, among them war-time Prime Minister Hideki Tojo and the other Class A war criminals. Sufficient cause in itself to infuriate Japan's Asian neighbors who suffered during Japanese occupation, in particular the Chinese and the Koreans, increasingly high-profile political visits fanned anger into wrath.

Imperial visits to the shrine began with the Meiji Emperor and were annual events. Emperor Hirohito visited the shrine in 1952, following restoration of Japanese sovereignty at the end of the Allied occupation. The current emperor has never visited the shrine but it is the visits of Japanese heads of government, not state, that have caused the greatest indignation. In 1975 Takeo Miki became the first post-war prime minister to visit the shrine, unofficially, on the thirtieth anniversary of the Japanese surrender. Prime Minister Yasuhiro Nakasone was the first to visit in official capacity in 1985, followed by Prime Minister Ryutaro Hashimoto in 1996, and Prime Minister Junichiro Koizumi on multiple occasions. Members of the ruling Liberal Democratic Party proposed to enshrine the Class A war criminals separately, but as a private religious corporation, albeit under the jurisdiction of the Tokyo Metropolitan government, Yasukuni has steadfastly refused. Surviving family members of soldiers, sailors, and airmen killed in the Pacific War lobby for a restoration of Yasukuni's public status to legitimize acknowledgement of a nation's debt.[262]

As the little troop of veterans completes its homage and makes its way to the parking lot, separate groups of Chinese and Korean tourists linger near the shrine entrance, taking in the spectacle. Most are young, too young to find other than amusement in the sight of nine old men playing soldier. But a number of those present are of an age to remember. The Koreans are more animated than the Chinese, but neither group does more than murmur and shake their heads. Like the Japanese veterans paying homage to their fallen comrades or Japanese leaders honoring a nation's dead, the foreign tourists draw their own lessons from the Yasukuni Shrine. These lessons are not reconcilable and never will be. Assuagement will come only with the distance of time and forgetfulness. Memories in Asia are long.

35

A GLEAM IN THE MISTS

23 May 1945
Luzon, Philippines

Dear Folks,

I have a silk Jap battle flag with all the Japanese signatures. I believe they have a party before battle, all the officers signing these flags. They are fine silk, usually are carried in the helmets...Haven't mailed [it] yet, but will as soon as things are reasonably certain. Up to now there has been too much "appropriating" by the mail clerks...At any rate, here is the key to the Jap writing on it: [hand-drawn picture of flag]

Area "A" is Jap writing to the effect that when this flag is raised, it is always raised for victory. Area "B" signifies that despite length of service, etc., soldiers never die, will live forever. This was taken from a "good" Jap officer on the outskirts of Baguio. I got it [following the taking of Baguio]...

Love, Bob

In 1974, after three decades of hiding, a Japanese officer emerged from the jungles on the remote Philippine island of Lubong and surrendered his sword to Ferdinand Marcos, then president of the Philippines. Like other soldiers in Guam and Saipan, the soldier had refused in 1945 to acknowledge his country's defeat, preferring decades of furtive, soul-wrenching isolation to the shame of surrender. His commander's last order in 1944 was to sustain guerrilla activities in Lubong until the Army returned, neither surrendering nor taking his own life. Once discovered, he agreed to emerge from hiding only after his former commanding officer, now a Tokyo bookseller, journeyed to Lubong, countermanded the earlier order, and declared his duty to Japan and the emperor satisfied. The soldier's first reaction upon hearing of his country's capitulation so much hardship ago was a gaping emptiness: "What have I been doing all these years?"[263]

When the Tokyo media published the account of the soldier, but before his name was released, a tremor of excitement ran through the Ishizuka family. Could the resurrected soldier be their long-missing son-brother-cousin? The family had received no evidence of his death, or life, other than a memorial wooden chit from the Imperial Army. The chit now held pride of place in the family's household Shinto shrine, alongside a faded yellow photograph of the lieutenant with two of his fellow soldiers and a larger charcoal sketch of Ishizuka in Manchurian army uniform. For several days expectancy bore false hope aloft. When the rediscovered soldier's name was released, Lieutenant Hiroo Onoda, the fall was as dispiriting as the ascent had been giddy. Now, another three decades to the month later, the family receives a telephone call from a ministerial official: Lieutenant Ishizuka's *Hinomaru* flag has been recovered.

The *Hinomaru*, or "disc of the sun" flag, is the national flag of Japan. It is a simple white banner with a centered red disk. American soldiers called it the "meatball." The flag carries fewer negative connotations than the "sunburst" flag with red disc and sixteen rays, originally the flag of the Japanese Imperial Navy, now the Maritime Self-Defense Force, and still a potent symbol of Japanese ultra-nationalism, evoking more virulent emotions than the Confederate battle flag in the American South. Japanese soldiers routinely carried, among other mementos for luck, a *hinomaru yosegaki* or "rising sun autographs" flag. Lieutenant Ishizuka's name on his flag runs vertically along the right-hand border with signatures of neighbors, family, and governmental officials radiating like rays around the center sun. Along the top and bottom of the flag are patriotic and personal inscriptions invoking valor, love of country, defeat of Japan's enemies, and a prayer for eternal good fortune in war. Among the signatures is the former mayor of the large town near Nikko, outside Tokyo, where Ishizuka taught school after his return from his first tour of duty in China and Southeast Asia.

Following a publicity generating lunch with senior politicians in the members' dining room of the ziggurat-topped neo-classical Japanese Diet building, we segued from photo-op to the backstage pilotage for which experienced politicians are justifiably renowned. The Health, Labor and Welfare Ministry in Tokyo handles veterans' affairs, including searches of the type I had initiated. Like any sprawling Japanese bureaucracy, public or corporate, its melodic unity spurns thematic improvisation, is impervious to tonal variation. Process is timeless; petitioner is ephemeral. A Westerner entering its precincts feels a little of the anxiety of Kafka's Joseph K. searching for the Court of Inquiry: the silent rippling regimentation of desk upon desk in tight defiles differentiated only by the length of the black hair visible on heads studiously bowed over numbingly repetitive work, all aware of your presence but pointedly ignoring it. In the fashion of a medieval Papal court, supplicants plead for favor by dispensation, not by taxpaying entitlement.

But unlike most bureaucracies in the world, Japanese ones, once having taken up the cudgels, perform their ordained duties with marked courtesy and efficiency. I was referred to the head of the veterans' affairs section by the governor of Saitama Prefecture, himself recently returned from battlefield visits in Guam and Saipan with aging constituents, among them Imperial Army veterans. Saitama is the administrative region, reorganized after the war, of which the town mayor memorialized on Ishizuka's flag would have been part. With my friend Dr. Yoshikiyo

Wada translating, the department head, an intent-looking young woman whose demeanor did justice to the gravity of her job, met us warmly in one of those Japanese micro-conference rooms apparently designed, as Churchill said of the reconstructed House of Commons, to encourage "a sense of crowd and urgency."

Having thus far encountered dead ends in our search for the identity of the flag's owner and his heirs, we intended to convene a press conference at which we would unveil the flag and request public assistance. The Ministry was appalled by this idea, albeit with the smiling, anodyne inscrutability of a Japanese "no," which is a "yes" with a slightly different intonation. It was explained that not all families relished revisiting a particularly humiliating and painful episode in Japanese life, even for the chance of personal closure. There was also the bureaucratic *bete noire in extremis* to consider: a partisan political dispute embroiling ministerial officialdom in the glare of public acrimony. In a country wrestling with the phoenix of remilitarization, even gestures as benignly intended as the return of a personal wartime artifact were subject to hijacking by the militarists at one pole and the pacifists at the other. Not wishing to risk embarrassment either to the family or those whose help we sought, I acquiesced in the less-public, more-circuitous route proposed by our hosts.

The department head cautioned that the prospects of success and failure were even, that of the 50 percent of families ultimately located at least a third refused the proffered gesture and that the search process would take a minimum of one year. I was asked whether I was prepared to return the flag even if the family, once located, refused to meet with me. I was disposed to consent; my Japanese colleagues demurred. Quid pro quo is the *lingua universalis*. Once again I acquiesced, leaving the flag in the care of the ministry and placing my trust in an altogether opaque process. My suspicions that ministerial officials were presenting an overly glum picture to hedge their bets were borne out when, fewer than six months after our meeting in Tokyo, I received a telephone call from Dr. Wada. The family had been located, they were anxious to meet and bring what information they possessed of Ishizuka's life, and they would authorize the ministry to release his service records to me.

"A little gleam of Time between two eternities," was how Carlyle described it. Two generations on from Lieutenant Ishizuka's death and death is providing the closure that life could not. The lieutenant never married, and his parents, brothers, and sisters have long since passed on, the last, his brother, in 1988. Only his sister-in-law, a nephew, and niece remain to appreciate the affirmation that reunion with a wartime flag brings. Bearing bags of *omiyagi*, traditional courtesy gifts, the Ishizuka family, led by two ministerial officials, bows its way into the reception room where we wait with the large flag in its elaborate box frame. The sister-in-law is stooped, hobbling, but alive with anticipation, wary of a room full of foreigners and officials. The niece and nephew, both in their early fifties, are visibly nervous yet punctilious in their observance of the rituals of Japanese courtesy. The nephew carries a flat object wrapped in what looks to be a sacramental cloth.

Spotting the framed flag on an easel at the other end of the room, the elderly woman casts to the wind the formalities of introduction and makes a beeline for her only extant link with a stolen youth. We follow. She inhales, shudders ever so slightly, and strokes the flag's frame as with glazed eyes she traverses emotional chasms that in our country have merited the laudation "Greatest Generation." She will not address us directly, from reticence not rudeness, and whispers to her nephew. "My aunt thanks you for bringing to our family and her brother-in-law the peace which we have missed until now," says the nephew through Dr. Wada. The nephew then unwraps the cloth, revealing the portrait and photographs brought from the home shrine. I bring out, at their request, a picture of my father and explain how the flag came into our possession. Whatever their innermost thoughts, the Japanese appear to find as remarkable as we the circle that has brought us together.

Watching the frail old woman, I wonder if it is possible to segregate the memory of loss from the circumstances of losing. Do the ignominy of a war lost and the knowledge of my father's role in her loss confound an otherwise pellucid memory? Bitterness felt by my father and other Allied soldiers during the war most often dissipated in the renewal of life resumed. Victory requires no rationalization; losing needs reaffirmation. In the American South, Confederate dress balls are still held 140 years after Appomattox. Post-war Germany underwent—and undergoes—the cultural equivalent of a zealot's scourging. Does an individual experience loss as a country does?

In his thoughtful book, *The Culture of Defeat*, Wolfgang Schivel-busch writes that modernity has made adaptation to defeat into a cultural, as opposed to a merely political, process. The extraordinary capacity of modern states to mobilize ever greater human and material resources for war ensures that the psychological burden of defeat will be spread throughout society. The culture of defeat thus becomes not about revenge; it becomes about making defeat feel like victory. What all defeated nations share, he argues, is a determination to affirm their moral superiority over the victor.[264] Japan remains at one and the same time resolutely pacifist and determinedly unwilling to confront the reality of its wartime experience, to admit moral deficiency. This is not simply a political failing; it is the price of cultural self-esteem. In Japan, mourning as a means of coming to terms with irretrievable loss remains intensely private. The public alternative is too discomfiting.

Before parting, the nephew with elaborate courtesy hands me a piece of yellowed paper containing several lines of hand-inscribed calligraphy. He explains that this is a famous *haiku* written by the eighth-century monk Akahito, a favorite of his uncle who made the calligraphic transcription before his final departure for the Southeast Asian front. I later have it translated:

> The mists rise over
> The still pools at Asuka.
> Memory does not
> Pass away so easily.

AFTERWORD

In 2002, following a decadal descent through un-knowing, not-knowing, to, at last, not-being, my father died of Alzheimer's disease. In rare and almost subliminally brief spurts of apparent illumination, his only active memories were those of ethereal flight in a wartime fighter plane. The intervening sixty years had all but vanished. I thought of da Vinci's famous comment on flight: "When once you have tasted flight, you will forever walk the earth with your eyes turned skyward, for there you have been, and there you will always long to return."

As my father quietly, almost serenely confronted what must have been eclipsing terror, I raged at the remorseless consuming darkness and at his refusal to rage with me. I recalled the words with which Dylan Thomas railed at his own father's fatalistic acceptance of a looming end, admonishing wild men who sang the sun in flight to rage against the dying of the light.[265] I flailed in fury at the injustice of a good man's end, a battle lost without ever having been joined. How could he explain that in the full knowledge of certain defeat, he was fighting to preserve his dignity? It was a final heroic rebuttal of darkness.

As with his death, I had too often misinterpreted his life. His native reticence I callowly interpreted as disengagement, his humility as timidity. I found in the detached abstraction of his wartime experience nothing more than my own complacent triumphalism. He understood but he was not a man to explain. He knew what he believed in, he knew what was right and he acted without grand gestures. It took his lifetime for me to value the strength that comes from quiet faith in transcendent purpose.

In *East of Eden*, John Steinbeck wrote of an afflicted time:

> There are monstrous changes taking place in the world, forc-
> es shaping a future whose face we do not know. Some of these
> forces seem evil to us, perhaps not in themselves but because
> their tendency is to eliminate other things we hold good…There
> is great tension in the world, tension toward a breaking point,
> and men are unhappy and confused. At such a time it seems nat-
> ural and good to me to ask myself these questions. What do I be-
> lieve in? What must I fight for and what must I fight against?[266]

If the scourges of our time—poverty, ignorance, terror, discrimina-
tion—are wrongs, then "aggressive fighting for the right," as Theodore
Roosevelt said, "is the noblest sport the world affords." The struggle
itself is heroic, but like all battles it presumes engagement. Progress is
the patient incremental accretion of "frail deeds" through a life's work, a
thread in a tapestry of infinite potential. It is a struggle to impart hope
where hope would not otherwise flourish.

The worthiness of a life is measured by the path it illumines for
those who follow. In a litany of debts I owe my father, a life well lived is
perhaps the greatest. But failed emulation risks the poet's censure: "He
follows his father, but with shorter strides." Perhaps simple recognition
is enough; to recall those who, as in Brooke's threnody, "…leave a white
unbroken glory, a gathered radiance, a width, a shining peace, under the
night."[267] Such was my father. I remember.

ACKNOWLEDGMENTS

The span of geography and chronology covered in this book has meant that any attempt at comprehensive acknowledgment would yield inadvertent omission and unintentional offence. I will therefore thank publicly all those whose assistance and input have been essential to the book's completion, assuring them that their exclusion by name eliminates any risk they might be taxed with the deficiencies of the work.

Every rule must support its exceptions and the exceptional efforts of a few individuals on my behalf merit mention. During my search for Lieutenant Ishizuka's family, Dr. Yoshikiyo Wada in Tokyo provided signal insights into the workings of the Japanese bureaucracy and untiring support in chasing down frequently fruitless leads. Dr. John Gilliam in Guam proved indispensable as an intellectual foil and traveling companion during extended investigative jaunts through Southeast and North Asia. And while the handwriting of The Greatest Generation was a more finely honed thing than that of its children, the interpretation of my father's letters bordered at times on the hieroglyphic. Kim Moreshita Garrido served as my untiring and intuitive Champollion.

It may be de rigueur to acknowledge the selfless indulgence of family in the antisocial process of research and writing, but the families of all the principal protagonists in the book, American, Japanese, and Chinese, were forced by my persistence often to revisit particularly painful memories. For their indulgence I can only offer heartfelt, affectionate thanks.

F. E. LaCroix
Manila
August 2008

SELECTED BIBLIOGRAPHY

THE SKY RAINED HEROES

This bibliography is by no means a complete record of all the works and sources I have consulted. I intend it merely to serve as a convenient tool for those who wish to learn more of the subjects discussed in this book.

Air Force Combat Units of World War II. Maurer, Maurer, ed. Washington, D.C.: U.S. Government Printing Office, 1961.

Bautista, Veltisezar. *The Filipino Americans from 1763 to the Present: Their History, Culture, and Traditions*. Bookhaus Publishers, 1998.

Becker, Jasper. *Hungry Ghosts: China's Secret Famine*. London: John Murray, 1996.

Bergerud, Eric M. *Fire in the Sky: The Air War in the South Pacific*. Boulder: Westview Press, 2001.

———. *Touched with Fire: The Land War in the South Pacific*. New York: Penguin, 1997.

Buruma, Ian. *Inventing Japan: 1853-1964*. New York: Modern Library, 2004.

Chang, Jung and J. Halliday. *Mao: the Unknown Story*. New York: Anchor Books, 2005.

Daugherty, Leo. *Fighting Techniques of a Japanese Infantryman, 1941-1945, Training, Techniques and Weapons*. St. Paul: MBI Publishing Company, 2002.

De Morga, Antonio, E.H. Blair and J.A. Robertson. *History of the Philippine Islands: Volume 1 and 2*. BiblioBazaar, LLC, 2006.

Fitzsimons, Peter. *Kokoda*. Sydney: Hodder Headline Australia, 2005.

Frei, Henry. *Guns of February: Ordinary Japanese Soldiers' Views of the Malayan Campaign & the Fall of Singapore 1941-42*. Singapore: Singapore University Press, 2004.

Hixson, Walter. *The American Experience in World War II*. New York: Routledge, 2002.

Ishimaru, Lt. Comdr. Tota. *Japan Must Fight Britain*. The Telegraph Press, 1936.

Latimer, Jon. *Burma: The Forgotten War*. London: John Murray Publishers Ltd., 2004.

Linn, Brian McAllister. *The Philippine War: 1899-1902*. Lawrence: University Press of Kansas, 2002.

Low, N.I. *When Singapore Was Syonan-to*. Singapore: Times Editions, 1998.

Owen, Frank. *The Fall of Singapore*. London: Penguin Books Ltd., 2002.

Philippines: A Country Study. Dolan, Ronald E., ed. Washington: GPO for the Library of Congress, 1991.

Rizal, José P. *Noli Me Tangere*. New York: Penguin Classics, 2006.

Rottman, Gordon L. *Japanese Army in World War II: The South Pacific and New Guinea, 1942-43*. Oxford: Osprey Publishing, 2005.

————. *Saipan & Tinian 1944: Piercing the Japanese Empire*. Oxford: Osprey Publishing, 2004.

Sakurai, Tadayoshi. *Human Bullets: A Soldier's Story of Port Arthur*. Tokyo: Teibi Publishing, 15th Edition, 1925.

Schivelbusch, Wolfgang. *The Culture of Defeat: On National Trauma, Mourning, and Recovery*, translated by Jefferson Chase. London: Granta, 2003.

Senso: The Japanese Remember the Pacific War: Letters to the Editor of Asahi Shimbun, edited by Frank Gibney. Armonk: M.E. Sharpe, 2006.

Silbey, David J. A *War of Frontier and Empire: The Philippines-American War: 1899-1902*. New York: Hill and Wang, 2008.

Slim, Field-Marshal Viscount William. *Defeat into Victory: Battling Japan in Burma and India, 1942-1945*. New York: Cooper Square Press, 1956.

Takeyama, Michio. *Harp of Burma*, translated by Howard Hibbett. Boston: Tuttle Publishing, 1966.

Tamayama, Kazuo and J. Nunneley, eds. *Tales By Japanese Soldiers*. London: Cassell Military Paperbacks, 2006.

Thant, Myant-U. *The River of Lost Footsteps: Histories of Burma*. New York: Farrar, Straus and Giroux, 2006.

The Army Air Forces in World War II: Volume 6, Men and Planes. Craven, Wesley Frank and James Lea Cate, eds. Washington, D.C.: New Imprint by the Office of Air Force History, 1983.

Ward, J.S.M. and W.G. Stirling. *Hung Society or the Society of Heaven and Earth*. Whitefish: Kessinger Publishing, 2003.

WWII Air Commandos, Volumes I & II. Produced by T. Kemp. Dallas: Taylor Publishing Company, 1994.

ENDNOTES

Part I

1. Robert Graves, *Good-Bye to All That: An Autobiography* (Anchor Books, 1958), 278.

2. D.M. Thomas, *The White Hotel* (London: Penguin Books, 1993), 250.

3. Rudyard Kipling, *The Irish Guards in the Great War* (New York: Sarpedon Publishers, 1997), 193.

4. Alexander Pope, "An Essay on Man, Epistle 1, X" in *The Poems of Alexander Pope*, John Butt, ed. (New Haven: Yale University Press), 515.

5. Throughout this book I use the terms "Malaysia" or "Malaya" to refer to what is commonly known today as Peninsular Malaysia or West Malaysia. The terms are used interchangeably although "Malaya," with its colonial overtones, is largely obsolete.

6. Leo Tolstoy, *War and Peace* (New York: Modern Library, 2002), 689 et. seq.

7. Algernon Charles Swinburne, *Poems and Ballads and Atalanta in Calydon* (London: Penguin Classics, 2000), 251.

8. The "Flying Tigers" was the nickname of the 1st American Volunteer Group, U.S. fighter pilots recruited in 1941-42 as private military contractors to fight within the Chinese Air Force under the command of U.S. General Claire L. Chennault.

9. Emily Bronte, *Wuthering Heights* (Oxford: Oxford University Press, 1998), 338.

10. Kipling, *The Irish Guards in the Great War*, Front Matter.

11. Bernard Schlink, *The Reader* (New York: Vintage International, 1999).

12. Tolstoy, *War and Peace*, 612.

Part II

1. I.J.N. Lt. Comdr. Tota Ishimaru, *Japan Must Fight Britain* (The Telegraph Press, 1936)

2. Tadayoshi Sakurai, *Human Bullets: A Soldier's Story of Port Arthur* (Tokyo: Teibi Publishing, 15th Edition, 1925), pp. 6-7.

3. Ibid., 222.

4. Frank Gibney, ed., *Senso: The Japanese Remember the Pacific War: Letters to the Editor of Asahi Shimbun*, (Armonk: M.E. Sharpe, 2006), 299.

5. Quoted in Henry Frei, *Guns of February: Ordinary Japanese Soldiers' Views of the Malayan Campaign & the Fall of Singapore 1941-42* (Singapore: Singapore University Press, 2004), 11. Ishizuka's family confirmed that this was virtually the identical letter he received in 1938.

6. Conrad Black, *Franklin Delano Roosevelt: Champion of Freedom* (New York: Public Affairs, 2003), 1123.

7. Ralph Waldo Emerson, *The Essential Writings of Ralph Waldo Emerson* (New York: The Modern Library, 2000), 556.

8. Ibid., 561.

9. Ibid., 562._____

10. "Life in a Lumber Camp," Wisconsin Historical Society, http://www.wisconsinhistory.org/teachers/lessons/secondary/lumber_camp.asp.

11. Ibid.

12. "La Bolduc: 'The Queen of Canadian Folksingers'," *The Virtual Gramophone: Canadian Historical Sound Recordings* (Library and Archives Canada), http://www.collectionscanada.gc.ca/gramophone/m2-1032-e.html.

13. Louis L'Amour, *Education of a Wandering Man* (New York: Bantam Books, 1990), 233.

14. "The Japanese Field Service Code, War Department, January 8, 1941," Extracted from the Tokyo *Gazette*, Vol. IV, no. 9, 343-6.

15. "The Imperial Precepts to the Soldiers and Sailors, 1882," The Imperial Precepts to Soldiers and Sailors (1882)/Kaiserliche Verordnung über die Volkserziehung (1890), http://www.ruhr-uni-bochum.de/gj/material/pdf/reader_ws0001_kapitel05.pdf.

16. Gibney, *Senso*, 23.

17. For insights into Japanese army training methods and techniques discussed in this chapter, I am indebted to Leo Daugherty, *Fighting Techniques of a Japanese Infantryman, 1941-1945, Training, Techniques and Weapons* (St. Paul: MBI Publishing Company, 2002) and to George Forty, *Japanese Army Handbook 1939-1945* (Stroud: Sutton Publishing, 2003)

18. Gibney, *Senso*, 23.

19. Tsuchikane Tominosuke, *Shingaporu e no michi: aru Konoe hei no kiroku* [The Road to Singapore: Diary of an Imperial Guard Soldier] (Tokyo: Sogeisha, 1977), Vol. 1, p. 101, quoted in Henry Frei, *Guns of February* 15.

20. Gibney, *Senso*, 27.

21. Frei, *Guns of February*, 19.

22. Salman Rushdie, *The Moor's Last Sigh* (New York: Vintage Books, 1997), 305.

23. Gibney, *Senso*, 30.

24. Sakurai, *Human Bullets*, 78.

25. Daugherty, *The Japanese Infantryman*, 29.

26. The Battle of the Yalu, 17 September 1894, *The Russo-Japanese War Research Society, February 1904-September 1905* (2002), http://www.russojapanesewar.com/yalu1894.html.

27. "The Japanese Field Service Code," *Tokyo Gazette*, 343-6.

28. Sakurai, *Human Bullets*, 141.

29. Ibid., 187.

30. Gibney, *Senso*, 60.

31. Sakurai, *Human Bullets*, 101.

32. Ibid., 32.

33. Frei, *Guns of February*, 27.

34. Gibney, *Senso*, 61.

35. Ibid.

36. Quoted in Kevin Uhrich, "The Other Holocaust," Los Angeles Readers, July 1, 1994, quoted in *Basic Facts on the Nanking Massacre and the Tokyo War Crimes Trial*, http://www.cnd.org:8006/mirror/nanjing/.

37. Gibney, *Senso*, 65.

38. Ibid., 61.

39. Ibid., 79.

40. Sakurai, *Human Bullets*, 174.

41. Gibney, *Senso*, 67.

42. Michio Takeyama, transl. by Howard Hibbett, *Harp of Burma* (Boston: Tuttle Publishing, 1966), 129-130.

43. Much useful information on the organization of the *gokaido* and its influence on the social, political and commercial development of Edo-period Japan is provided in: Thomas A. Stanley and R.T.A. Irving, "The Five Roads," *Nakasendo Way* (Walk Japan, Ltd., 2008), http://www.nakasendoway.com/5roads.xhtml.

44. Nikko Toshogu Shrine website, http://news-sv.aij.or.jp/zairyou/s3/nikko.htm.

45. I have borrowed liberally from the vivid evocations of the gokaido in this era contained in: Lucia St. Clair Robson, *The Tokaido Road: A Novel of Feudal Japan* (New York: Ballantine Books, 1991).

46. Stanley and Irving, "The Five Roads," *Nakasendo Way*, http://www.nakasendoway.com/g002.xhtml.

47. *Samurai: Social Structure, The Castes*, http://www.pvv.ntnu.no/~leirbakk/rpg/mythus/mythus_samurai.html.

48. Umberto Eco, transl. by William Weaver, *Travels in Hyperreality: Essays*, (London: Picador, 1987), 258.

49. William Manchester, *Goodbye, Darkness: A Memoir of the Pacific War* (New York: Back Bay Books, 2002), 393.

50. Tom Brokaw, *The Greatest Generation* (New York: Random House, 2004), 11.

51. Tokihisa Sumimoto, "Religious Freedom Problems in Japan: Background and Current Prospects," *The International Journal of Peace Studies*, vol. 5, no. 2 (2000), http://www.gmu.edu/academic/ijps/vol5_2/sumimoto.htm.

52. Japanese historian Yuiken Kawawata, quoted in Sumimoto, "Religious Freedom Problems in Japan."

53. Sumimoto, "Religious Freedom Problems in Japan."

54. Kenji Ueda, "Shinto," in Noriyoshi Tamaru and David Reid, *Religion in Japanese Culture* (Tokyo: Kodansha International, 1996), 28.

55. Monique Truong, *The Book of Salt*, (New York: Mariner Books, 2004), 198.

56. Charles Lutton, "Pearl Harbor: Fifty Years of Controversy," *The Journal of Historical Review, vol. 11, no. 4, 431-467.*

57. Frei, *Guns of February*, 35.

Part III

1. Extracted from online biography of General Tomoyuki Yamashita, http://www.britain-at-war.org.uk/WW2/Malaya_and_Singapore/html/body_general_yamashita.htm.

2. Frei, *Guns of February*, 46 et seq.

3. Ibid., 100.

4. Ibid., 99.

5. Quoted in LCDR Alan C. Headrick, USNR, "Bicycle Blitzkrieg: The Malayan Campaign and the Fall of Singapore," *HyperWar Foundation* (1994), http://www.ibiblio.org/hyperwar/PTO/RisingSun/BicycleBlitz/index.html.

6. Frei, *Guns of February*, 66.

7. Quoted in Forty, *Japanese Army Handbook 1939-1945.*

8. Sakurai, *Human Bullets*, 149-150.

9. Ibid., 150.

10. James Clavell, *King Rat* (New York: Dell Publishing, 1986).

11. N.I. Low, *When Singapore Was Syonan-to* (Singapore: Times Editions, 1998) 118-119.

12. Jasper Becker, *Hungry Ghosts: China's Secret Famine* (London: John Murray, 1996), 211–219.

13. Samuel P. Huntington, *The Clash of Civilizations and the Remaking of World Order* (New York: Simon & Schuster, 1998), 170.

14. N.I. Low, *When Singapore Was Syonan-to*. 16.

15. Ibid.

16. "Between October 1942 and November 1944 some 61,000 Allied POWs and 270,000 conscripted laborers – Malays, Indonesians, Thais, and Burmese – were put to work on Japan's ill-fated railroad planned to link Thailand and Burma. More than 100,000 died as a result of brutal treatment by the Japanese army." Quoted in Gibney, *Senso*, x.

17. N.I. Low, *When Singapore Was Syonan-to*. 54.

18. Ibid., 11.

19. Ibid., 84-85.

20. Ibid., 55.

21. Acts 8.23, *The Bible: Authorized King James Version with Apocrypha* (Oxford: Oxford University Press, 1998), 184.

22. C. Loring Brace, "The Samurai and the Ainu," *Science Frontiers Online, no. 65 (1989)*, http://www.science-frontiers.com/sf065/sf065a01.htm.

23. Ibid.

24. Frei, *Guns of February*, 162.

25. N.I. Low, *When Singapore Was Syonan-to*, 122.

26. Ibid., 109.

27. Ibid., 111.

28. Ibid., 118.

29. Dean Acheson, *Present at the Creation: My Years at the State Department* (New York: W. W. Norton & Company, 1987), 662.

30. "Chinese Secret Society, Hung Society," *ChinatownConnection.com*, http://www.chinatownconnection.com/chinese-secret-society.htm.

31. An excellent colonial-period source on the origins and history of Chinese secret societies, and one on which I have drawn, is J.S.M. Ward and W.G. Stirling, *Hung Society or the Society of Heaven and Earth* (Whitefish: Kessinger Publishing, 2003).

32. R. Elberton Smith, quoted in Frank N. Schubert, "Mobilization: The U.S. Army In World War II, The 50th Anniversary, *U.S. Army Center of Military History*, http://www.history.army.mil/documents/mobpam.htm.

33. Ibid.

34. Colonel Charles F. Brower, *George C. Marshall: A Study in Character*, http://famousamericans.net/georgemarshall.org/.

35. Quoted in Brower, *George C. Marshall: A Study in Character*.

36. Time Archive, "George C. Marshall," *Time*, January 3, 1944.

37. The full extent of innovation in the field of rocketry is affectionately catalogued by an unofficial NASA historian, Cliff Lethbridge of Spaceline, Inc., to whose work I am indebted for much of the background information contained in this section. Of particular relevance is: Cliff Lethbridge, "History of Rocketry, Chapters 3-6," Spaceline.org.,http://www.spacearium.com/special/spaceline/spaceline.org/rockethistory.html.

38. Ibid.

39. Ibid.

40. Ibid.

41. Wesley Frank Craven and James Lea Cate, eds., *The Army Air Forces in World War II: Volume 6, Men and Planes* (Washington, D.C.: New Imprint by the Office of Air Force History, 1983), 560.

42. Ibid., 567.

43. General Henry H. "Hap" Arnold, Commanding General of the U.S. Army Air Forces, 1941-1945.

44. General Jonathan M. Wainwright IV, Commander of the Allied forces in the Philippines at the time of their surrender to the Japanese in 1942.

45. Craven and Cate, *The Army Air Forces in World War II*, 569.

46. Ibid., 575-576.

47. Ibid., 456. The original nine schools were: Spartan School of Aeronautics, Tulsa, Okla.; Santa Maria School of Flying, Santa Maria, Calif.; Dallas Aviation School and Air College, Dallas, Tex.; Ryan School of Aeronautics, San Diego, Calif.; Alabama Institute of Aeronautics, Tuscaloosa, Ala.; Grand Central Flying School, Glendale, Calif.; Parks Air College, East St. Louis, Ill.; Lincoln Airplane and Flying School, Lincoln, Neb.; and Chicago School of Aeronautics, Glenview, Ill.

48. Eric M. Bergerud, *Fire in the Sky: The Air War in the South Pacific* (Boulder: Westview Press, 2001), 362.

49. Ibid., 519.

50. Craven and Cate, *The Army Air Forces in World War II*, 569.

51. Ibid., 571.

52. Background information for this section was provided by "The Link Trainer in WWII," *Wing Tips: A Publication of the Vintage Flying Museum in Fort Worth, Texas*, Summer (2007), http://www.vintageflying-museum.org/newsletter/wingtips_09_07.pdf, and "The Link Flight Trainer: A Historic Mechanical Engineering Landmark," *ASME International, History and Heritage Committee, Roberson Museum and Science Center*, May (2000), http://files.asme.org/ASMEORG/Communities/History/Landmarks/5585.pdf.

53. David Brooks, *Bobos in Paradise: The New Upper Class and How They Got There*, (New York: Touchstone, 2001), 24.

54. Quoted in "Biography: John Llewellyn Lewis," *Answers.com*™, http://www.answers.com/topic/john-l-lewis.

55. Ibid.

56. Craven and Cate, *The Army Air Forces in World War II*, 572.

57. Ibid., 572-573.

58. Gibney, *Senso*, 6.

59. Ibid., 5.

60. Ibid.

61. Ibid., 6.

62. Ibid.

63. Ibid.

64. Forty, *Japanese Army Handbook 1939-1945*, 6.

65. Gibney, *Senso*, 5.

66. Forty, *Japanese Army Handbook 1939-1945*, 5-6.

67. Transl. by George Arrington, *Translation – Imperial Rescript on Education of the Emperor Meiji* (2002), http://www.danzan.com/HTML/ESSAYS/meiji.html.

68. Gibney, *Senso*, 183-185.

69. Ibid.

70. Ibid., 188-189.

71. Ibid., 299-300.

72. Ibid., 7.

73. Craven and Cate, *The Army Air Forces in World War II*, 600.

74. Ibid., 608.

75. Ibid., 610.

76. Ibid., 615.

77. Bergerud, *Fire in the Sky*, 360.

78. Ibid.

79. Ibid., 358.

80. *Army Air Forces Statistical Digest (World War II)*, (Office of Statistical Control, Headquarters, Army Air Forces, December 1945)

81. Rick Marschall, *Milton Caniff, Rembrandt of the Comic Strip* (Flying Bultress Publications, 1981).

82. Coulton Waugh and M. Thomas Inge, *The Comics* (Jackson: University Press of Mississippi, 1991), 275.

83. Michael O'Leary, "AIR COMMANDO Mustang," *Air Classics*, Sep 2006, in BNET Business Network, http://findarticles.com/p/articles/mi_qa3901/is_200609/ai_n17196318.

84. Extracted from the First Air Commando Association newsletter, Fall 2000, quoted online from an exchange of correspondence between Philip G. Cochran and Milton Caniff, http://www.specialoperations.net/CochranLtr.htm.

85. *WWII Air Commandos, Volume II*, produced by T. Kemp (Dallas: Taylor Publishing Company, 1994), 4.

86. Craven and Cate, *The Army Air Forces in World War II*, xxxiv.

87. Dan Schneider, *Mouth-To-Mouth For Mickey: Spillane's Long Foreshadow*, 2002, http://www.cosmoetica.com/B61-DES29.htm.

88. Ibid.

89. Respectively the British prime minister and the Irish taoiseach.

90. John E. Semonche, *The Internment of the Japanese in World War II and its Aftermath*, http://www.dlt.ncssm.edu/lmtm/docs/jap_intern/script.pdf. Note: The attribution of the $400 million estimate to the Federal Reserve Bank of San Francisco is disputed. What is not disputed is that the actual losses incurred by Japanese-Americans as a result of internment greatly exceeded the compensation received.

91. "Research on 100th/442nd Regimental Combat Team," *National Japanese American Historical Society*, http://www.njahs.org/research/442.html.

92. "U.S. Supreme Court: Korematsu v. United States," *Answers.com*, http://www.answers.com/topic/korematsu-v-united-states.

93. John Milton, Paradise Lost (New York: Penguin Classics, 2003), bk. X, I. 232.

94. Quoted in D. M. Giangreco, "'Spinning' the Casualties: Media Strategies During the Roosevelt Administration," (U.S. Army Command and General Staff College, December 2004 Newsletter), http://www.shafr.org/newsletter/2004/december/giangreco.htm.

95. Maurer, Maurer, ed., *Air Force Combat Units of World War II* (Washington, D.C.: U.S. Government Printing Office, 1961), 121-122, 460-461.

96. The official history of the Air Commandos, *WWII Air Commandos, Volumes I and II*, has been an invaluable source of background material on the development and wartime operation of the Air Commandos.

97. Quoted in *WWII Air Commandos, Volume II*, 4.

98. Ibid., Volume I, Introduction.

99. Anti-malarial prophylaxis thought by many soldiers to induce impotence and for this reason unpopular.

100. Manchester, *Goodbye, Darkness*, 210.

101. M.S. Medina, "Spam Celebrates 70 Year Anniversary!," *Associated Content*, 2008, http://www.associatedcontent.com/article/301668/spam_celebrates_70_year_anniversary.html?page=2&cat=22. For the nostalgic and the peckish, a comprehensive menu of SPAM-derived menu options is provided on the SPAM site of the Hormel Foods website: http://www.hormelfoods.com/brands/spam/.

102. Mark Twain, *Innocents Abroad* (New York: Signet Classics, 1966), 196.

103. Edmund White, *The Flâneur: A Stroll through the Paradoxes of Paris* (New York: Bloomsbury Publishing, 2001), 34.

104. Luis Sepulveda, *The Old Man Who Read Love Stories*, (New York: Harvest Books, 1995), 131.

105. Eric Bergerud, *Touched with Fire: The Land War in the South Pacific*, (New York: Penguin, 1997), 114.

106. "The History of Quality–World War II," *Basic Concepts* (American Society for Quality), http://www.asq.org/learn-about-quality/history-of-quality/overview/wwii.html.

107. Frei, *Guns of February*, 17.

108. "The Battle for Leyte Gulf, 23-26 October 1944," http://www.angelfire.com/fm/odyssey/LEYTE_GULF_Summary_of_the_Battle_.htm.

109. Major Thomas C. Hardman, "Air Strategy in Luzon," quoted in *The Jungle Air Force of World War II, 1942-1945*, http://www.enter.net/~rocketeer/13thaaf/13thaf_0645.html.

110. Quoted in Howard Kelley, "The 32nd Infantry Division in World War II, 'The Red Arrow'," http://members.aol.com/Sarge000tb/32-ww2e.html.

111. Joseph Heller, *Catch-22*, (London: Vintage, 1994), 73.

112. Ibid., 298.

113. Bernard Baruch, "Priorities, The Synchronizing Force," *Harvard Business Review* (Spring, 1941), 261-270.

114. Quoted in Kevin Conley Ruffner, "The Black Market in Postwar Berlin," *Prologue Magazine*, Vol. 34, No. 3, (Fall 2002).

115. Ibid.

116. Ibid.

117. Stephen Ellis, "Senate Democratic Policy Committee: Oversight Hearing on Iraq Contracting Practices," *Taxpayers for Common Sense*, February 2004.

118. Garrett Moritz, "Coupons and Counterfeits: World War II and the U.S. Black Market," *eiNET.net*, http://www.gtexts.com/college/papers/j2.html.

119. Robert Higgs, "Wartime Prosperity? A Reassessment of the U.S. Economy in the 1940s," *The Journal of Economic History*, Vol. 52, No. 1, (Mar., 1992), 41-60.

120. P.D. James, *Devices and Desires*, (London: Vintage, 2004).

121. Ronald E. Dolan, ed., "José Rizal and the Propaganda Movement," *Philippines: A Country Study* (Washington: GPO for the Library of Congress, 1991).

122. Ibid.

123. José P. Rizal, *Noli Me Tangere*, (New York: Penguin Classics, 2006).

124. José P. Rizal, *El Filibusterismo*, (Instituto Nacional de Historia, 1990).

125. Dolan, "The Katipunan," *Philippines: A Country Study*.

126. Dr. Bernardita Reyes Churchill, "History of the Philippines Revolution: The Katipunan Revolution," http://www.ncca.gov.ph/culture&arts/cularts/heritage/research/research-history.htm.

127. Kevin Hymel, "Puerto Rico and the Philippines: The Lesser Known Campaigns of the Spanish-American War," The Army Historical Foundation, 2006-2007, http://www.armyhistory.org/armyhistorical. aspx?pgID=868&id=97&exCompID=32.

128. Ibid.

129. Ibid.

130. Ibid.

131. Dolan, "The Malolos Constitution and the Treaty of Paris," *Philippines: A Country Study.*

132. Dolan, "War of Resistance," *Philippines: A Country Study.*

133. Ibid.

134. James A. Blount, "The Philippine-American War: McKinley's Benevolent Assimilation Proclamation," *American Occupation of the Philippines 1898/1912*, http://www.msc.edu.ph/centennial/benevolent.html.

135. Isagani A. Cruz, "The Pathetic Record of Our Public Schools," *Philippine Daily Inquirer*, October 17, 2004, http://isaganicruz.blogspot. com/2004/10/pathetic-record-of-our-public-schools.html.

136. Menardo L. Lumapak, "Chapter 4. World War II in Biliran Town," from Rolando O. Borrinaga, ed., *Sunset in Biliran: Japanese and Filipino Accounts of World War II in Northern Leyte*, http://www.geocities. com/rolborr/sunintro.html.

137. Quoted in SGM Herbert A. Friedman, "Japanese PSYOP During WWII," http://www.psywarrior.com/JapanPSYOPWW2.html.

138. Hiroyuki Miyawaki, "Linguistic imperialism: Japanese language policy in Asia until 1945," Miyagi Gakuin Women's College, Sendai, Japan, http://ec.hku.hk/kd96proc/authors/papers/miyawaki.htm.

139. Ibid.

140. Veltisezar Bautista, "From Philippine Independence to Ramos Regime," *The Filipino Americans from 1763 to the Present: Their History, Culture, and Traditions* (Bookhaus Publishers, 1998).

141. José P. Rizal, *Mi Ultimo Adios*, from an English translation distributed at the Rizal Memorial, Rizal Park in Manila.

142. Transcript of "MacArthur's Speeches: Radio Message from the Leyte Beachhead," *The American Experience, PBS Online*, http://www.pbs.org/wgbh/amex/macarthur/filmmore/reference/primary/mac-speech03.html.

143. Charles R. Anderson, "The U.S. Army Campaigns of World War II: Leyte," *HyperWar Foundation*, http://www.ibiblio.org/hyperwar/USA/USA-C-Leyte/index.html.

144. Bergerud, *Fire in the Sky*, 144.

145. "History of the American Red Cross," American Red Cross of the Greater Lehigh Valley, 2007, http://www.redcrosslv.org/history.html.

146. "Remembering the Millions Who Helped During WWII," *Trail-news*, American Red Cross, Oregon Trail Chapter, Summer 2004, http://www.redcross-pdx.org/news/Trail_News_Archive/TrailNews_Summer_2004.pdf.

147. "Milestones: American Red Cross Blood Services," *American Red Cross Blood Services – New England Region*, 200-2002, http://www.newenglandblood.org/medical/milestones.htm.

148. H.G. Wells, *The World Set Free* (Whitefish: Kessinger Publishing, 2004), 46.

149. Douglas Martin, "Saburo Sakai Is Dead at 84; War Pilot Embraced Foes," *The New York Times*, October 8, 2000, http://www.mishalov.com/Sakai.html.

150. Christian Jaki, "Junkers Ju 87 G-2, flown by Stuka Colonel Hans-Ulrich Rudel," *The Luftwaffe in Scale*, http://www.rlm.at/cont/gal12_e.htm.

151. Alfred F. Hurley, *Billy Mitchell: Crusader for Air Power* (Bloomington: Indiana University Press, 1975), 93.

152. Not to be confused with Bataan Province in the Central Luzon Region, starting point of the infamous Bataan Death March.

153. "Situation Normal, All Fucked Up"

154. James K. Sunshine, quoted in David Steinert, "The Function of a Field Hospital in the Chain of Evacuation During WWII," 2000, http://home.att.net/~steinert/beachhead_hospital.htm.

155. Judith A. Bellafaire, "The Pacific Theater," *The Army Nurse Corps: A Commemoration of World War II Service*, 28, http://www.history.army. mil/books/wwii/72-14/72-14.HTM.

156. "That Men Might Live! The Story of the Medical Service–ETO," (Paris: Stars and Stripes, 1944-1945), in LoneSentry.com, http://www. lonesentry.com/gi_stories_booklets/medical/index.html.

157. Charles M. Wiltse in Kathi Jackson, *They Called Them Angels: American Military Nurses of World War II* (University of Nebraska Press, 2006), 181.

158. Bellafaire, *The Army Nurse Corps*, 26.

159. Steinert, "The Function of a Field Hospital in the Chain of Evacuation During WWII."

160. "Battle of Brisbane: 'Overpaid, Oversexed and Over Here'," Digger History: *An Unofficial History of the Australian & New Zealand Armed Forces*, http://www.diggerhistory.info/pages-battles/ww2/battle-brisbane.htm.

161. Ibid.

162. Ibid.

163. Larry Parker, "Nomonhon and Okinawa: The First and Final Battles of the Pacific War," *MilitaryHistoryOnline.com*, 2005, http://www. militaryhistoryonline.com/wwii/articles/nomonhanokinawa.aspx.

164. Field-Marshal Viscount William Slim, *Defeat into Victory: Battling Japan in Burma and India, 1942-1945* (New York: Cooper Square Press, 1956), ix-x.

165. Jon Latimer, *Burma: The Forgotten War*, (London: John Murray Publishers Ltd., 2004).

166. Kazuo Tamayama and John Nunneley, eds., *Tales By Japanese Soldiers* (London: Cassell Military Paperbacks, 2006), Back Cover.

167. Slim, *Defeat Into Victory*, 516.

168. Ibid., 518.

169. Ibid., 520. Jan Christiaan Smuts (1870-1950), South African Boer independence fighter turned British Commonwealth statesman, Prime Minister of the Union of South Africa and British Field Marshal.

170. Ibid., 30, et seq.

171. *WWII Air Commandos, Volume II, 89.*

172. *WWII Air Commandos, Volume I, 42*

173. Ibid., 98

174. Quoted in Barbara Crossette, *The Great Hill Stations of Asia* (Boulder: Westview Press, 1998), v.

175. Robert Ross Smith, "Chapter V, The Enemy," *U.S. Army in World War II: Triumph in the Philippines,* (HyperWar Foundation, 94-96), http://ibiblio.org/hyperwar/USA/USA-P-Triumph/USA-P-Triumph-5.html.

176. Ibid., 92.

177. Ibid., 93.

178. Ibid., 91.

179. Tamayama and Nunneley, *Tales By Japanese Soldiers,* 178.

180. Ibid., 170.

181. Ibid., 198.

182. Ibid., 200.

183. Craven and Cate, *The Army Air Forces in World War II.*

184. Ibid.

185. *WWII Air Commandos, Volume I, 102.*

186. Sakurai, *Human Bullets,* 91.

Part IV

1. Gibney, *Senso,* 34.

2. T.S. Eliot, "Quartet No. 1: Burnt Norton," *Four Quartets,* II, http://www.tristan.icom43.net/quartets/index.html.

3. Norman Mailer, *The Naked and the Dead: 50th Anniversary Edition* (New York: Picador, 2000), 247.

4. Ibid., 248.

5. Gibney, *Senso,* 48.

6. Ibid., 24.

7. Masami Ito, "Yasukuni Shrine: Yasukuni in Spotlight as Aug. 15 Nears," *The Japan Times Online*, Aug. 5, 2008, http://search.japantimes.co.jp/cgi-bin/nn20080805i1.html.

8. Jennifer Rosenberg, "The War is Over...Please Come Out," *About.com: 20th Century History*, http://history1900s.about.com/od/worldwarii/a/soldiersurr.htm.

9. Daniel Moran, "The Culture of Defeat: On National Trauma, Mourning, and Recovery, by Wolfgang Schivelbusch," *Center for Contemporary Conflict, Strategic Insights*, Vol. 3, Issue 6, June 2004.

10. Dylan Thomas, *The Poems of Dylan Thomas, New Revised Edition* (New York: New Directions Publishing Corporation, 2003), 162.

11. John Steinbeck, *East of Eden*, (New York: Penguin, 2002), 130-131.

12. Rupert Brooke, "1914, A Sonnet Sequence, IV., The Dead," *The Collected Poems of Rupert Brooke* (BiblioBazaar, LLC, 2006), 110.